B

Reach HIGHER

Program Authors
Nancy Frey
Lada Kratky
Nonie K. Lesaux
Sylvia Linan-Thompson
Deborah J. Short
Jennifer D. Turner

Australia · Brazil · Mexico · Singapore · United Kingdom · United States

National Geographic Learning,
a Cengage Company

Reach Higher 2B

Program Authors: Nancy Frey, Lada Kratky, Nonie K. Lesaux, Sylvia Linan-Thompson, Deborah J. Short, Jennifer D. Turner

Publisher, Content-based English:
Erik Gundersen

Associate Director, R&D: Barnaby Pelter

Senior Development Editors:
Jacqueline Eu
Ranjini Fonseka
Kelsey Zhang

Director of Global Marketing: Ian Martin

Heads of Regional Marketing:
Charlotte Ellis (Europe, Middle East and Africa)
Kiel Hamm (Asia)
Irina Pereyra (Latin America)

Product Marketing Manager: David Spain

Senior Production Controller: Tan Jin Hock

Senior Media Researcher (Covers): Leila Hishmeh

Senior Designer: Lisa Trager

Director, Operations: Jason Seigel

Operations Support:
Rebecca Barbush
Drew Robertson
Caroline Stephenson
Nicholas Yeaton

Manufacturing Planner: Mary Beth Hennebury

Publishing Consultancy and Composition:
MPS North America LLC

ISBN: 978-0-357-36683-7

National Geographic Learning
200 Pier Four Blvd
Boston, MA 02210
USA

Locate your local office at **international.cengage.com/region**

Visit National Geographic Learning online at **ELTNGL.com**
Visit our corporate website at **www.cengage.com**

Printed in Mexico
Print Number: 06 Print Year: 2022

4FCS0000696210

Contents at a Glance

Table of Contents

Everything Changes

Unit 5

? BIG QUESTION

Why is nature always changing?

Extra phonics support with **READ ON YOUR OWN**

Dare to Invent

SCIENCE

- Changes and Patterns in Nature
- Seasons and Weather

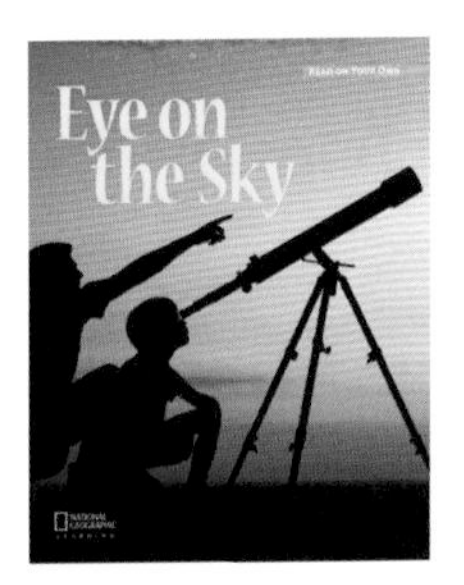

Eye on the Sky

Table of Contents

Better Together

Unit 6

? BIG QUESTION

Why is it good to work together?

Extra phonics support with **READ ON YOUR OWN**

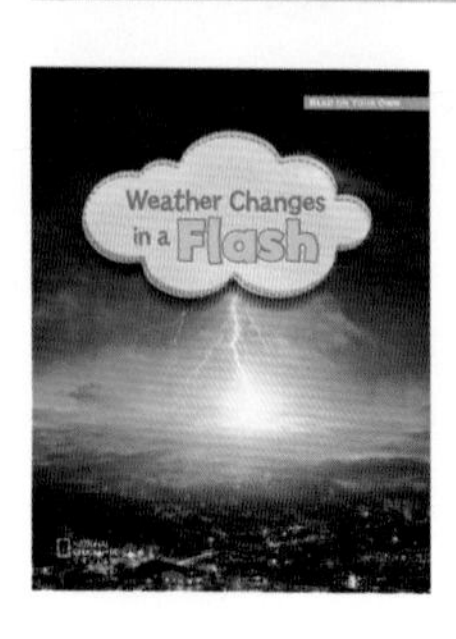

Weather Changes in a Flash

Look Out For Animals

SOCIAL STUDIES

- Cooperation
- Working for the Common Good

Part 2

Weather Wise

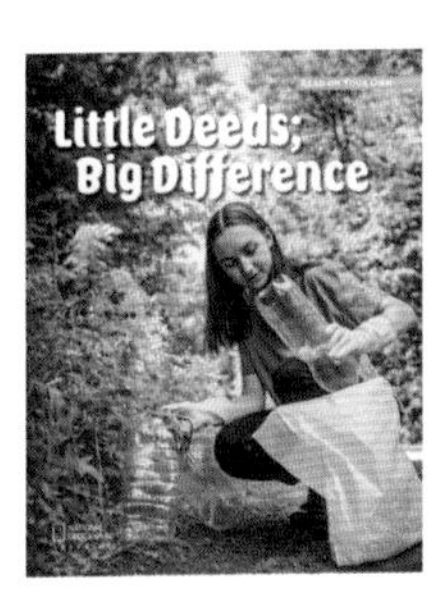

Little Deeds, Big Difference

Table of Contents

Best Buddies

Unit 7

? BIG QUESTION

How do living things depend on each other?

Extra phonics support with **READ ON YOUR OWN**

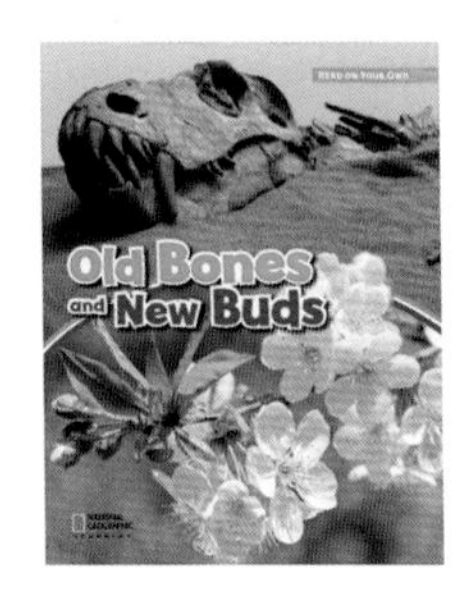

Old Bones and New Buds

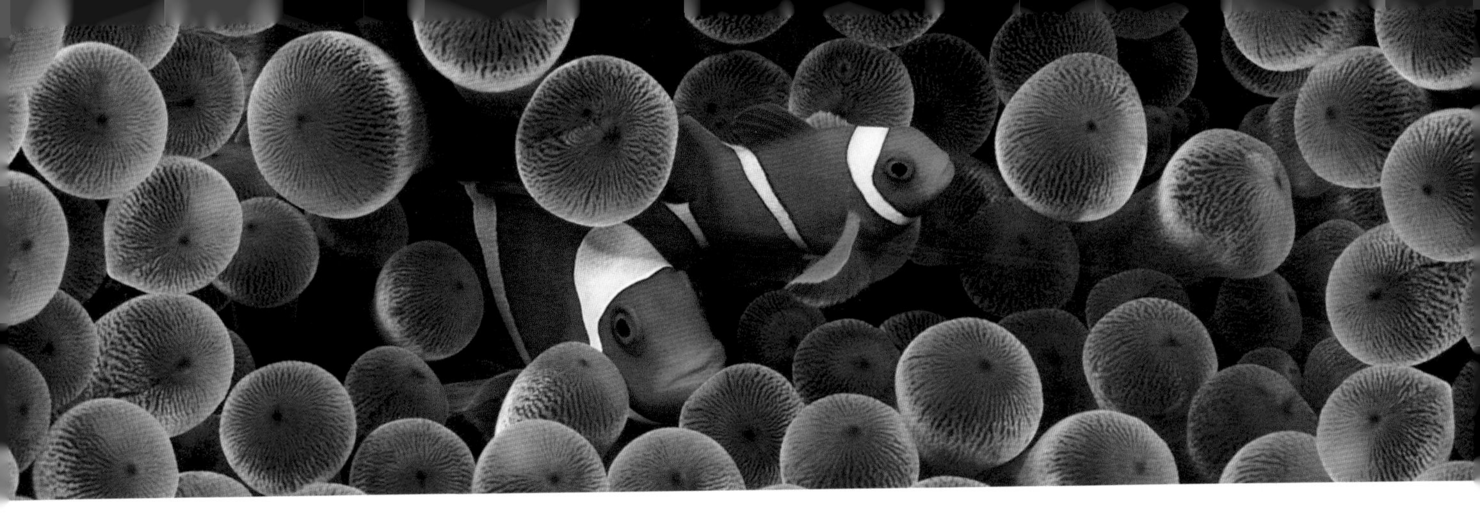

SCIENCE

- Animals and their Basic Needs
- Partnerships in Nature

Part 2

Bird Watchers

Table of Contents

Our World

Unit 8

? BIG QUESTION

What does the world mean to you?

Extra phonics support with **READ ON YOUR OWN**

Animals at Home

SOCIAL STUDIES

- Customs, Symbols, Celebrations, Landmarks
- National Identity

Part 2

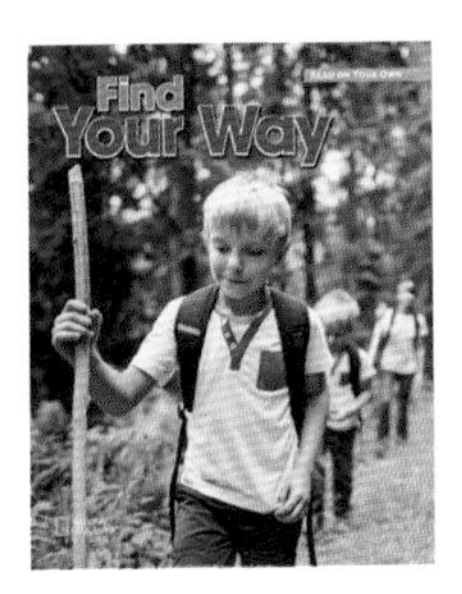

Find Your Way

Genres at a Glance

Fiction

Folk Tale

Realistic Fiction

Poetry

Poem

Song Lyrics

Drama

Play

Nonfiction

Human-Interest Feature

Literary Nonfiction

Photo-Essay

Profile

Science Article

Unit 5

Everything Changes

BIG Question

Why is nature always changing?

ONTARIO, CANADA
Brother and sister looking at a maple leaf in autumn through magnifying glasses

Unit at a Glance

- **Language Focus**: Engage in Discussion, Make Comparisons
- **Reading Strategy**: Visualize
- **Phonics Focus**: Vowel Sounds and Spellings: *air, are, ear*; Silent consonants: *gn, kn*
- **Topic**: Changes in Nature

Share What You Know

Do It!

1. **Draw** a picture of your favorite time of year. Work with a partner.
2. **Share** your picture with the class.
3. **Place** all of the pictures in order of the seasons. Work with the whole class.

PART 1 **Language Focus**

Words to Know
both
do
why

Engage in Discussion

Listen and read along.

Dialogue 

Day and Night

 I think day is better than night.

 **Why do** you think so?

 Because it is bright.

 I think night is better than day.

 Why do you think so?

 It's hard to say! I like planet Mars— I love all the stars!

 And I love the Milky Way! I guess I like **both** night and day.

Science Vocabulary

Key Words

The **moon** and **stars** come out at night.

Day **begins**.

The sun moves high in the sky. **Shadows** get short.

What changes happen on Earth every day?

Day **ends**. **Night** begins.

The sun sets.

The sun moves lower in the sky. Shadows get long.

Talk Together

What do you see during the day? How is it different from what you can see at night?

Theme

The **theme** of a story is its main message. Look for clues about the theme of the story below.

A Night Under the Stars

Theme Chart

Title	Characters
"A Night Under the Stars" makes me think about camping.	Thomas and his dad have fun spending time together.
Setting	**Plot**
Thomas and his dad are in their backyard at night.	Thomas and his dad set up their tent and tell scary stories. Then they fall asleep and wake up at dawn.

Theme: Sleeping under the stars is fun.

Write the ideas you get from the title here.

Write about the characters here.

What is the message of the story? Write it here.

Write the ideas you get from the setting here.

Write the story events here.

Talk Together

Tell your partner about your favorite story. Write the details in a theme chart. Work together to find the theme of the story.

More Key Words

appear
verb

The whale **appears** above the water.

motion
noun

The man is in **motion**.

observe
verb

He **observes** the insect.

pattern
noun

Orange, gray, and blue tiles make a **pattern** on this floor.

repeat
verb

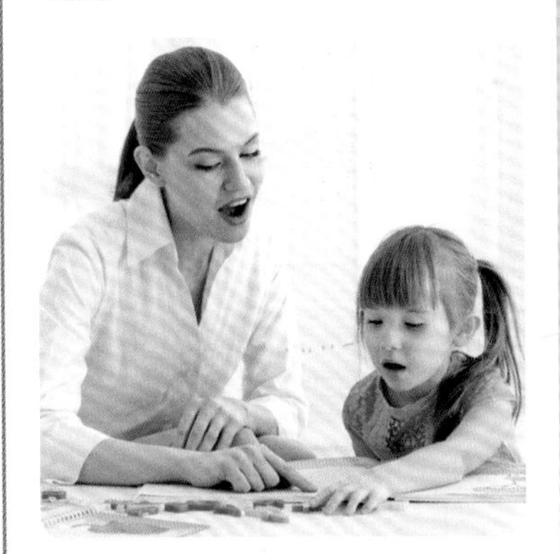

She has to **repeat** what she said because her teacher did not hear her.

Talk Together

Make an Expanded Meaning Map for each **Key Word**. Compare your maps with a partner's.

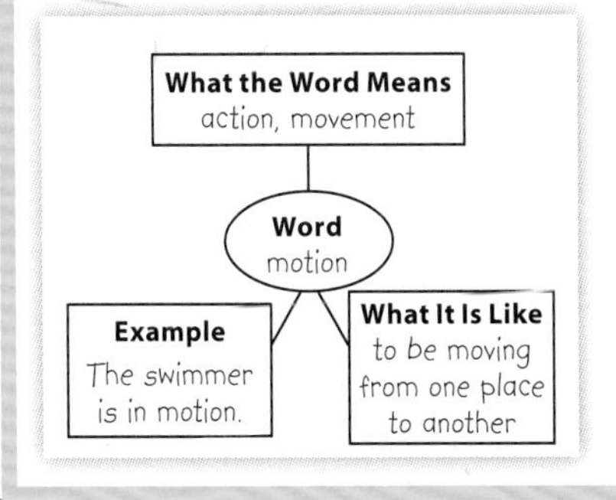

PART 1 **Reading Strategy**

Learn to Visualize

As you read, try to **visualize**, or form pictures in your mind. Look for words that tell how things look, taste, smell, feel, and sound.

Try to **visualize** what Thomas does.

How to Visualize

1. As you read, look for words that describe how things look, taste, smell, feel, and sound.

2. Use the words to create pictures in your mind.

3. Draw the picture. Show how you see things in your mind.

I read _____.

I think it _____ like _____.

I draw _____.

Talk Together

Language Frames

I read ______ .

I think it ______ like ______ .

I draw ______ .

Read Carmen's story. Read the sample visualization. Then use **Language Frames** to tell a partner how you visualized things in the story.

Story

Playtime in the Park

My friend Thomas likes to play in the park every **day** after school. He loves to play on the swings. The **motion** of his legs and body make him go really high.

Thomas always notices things. He **observes** how the park changes from spring to summer. As time goes on, he notices a **pattern**.

In spring, tulips **appear** in the green grass. Thomas calls me and asks, "Why are you inside? Don't you want to come out and play?" I run outside. We play tag and hide-and-seek.

In summer, the grass is still green, but the tulips are gone. We try to **repeat** the games we play in spring, but we get too hot. Then we lie in the **shadow** of a large oak tree.

"Is there anything else we can do?" he asks.

"I know," I say. "Let's run through the sprinklers!" Then we play until it is almost **night**.

Sample Visualization

"I read about Thomas playing on a swing in the park.

I think it feels like the wind is rushing past him as he swings through the air.

I draw a boy smiling as he swings on the swing."

= A good place to visualize

PART 1 **Phonics Focus**

Vowel Sounds and Spellings: *air, are, ear*

chair

hare

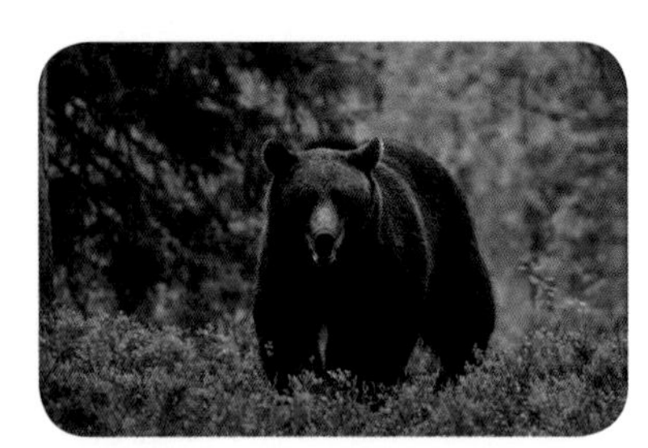
bear

Listen and Learn

Listen to each group of words. Choose the two words in each group with the vowel sound you hear in the word *air.*

1. fair	fur	flare
2. scare	bear	bar
3. hair	her	bare
4. were	wear	rare
5. flair	fly	flare
6. star	stare	stair

Talk Together

Listen and read. Find the words with the vowel patterns *air, are,* or *ear.*

Over to You

The Pattern of Night and Day

The day ends. The sun is low in the sky. Shadows get long. The air feels cool. Twinkling stars appear in the dark sky. The moon rises slowly over the hills. It lights up the ground.

A hare hops along. It feeds on both grasses and plants. A fox stares into the darkness. A pair of mice dare to rush from bush to bush. They have to take care. An owl is looking for food. It will swoop down if it sees motion.

What do other animals do? Bees are quiet in their hives. A bear snores in its den. A mare sleeps in the barn. A dog curls up at the foot of a bed.

Slowly, the moon disappears from the sky. The sun begins to rise. Birds wake up to the new day. This pattern of day and night will repeat over and over.

Work with a partner.
Find words with the vowel patterns *air, are,* and *ear.* Sort the words by their vowel patterns. Then use one of each in a sentence of your own.

Read "The Pattern of Night and Day" with a partner. Practice reading words with the vowel patterns *air, are,* or *ear.*

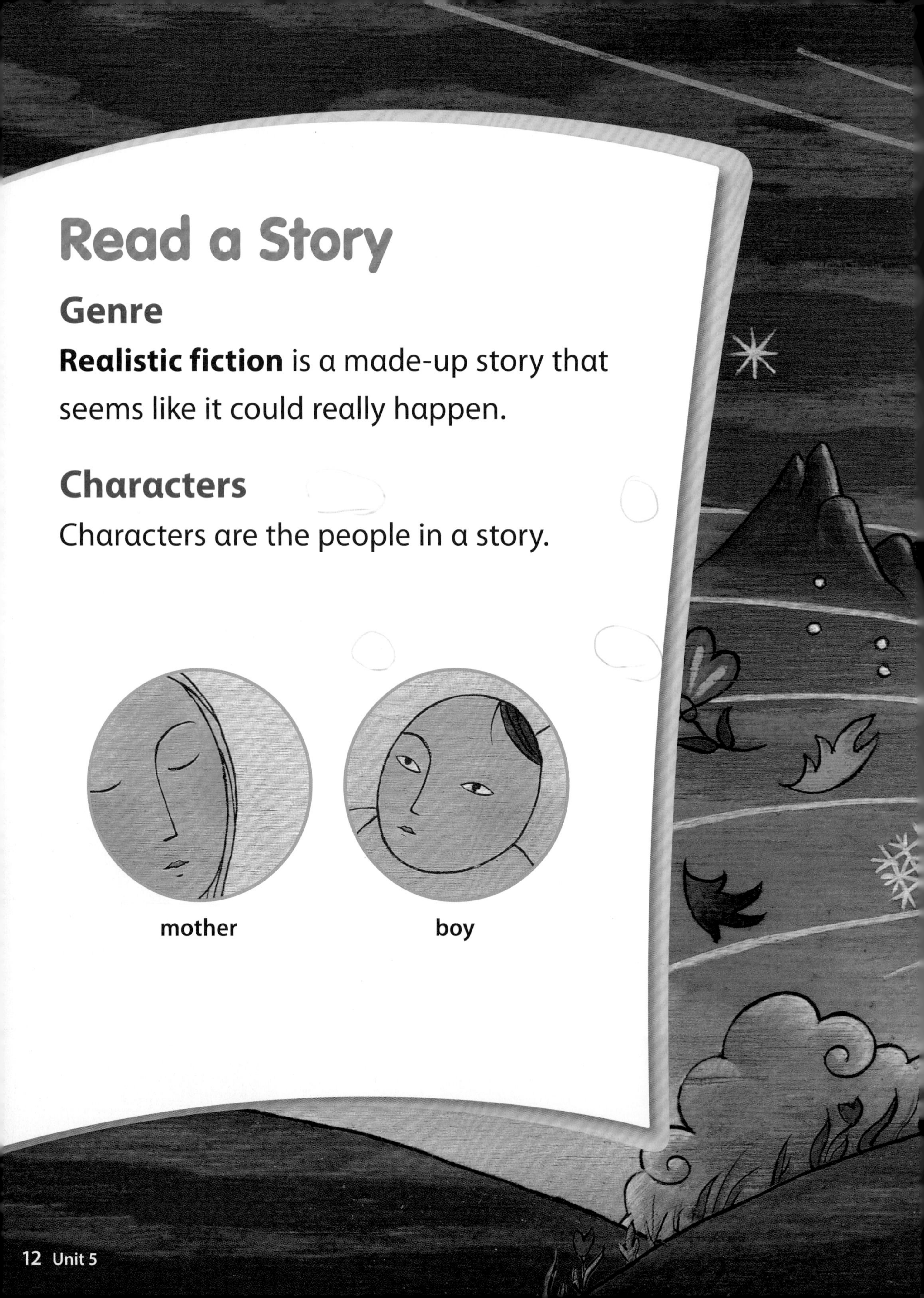

Read a Story

Genre

Realistic fiction is a made-up story that seems like it could really happen.

Characters

Characters are the people in a story.

mother

boy

When the Wind Stops

by **Charlotte Zolotow**

illustrated by **Stefano Vitale**

Set a Purpose

A boy **wonders** why the **day** must **end**. Find out what he learns.

The bright sun had shone all **day**, and now the day was **coming to an end**. The sun **sank lower** into the **glowing** pink clouds. The little boy was sorry to see the day **end**.

wonders thinks about
coming to an end almost over
sank lower went down
glowing bright

Later, his mother came to say good **night**.

"Why does the **day** have to **end**?" he asked her.

"So night can **begin**," she said. "Look."

Through the window, the little boy could see **a pale sliver of moon** in the **darkening sky** behind the branches of the pear tree.

a pale sliver of moon some of the moon
darkening sky sky that was getting darker

"But where does the sun go when the **day ends**?" the little boy asked.

"The day **doesn't** end," said his mother. "It **begins somewhere else**. The sun will be shining there, when **night** begins here. Nothing ends."

"Nothing?" the little boy asked.

"Nothing," his mother said. "It begins in another place or in a different way."

doesn't does not

somewhere else in another place

Before You Continue

1. **Explain** What does the boy learn about day and **night**?
2. **Visualize** Picture the boy and his mother talking about the end of the **day**. Where are they? What do you see?

▸ **Predict**
Look at the pictures. What questions will the little boy ask next?

The little boy lay in bed, and his mother sat beside him.

"Where does the wind go when it stops?" he asked.

"It **blows away** to make the trees **dance** somewhere else."

blows away goes to another place
dance move and shake

“Where does the **dandelion fluff** go when it blows away?”

“It carries the seeds of new dandelions to someone’s **lawn**.”

“Where does the mountain go after the top?”

“It goes down to where it becomes the **valley**.”

dandelion fluff soft, white part of a dandelion flower ▶

lawn grass

valley low place between the mountains

"Where does the rain go when a storm **is over**?"
"It goes into clouds to make other storms."

is over ends

"Where do clouds go when they move across the sky?"

"They go to **make shade** somewhere else."

make shade make **shadows**

Before You Continue

1. **Confirm Prediction** What did the boy ask? Was your prediction correct?
2. **Visualize** Think about trees "dancing." What else do you see, hear, and feel when you read about the wind blowing?

Predict

Look at the pictures. What part of nature will the boy learn about next?

"What about the leaves when they **turn color and fall**?"

"They go into the ground to become part of new trees with new leaves."

turn color and fall change colors and fall off the trees

“But when the leaves fall, that is the end of something!” the little boy said. “It is the end of autumn.”

“Yes,” his mother said. “The end of autumn is when the winter **begins**.”

“And the end of winter . . . ?” the little boy asked.

“The end of winter, when the snow **melts** and birds come back, is the beginning of spring,” his mother said.

The little boy smiled.

melts turns into water

"It really does go on and on," he said. "Nothing **ends**."

He looked out at the sky. The sun was gone completely and the **lovely** pink clouds had **disappeared**. The sky was dark and purple-black, and high above the branches of the pear tree shone a thin **moon**.

lovely pretty
disappeared gone; left

"Today is over," his mother said, "and it's time for sleep. Tomorrow morning, when you wake, the **moon** will be **beginning** a **night** far away, and the sun will be here to begin a new **day**." ❖

▸ Before You Continue

1. **Confirm Prediction** What does the boy learn about nature? Was your prediction correct?
2. **Character** How does the boy feel about what he has learned? How can you tell?

Meet the Author

Charlotte Zolotow

AWARD WINNER

CHARLOTTE ZOLOTOW (1915–2013) was the author of over 70 picture books for children and a lifelong champion of honest, true-to-life literature for young readers. Zolotow's work offered even the youngest children a realistic but compassionate view of topics like anger, envy and death. Her long and distinguished career as a writer and an editor was based on expressing her sense of what the experience of childhood was like, from the child's point of view. She said, "I remember actually thinking, when I was a child, that I would remember things that had happened, things that seem important to me but seemed to go unnoticed by the adults around me."

Writing Tip

Charlotte Zolotow used details such as "lovely pink clouds" and "purple-black" sky to help you see and feel what is happening in the story. Write your own sentence about nature. Be sure to use a lot of details!

PART 1 **Think and Respond**

Talk About It

1. Name one thing in the story that is **realistic**. Read that part of the story aloud and then talk about it.

   _____ could happen in real life.

2. The boy's mother says, "Nothing **ends**." What does she mean? **Discuss** your ideas with a partner.

   I think _____ because _____.
   I don't think _____ because _____.

3. Pretend you are the boy. What do you see from your window before you go to bed? Use words and pictures from the story to create a picture in your mind. Tell a partner what you see, hear, and smell.

   I see _____.
   I hear _____.
   I smell _____.

Write About It

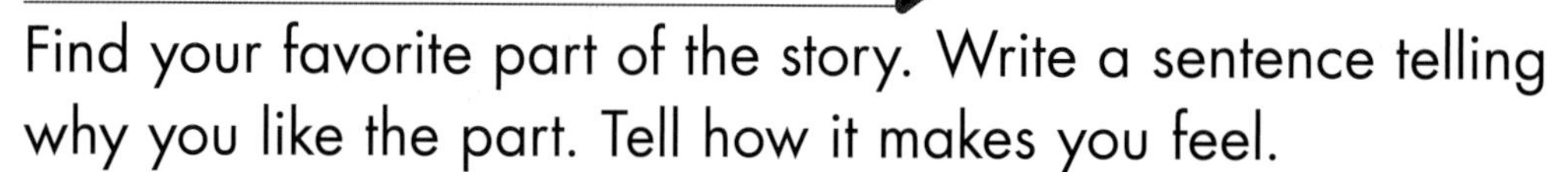

Find your favorite part of the story. Write a sentence telling why you like the part. Tell how it makes you feel.

Today we read _____.
I like _____ because _____.
It makes me feel _____.

Reread and Describe

Theme

What is the theme of "When the Wind Stops"?

Theme Chart

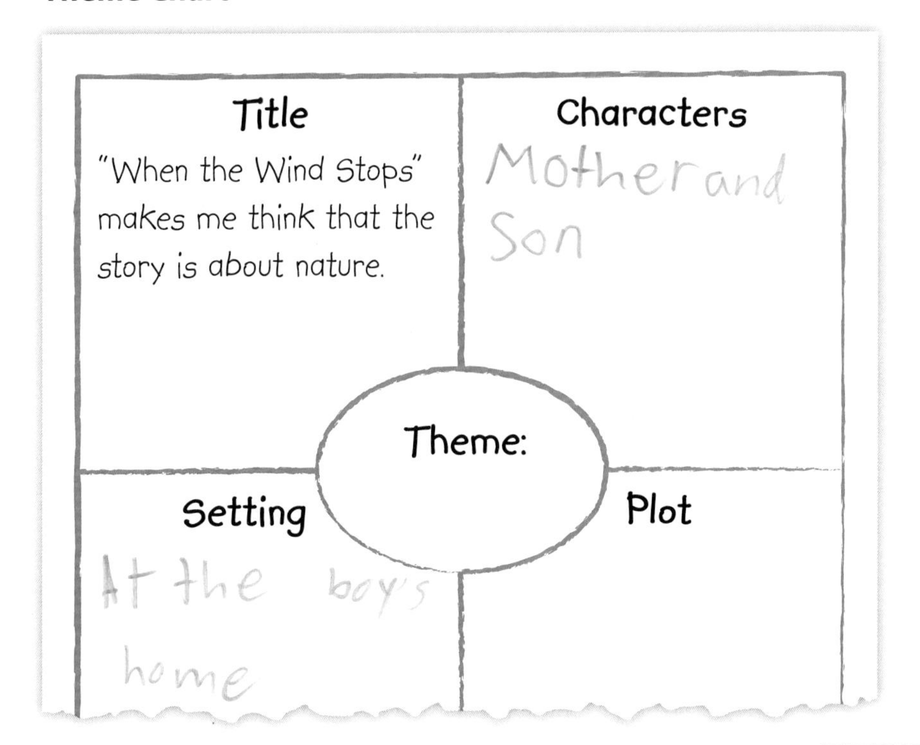

Now use your theme chart. Tell your partner about the theme of "When the Wind Stops."

The theme of the story is ______.

Fluency

Practice reading with the correct expression. Rate your reading.

PART 1 **Word Work**

Antonyms

Antonyms are words with opposite meanings. Look at the pictures below. Read the antonyms. Then compare their meanings.

begin: When something starts, it **begins**.

Day **begins** at sunrise.

end: When something stops, it **ends**.

Day **ends** at sunset.

Try It Together

Read the passage from "When the Wind Stops." Then answer the questions.

> Later, his mother came to say good night. "Why does the **day** have to **end**?" he asked her. "So night can begin," she said. "Look."

1. Find an antonym for **day**. Use it in a sentence.
2. Find an antonym for **end**. Use it in a sentence.

Making Connections Now read this article to find out why some changes in nature happen.

Genre A **science article** is nonfiction. It can tell how something in nature works. It might also have an **experiment** you can try to see how things work.

Day and Night

by Glen Phelan

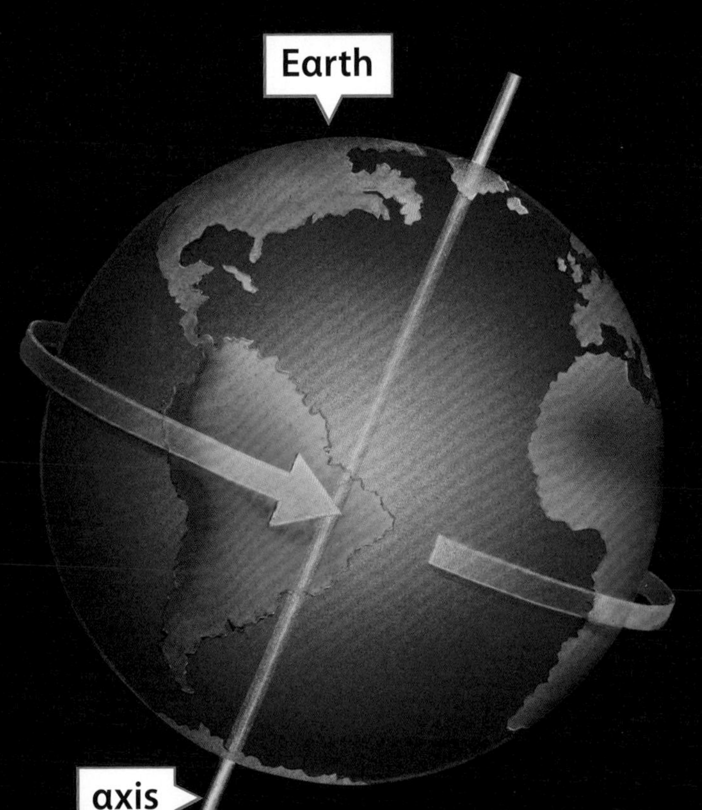

▲ Earth spins on an **imaginary** line. It is called an axis. This diagram shows how.

Around and Around

The **planet** we live on seems to **stand still**, yet Earth is always moving. It rotates, or spins, around and around. You cannot feel Earth rotate because you are moving along with it.

planet world
stand still not move
imaginary pretend

Before You Continue

1. **Use Text Features** How does the diagram help you understand the way **Earth** spins?
2. **Clarify** Why does it seem like Earth is standing still even though the planet is really moving?

Because **Earth** spins, only one part can **face** the sun at a time. When the sun reaches the part facing it, it makes day. The other part of Earth **doesn't** get any sun at that time, so it is **night**.

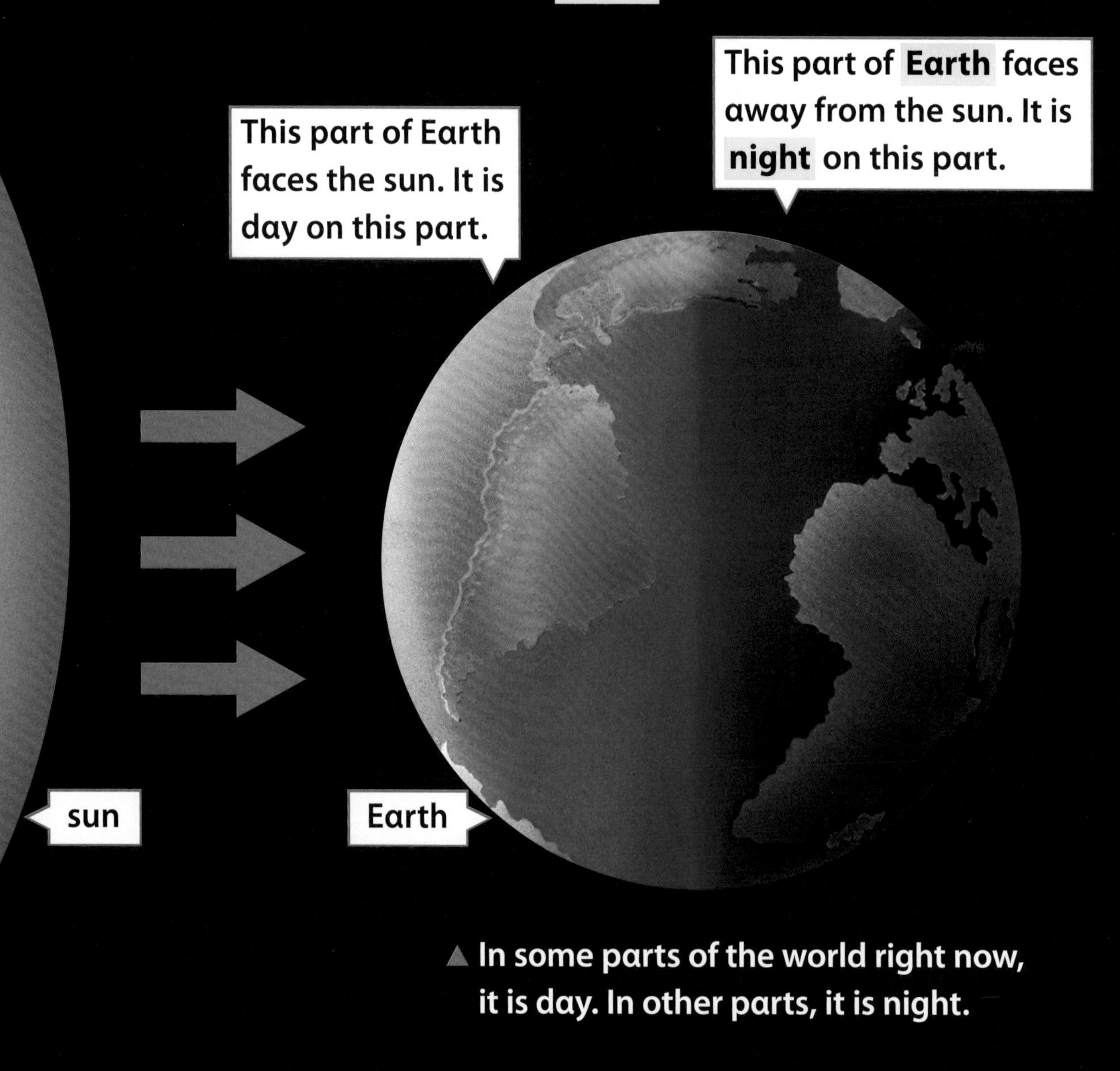

▲ In some parts of the world right now, it is day. In other parts, it is night.

face turn toward
doesn't does not

Sunrise and Sunset

From **Earth**, it looks like the sun moves across the sky. But the sun does not move. Earth moves. When Earth starts to face the sun, the sun looks like it **rises** into the sky. When Earth starts to turn away from the sun, the sun looks like it goes down.

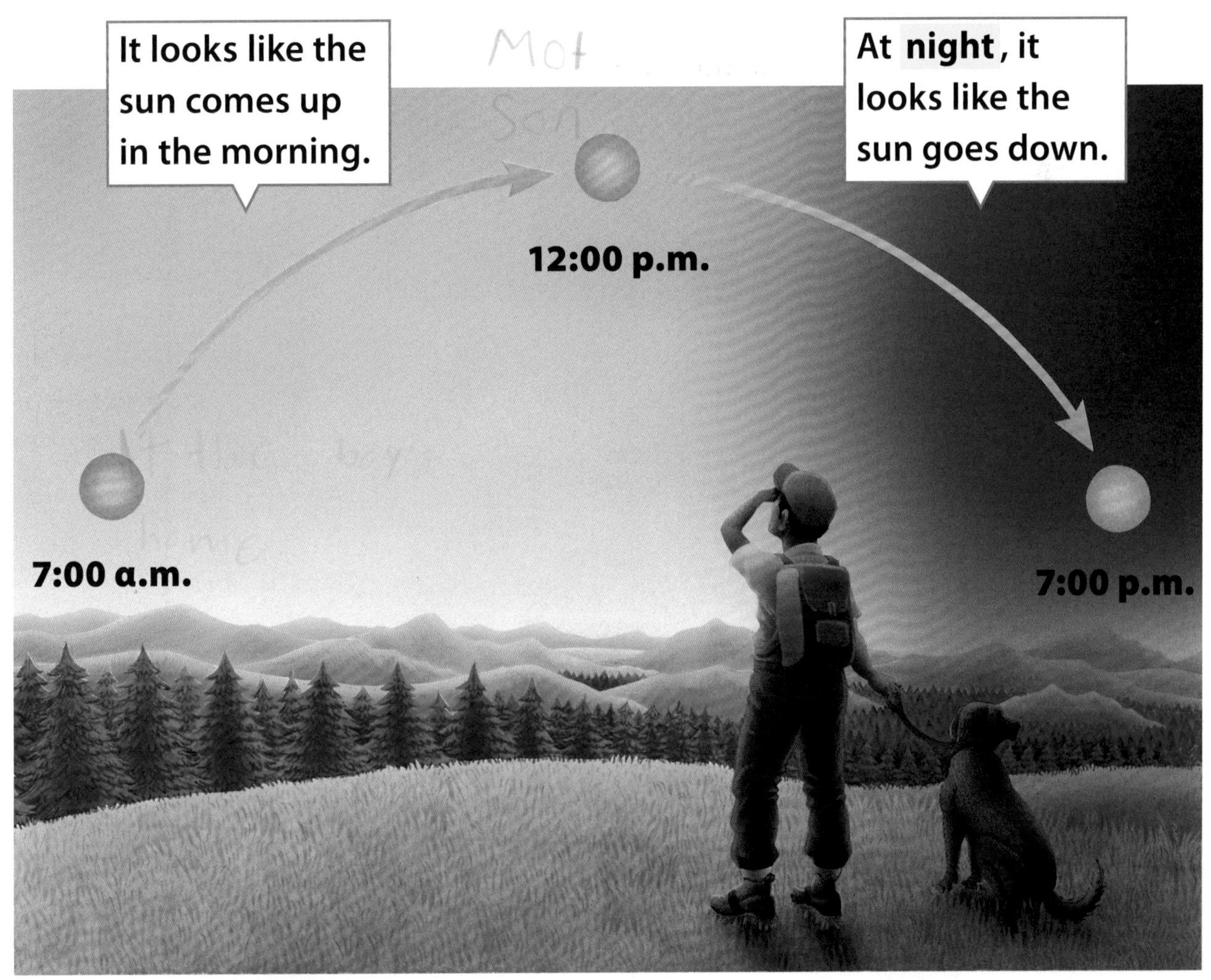

▲ As **Earth** spins, it looks like the sun moves across the sky.

Sunrise When the Sun Comes Up
Sunset When the Sun Goes Down
rises goes up

▸ Before You Continue

1. **Visualize** Point to a spot on land in the diagram. Move your finger up. Describe how the sky looks at that time.
2. **Explain** Why does it look like the sun is moving down in the sky at sunset?

From Day to Night: An Experiment

Try this experiment to see how day turns to **night**.

You will need:

- a partner
- a flashlight
- a ball

1. Partner 1 holds the ball.
2. Partner 2 shines the flashlight on the ball.
3. Partner 2 asks someone to turn off the classroom lights.
4. Partner 1 slowly rotates the ball as Partner 2 shines the light on it.

What Happens?

Light shines on different parts of the ball as it turns. Now pretend the ball is **Earth** and the flashlight is the sun. When one part of Earth faces the sun, it is daytime. When it turns away from the sun, it is **night**. So when day **begins** on your side of the world, night begins for someone on the other side! ❖

In China, it is night. But in the United States, it is day.

Before You Continue

1. **Clarify** How does the experiment help you understand day and night?
2. **Use Text Features** What helps you know what to do in the experiment?

Compare Author's Purpose

The authors of "When the Wind Stops" and "Day and Night" both had more than one reason for writing. **Compare and explain their purposes** to complete the chart.

Comparison Chart

Charlotte Zolotow	Glen Phelan
• to tell about patterns in nature • •	• to explain how day becomes night • •

Write more reasons for writing from "When the Wind Stops" here.

Write more reasons for writing from "Day and Night" here.

Talk Together

What is another **pattern** from the world of nature? Draw a series of pictures to show one of the cycles in nature. Explain your pictures to the class. Use **Key Words**.

Kinds of Sentences

A group of words that tells a complete thought is a sentence. There are four **different kinds of sentences**.

Grammar Rules Kinds of Sentences

• A **statement** tells something. It ends with a **period**.	It is morning. The day is just beginning.
• A **question** asks something. It ends with a **question mark**.	Where did the moon and stars go?
• An **exclamation** shows strong feeling. It ends with an **exclamation mark**.	What a great day!
• A **command** tells someone to do something. It ends with a **period**.	Make your bed, please.

Read Kinds of Sentences

Read this passage. Find two different kinds of sentences. Then make up your own sentence.

> The little boy lay in bed, and his mother sat beside him. "Where does the wind go when it stops?" he asked. "It blows away to make the trees dance somewhere else."

Write Kinds of Sentences

Pretend you are looking out a window at the world. Write two different kinds of sentences about what you see. Read your sentences to a partner.

PART 2 **Language Focus**

Words to Know
and
but
different
have

Make Comparisons

Listen and sing.

Autumn and Winter

Song  

Both autumn **and** winter **have** weather that's colder
Than summer and spring, when warm days are long.
In autumn it's chilly, **but** in winter it's snowy.
In fall, leaves are falling. In winter, they're gone.

I love fall and winter because they are **different**.
In winter we sled, but in autumn, we run.
Both autumn and winter have one thing in common:
Both seasons are favorites for all kinds of fun.

Tune: "Cockles and Mussels"

Science Vocabulary

Key Words

Weather and temperature change with the **seasons**.

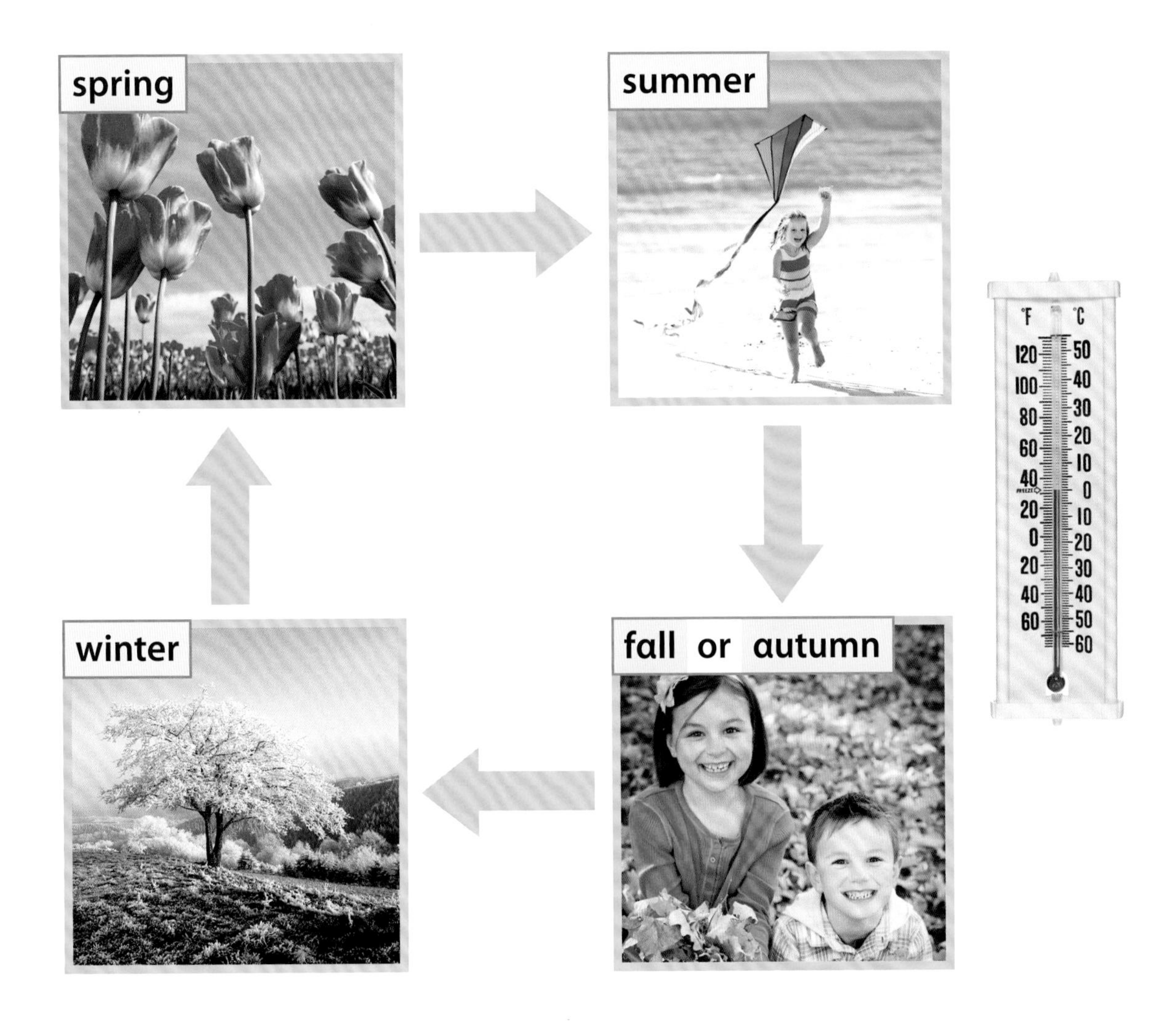

Talk Together

Look at the photos. What happens in each season? What changes with each season?

Compare and Contrast

To **compare**, look for how things are alike. To **contrast**, look for how things are different. Compare and contrast the animals below.

Comparison Chart

Look for how the animals are alike and different.

Talk Together

With your partner, choose two picture cards. Talk about what is the same and what is different. Together, fill in a comparison chart.

More Key Words

affect
verb

The hot sun **affects** ice cream. It makes ice cream melt.

explain
verb

She **explains** the math problem to her student.

happen
verb

They watch what **happens** in the game.

measure
verb

He **measures** the doorway to see how big it is.

reason
noun

Hard work and practice are the **reasons** she is a good musician.

Talk Together

Make a Word Web of examples for each **Key Word**. Compare your webs with a partner's.

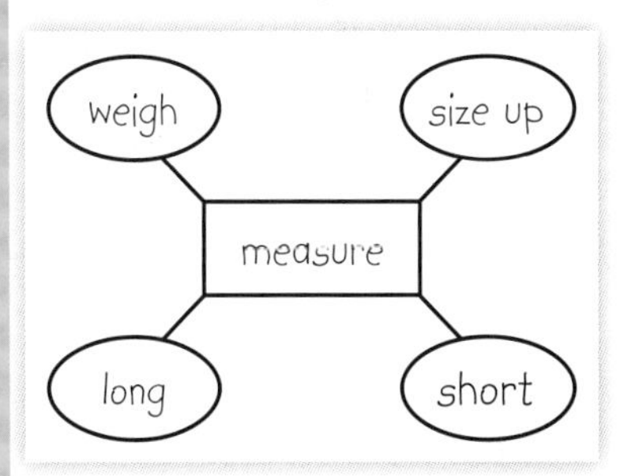

PART 2 **Reading Strategy**

Learn to Visualize

As you read, try to **visualize**, or form pictures in your mind.

Try to **visualize** what Abby and Leon are talking about.

How to Visualize

1. As you read, look for words that describe how things look, sound, smell, taste, and feel.
2. Use the words to create pictures in your mind.
3. Draw the picture. Ask yourself: *How does this help me understand what I read?*

I read ______.

I see ______.

I draw ______. Now I understand ______.

Language Frames

- I read ______ .
- I see ______ .
- I draw ______ . Now I understand ______ .

Talk Together

Read the letter that Leon writes to Abby. Read the sample visualization. Then use **Language Frames** to tell a partner how you visualized things in the letter.

Letter

July 15, 2019

Dear Abby,

The **reason** I am writing is to tell you about my vacation. We are staying in the same beach town we stayed in last **winter**, but it is very different in **summer**. Let me **explain**. On summer mornings, crowds of people flock to the beach to swim. When that **happens**, it's hard to find room to put down a towel!

Sample Visualization

"I read about Leon's vacation at the beach.
I see a sunny, crowded beach.
I draw a white beach crowded with swimmers.
Now I understand why it is hard for Leon to find a place to put his towel."

In winter, clouds often block the sun. The sky is not blue. It is gray. This **affects** the number of tourists who come to the beach. I think the beach looks prettier when there are just a few people.

The two **seasons** at the beach are alike in one way. During both seasons, we buy food at the local market and have fresh fish to cook and eat.

I like both seasons at the beach. I wish you were here in summer!

Your friend,

Leon

= A good place to visualize

PART 2 **Phonics Focus**

Silent Consonants: *gn, kn*

gnome

knee

Listen and Learn

Listen to each sentence. Choose the word with the silent letter *g* or *k* that best completes the sentence.

1. The ______ told us to stop.

know
sign
knock

2. He is able to tie a strong ______.

knife
gnat
knot

3. The paper has pretty ______.

knits
signs
designs

4. Turn the ______ and open the door.

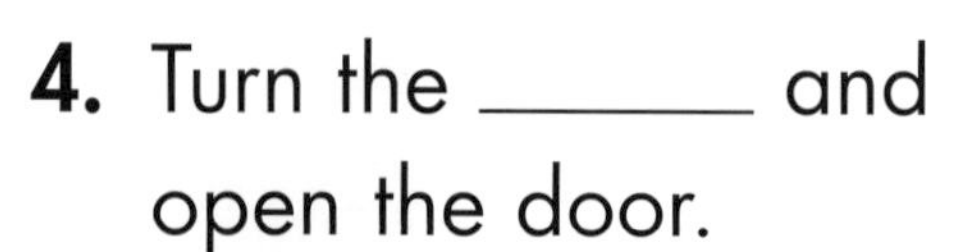

knob
kneel
knew

Talk Together

Listen and read. Find the words with silent letters *g* or *k*.

Over to You

Which Season Is Best?

Which season do you like best? Do you know? In summer, it's nice and warm. Everything is green. You can go swimming. You can play in the park. But maybe you live where it gets really hot. Maybe you don't like all that heat. Then you might like a different season.

In some places, snow can cover your yard in winter. People can ski and ice-skate. That's fun. But winter can get very cold. A cold wind can feel like the cut of a knife. Other places get a lot of rain in winter. All that rain or snow might make you gnash your teeth. In that case, you might like spring or autumn. They are not too hot or too cold. Spring means new buds on trees. It means cute birds in nests. Falling leaves are a sign that it's autumn.

Weather can affect your mood. Do you know which season makes you feel the happiest?

Work with a partner.

Find the words with silent *g* or silent *k*. Take turns using the words in oral sentences.

Read "Which Season Is Best?" with a partner. Practice reading words with silent letters *g* and *k*.

Read a Poem

Genre

A **poem** uses words in a special way to tell about ideas. This poem gives facts about the seasons.

Text Features

A **diagram** uses pictures, arrows, and labels to show how something works.

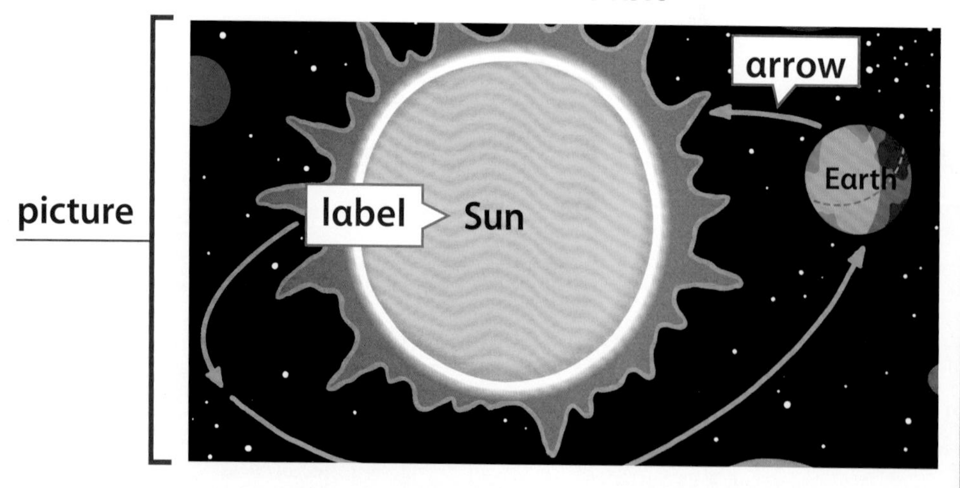

What Makes the Seasons?

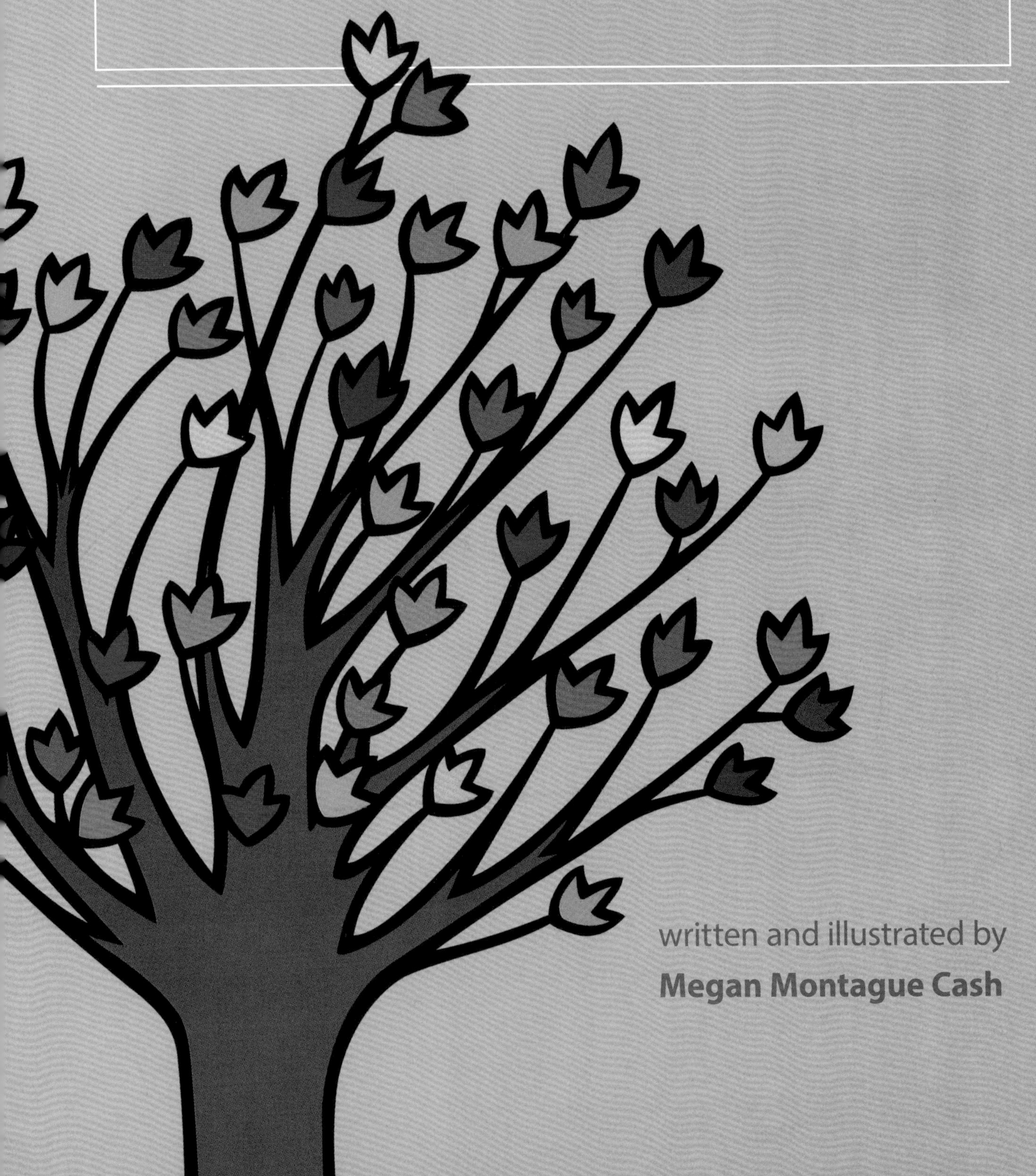

written and illustrated by

Megan Montague Cash

▸ **Set a Purpose**

Find out what **happens** when the **seasons** change.

The day began with sprinkling rain

tapping at the windowpane.

Rain has turned the sky to gray.

Our snowman friend has gone away.

Fresh green leaves are peeking out.

What makes this their time to **sprout**?

tapping at the windowpane hitting against the window

sprout begin to grow

Spring's mild weather wakes the seeds,

bringing **showers** each seed needs.

Spring was here but couldn't stay.

Spring left on a **summer** day.

mild warm and wet
wakes the seeds gets the seeds ready to grow
showers rain

Plants that once were **hardly there**

now have flowers everywhere.

Each tree and weed and lima bean

shows its favorite **shade** of green.

hardly there very small
shade kind

Why is this a growing **season**?

Plants grow tall, but **what's the reason**?

Plants grow best in **summer** light,

when days are long and warm and bright.

what's the reason why do the plants grow tall

Before You Continue

1. **Details** What **happens** in **spring**? What happens in **summer**? How can you **measure** the changes?
2. **Visualize** Look at the pictures. Tell how summer feels, looks, and smells.

▸ Predict

What will **happen** when the **summer** is over?

But when the **summer** days are done,

the **autumn** days have just begun.

The sun **grows dim**, the wind blows cold.

Green leaves turn to red and gold.

The colored leaves **dance all around**.

But why do leaves fall to the ground?

grows dim is not as bright

dance all around move in the wind

In all the leaves on all the trees

are **teeny tree food factories**.

Leaves use sun to make the food.

When there's less sun, leaves **come unglued**.

teeny tree food factories small parts that make food for the tree

come unglued fall from the tree

The **weather** brought a change last night.

Winter turned the world to white.

Puffy flakes swirled high and low.

Snow makes **flurries**. What makes snow?

In chilly clouds the raindrops **freeze**.

It's one of winter's recipes.

flurries snowflakes that blow around in the wind

freeze turn cold and hard

It's one of winter's recipes. It is something that **happens** in **winter**.

Winter is a time for sleep.

Trees are resting. Seeds will keep.

Many **creatures** sleep and wait.

Winter's time to **hibernate**.

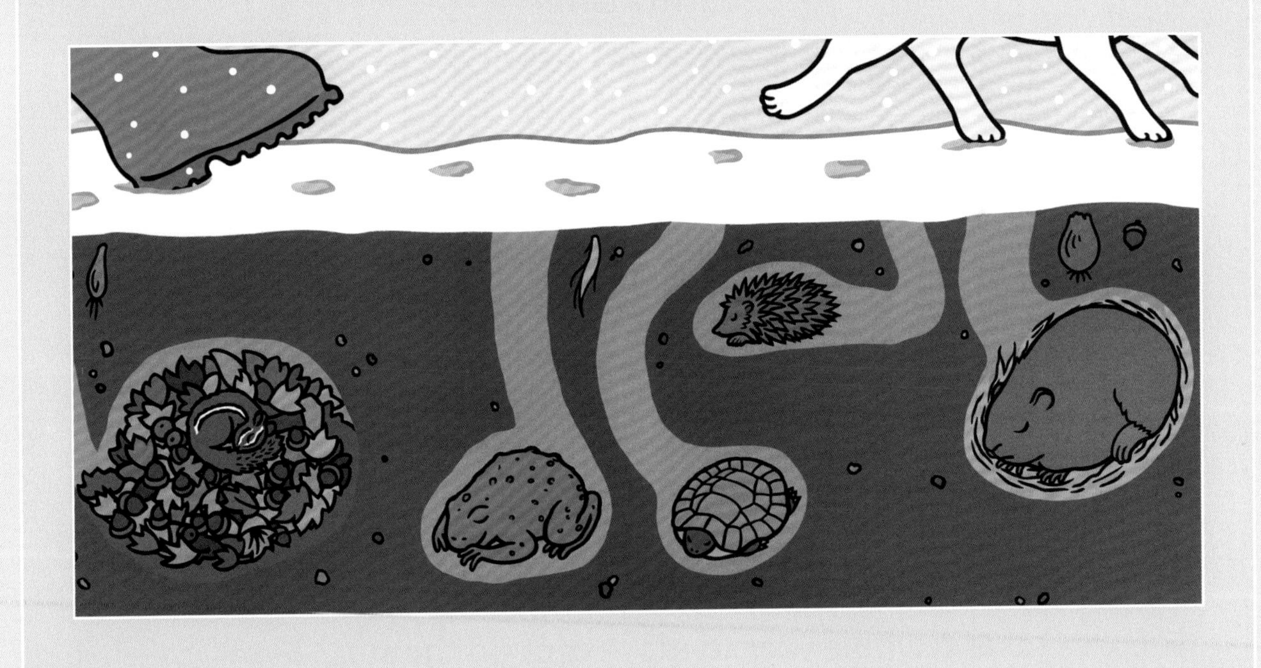

creatures animals and insects
Winter's Winter is
hibernate sleep until **spring** comes again

Before You Continue

1. **Confirm Prediction** What **happens** in the poem when **summer** is over? Was your prediction correct?
2. **Visualize** Think about the snowflakes. Which words in the poem help you picture and feel them?

Predict

Look at the diagram below. What causes the seasons to change?

But what **controls** the **season's** change?

And what makes **weather rearrange**?

Earth's yearly trip around the sun

affects the seasons one by one.

Earth's Orbit

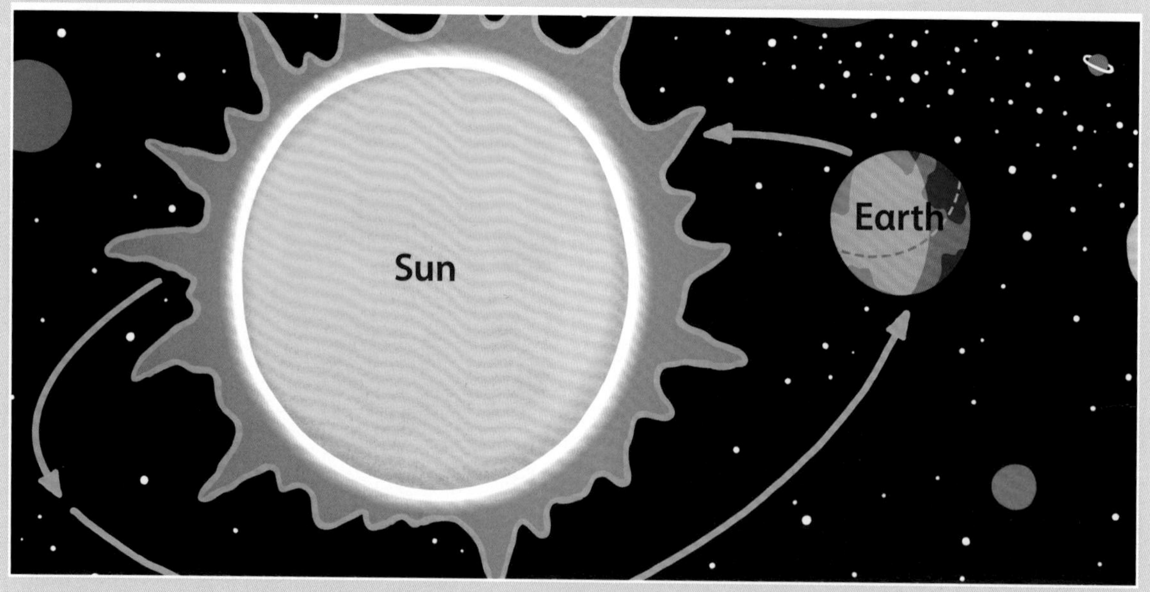

▲ Earth takes a whole year to move around the sun.

controls makes; causes
rearrange change from **season** to season
Orbit Path Around the Sun

In **summer** when the days are long

the sun shines down both hot and strong.

While **winter** has the shortest days —

less time for Earth to get **warm rays**.

warm rays sunshine

Earth's Hemispheres

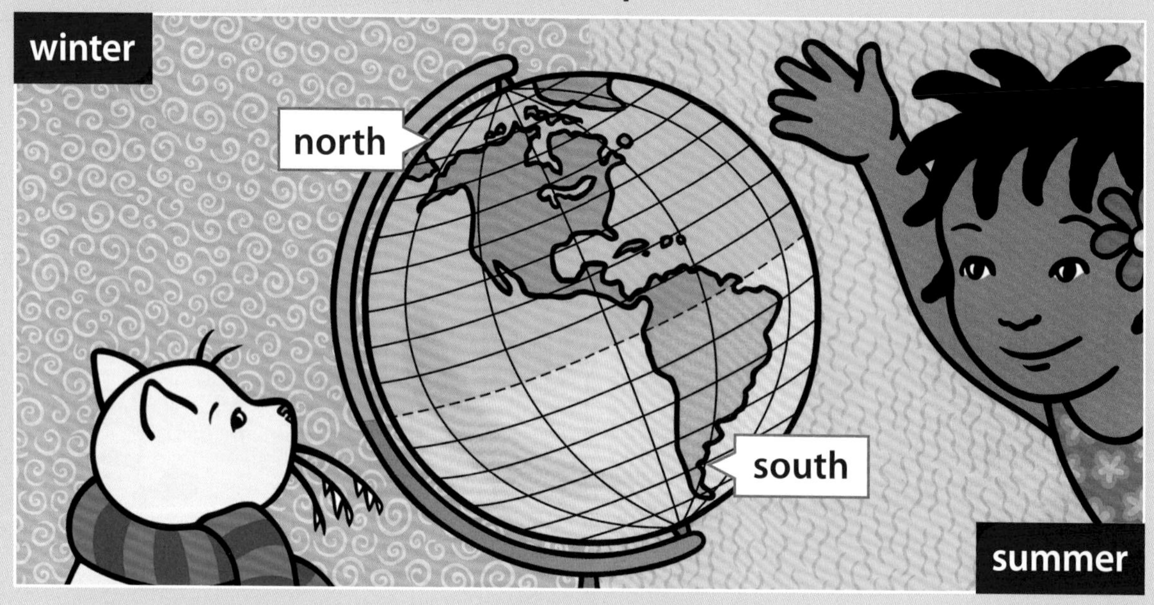

But when you have a **summer** day,

it's **winter half the world away**.

If summer **blossoms** open wide,

it's winter on Earth's other side.

Earth's Hemispheres The Two Main Parts of Earth

half the world away on the other side of Earth

blossoms flowers

Seasons change four times a year.

When each one ends, **the next one's here**.

Enjoying changes one by one

makes the seasons so much fun. ❖

the next one's here another **season** begins

Before You Continue

1. **Confirm Prediction** What causes the seasons to change?
2. **Make Comparisons** Find words in the poem about how **summer** and **winter** are different. Describe each season to a partner.

Talk About It 

1. **Poems** use words in an interesting way. Find your favorite lines in the poem. What do you find interesting about them?

   I like it when the author says, "____."
   It is interesting because ____.

2. **Compare** the **weather** in **spring** and **summer**. How is it alike? How is it different? Give examples from the text.

   Spring and summer are alike because ____.
   They are different because spring weather is ____, but summer weather is ____.

3. Tell about a **season**. Use words from the poem to help a partner picture it. Have a partner guess the season.

   In this season, I see ____. *I hear ____.*
   The season is ____.

Write About It

Work with a partner to write a poem about your favorite season. Tell how the season looks, sounds, feels, smells, and tastes.

> **Autumn** *looks ____.*
> *It sounds ____.*
> *It smells ____.*

Compare and Contrast

Think about the ideas in "What Makes the Seasons?" How are the **seasons** alike? How are they different?

Comparison Chart

	Spring	Summer	Fall	Winter
Leaves	sprout			
Raindrops	fall			
Snow	melts			
Days	get longer			

Now use your comparison chart. Tell your partner how the seasons are alike and different in "What Makes the Seasons?"

Spring and summer are alike because ______.
Winter and spring are different because ______.

Fluency

Practice reading with the correct intonation. Rate your reading.

PART 2 Word Work

Multiple-Meaning Words

Some words have **more than one meaning**. You can use other words near the word to figure out the right meaning.

Fall is a multiple-meaning word. Look at these examples.

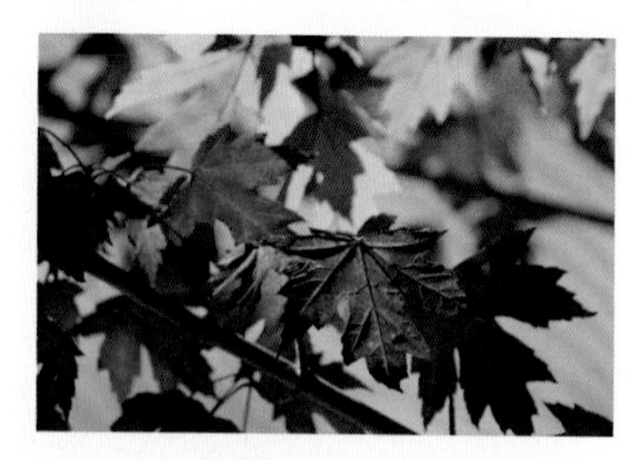

In the **fall**, the leaves change colors.
Meaning: the season before winter

Be careful not to **fall**!

Meaning: to trip or slip

Try It Together

Read this passage. Then answer the questions.

In the **spring**, my family always plants a garden. First, we put the seeds in the ground. After a while, new plants **spring** up from the dirt!

1. What does **spring** mean in the first sentence?
2. What does **spring** mean in the third sentence: "a season" or "grow quickly"?

Making Connections Read about an amazing change that **happens** to some frogs each **winter**.

Genre A **science article** is nonfiction. It can **explain** something about nature.

NATIONAL GEOGRAPHIC EXCLUSIVE

A Winter Wonder

by ***Tyrone Hayes, PhD***

Hi! My name is Dr. Tyrone Hayes. I **study** frogs and toads. I work in a **lab** and sometimes in muddy ponds.

Dr. Tyrone Hayes studies frogs and toads. ▶

study learn about

lab special room where scientists work ▶

▶ Before You Continue

1. **Visualize** What do you think Dr. Hayes feels, smells, and hears when he is at work?
2. **Make Inferences** How do you think Dr. Hayes feels about his work? **Explain**.

We know that **weather** changes with each **season**. Did you know that some frogs change with the seasons, too?

Winter can be a hard season for frogs. It's so cold that many ponds **freeze**. Insects that frogs eat can be hard to find, too.

But winter is no problem for the North American wood frog! It has **an unusual** way to survive the **harsh** winter. Each winter, the wood frog lets its body freeze. Then it sleeps all winter long.

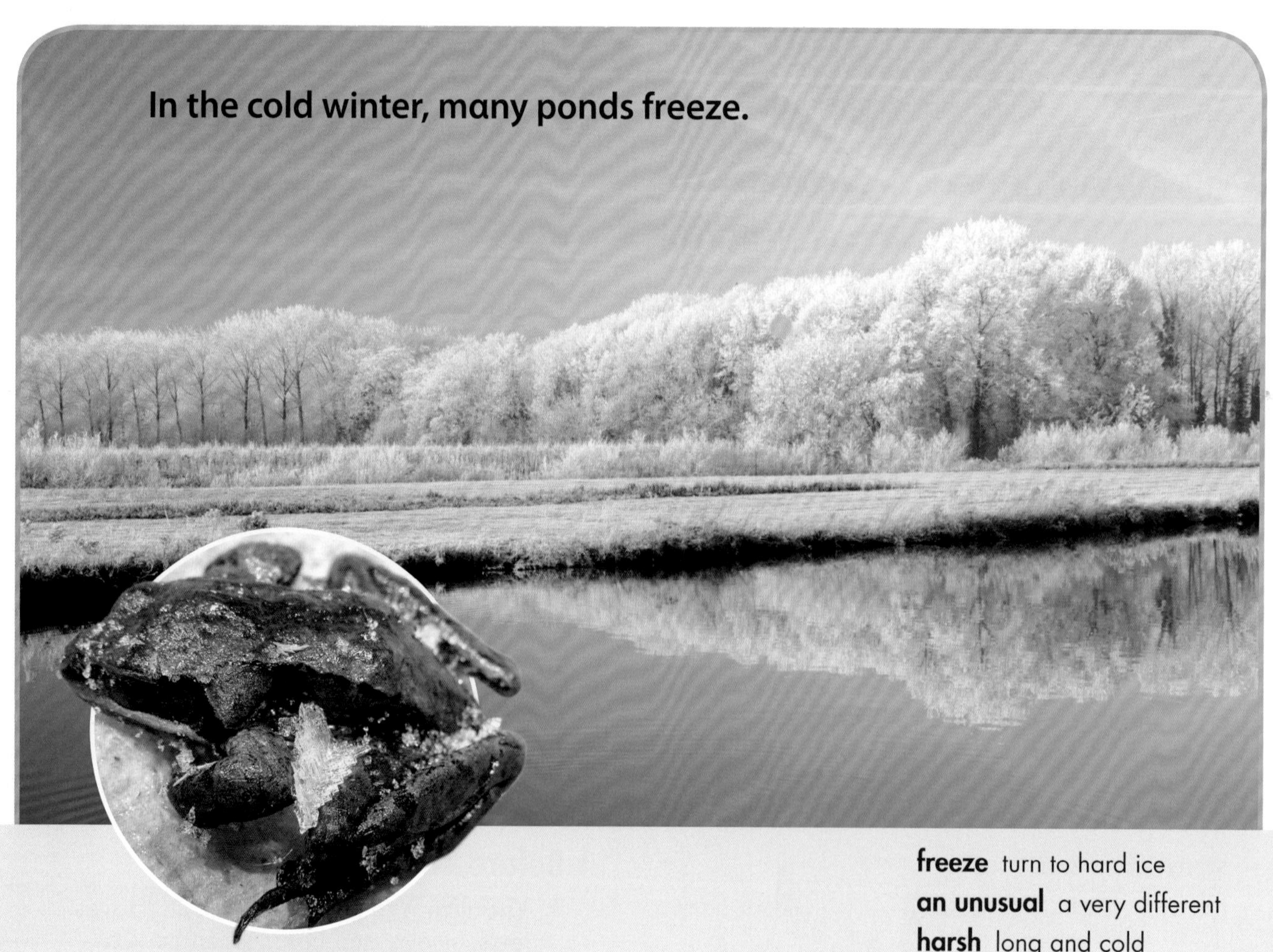

In the cold winter, many ponds freeze.

▲ A North American wood frog freezes each **winter**.

freeze turn to hard ice
an unusual a very different
harsh long and cold

Soon the warm **spring** comes. That's when the frog wakes up! **Its body thaws.** Then it hops away until **winter** comes again.

This **unique** frog is **truly amazing**! ❖

In the **spring**, the wood frog wakes up again. ▶

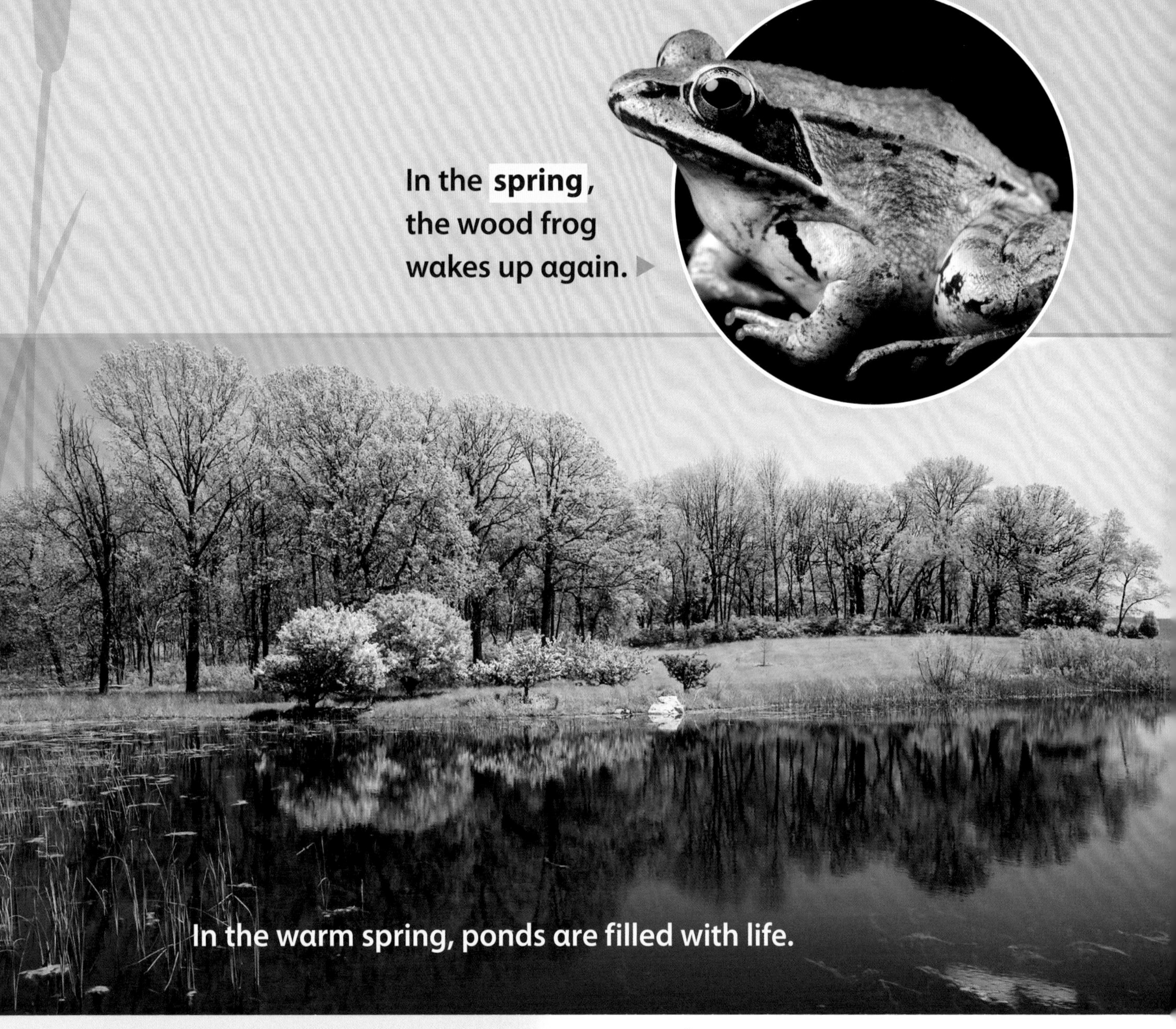

In the warm spring, ponds are filled with life.

Its body thaws. The ice on its body melts.
unique special
truly amazing very surprising

▶ Before You Continue

1. **Make Comparisons** Look at the photos on pages 64–65. Tell how the pictures are the same and how they are different.
2. **Main Idea** What is so unusual about the wood frog?

PART 2 **Respond and Extend**

Compare Genres

"What Makes the Seasons?" is a poem. "A Winter Wonder" is a science article. How are the two texts the same? How are they different? Work with a partner to complete the Venn diagram.

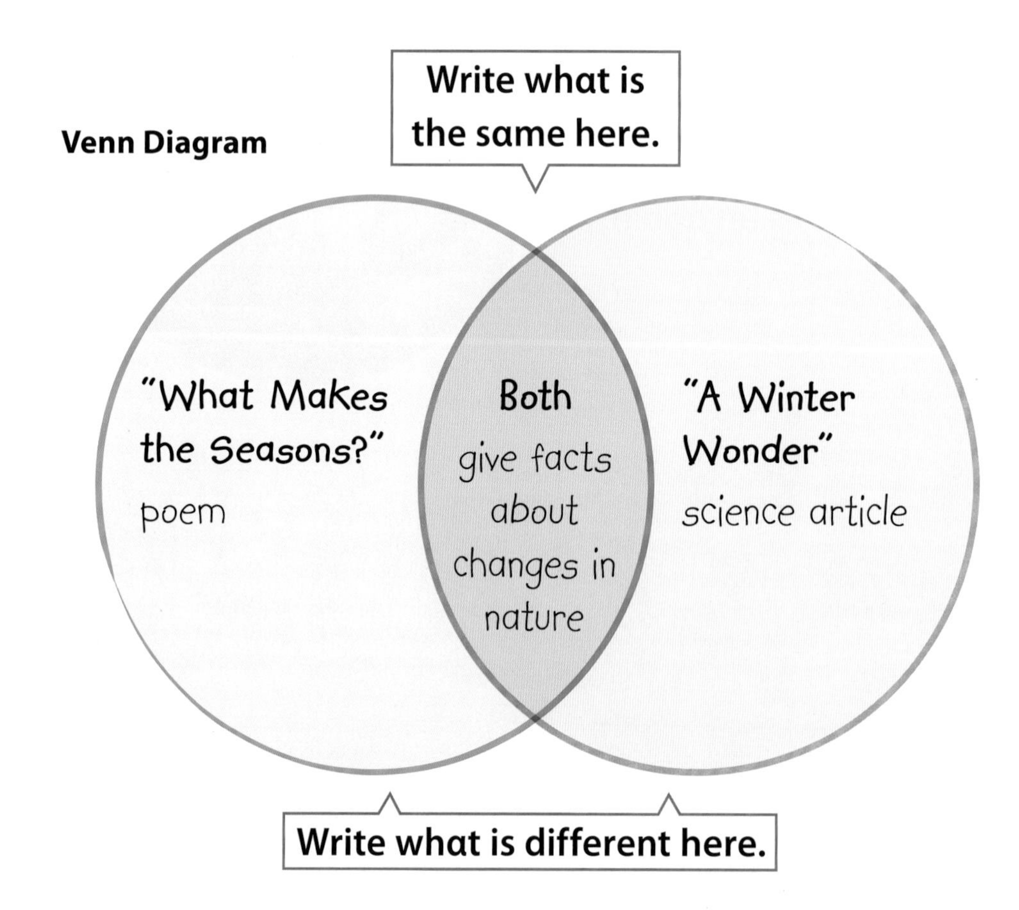

Talk Together

Why is nature always changing? Take turns choosing picture cards with a partner. Use **Key Words** to **explain** what **happens** during the **season** on the card you picked.

Questions

You can ask **questions** to get information. All questions begin with a capital letter and end with a question mark.

Grammar Rules Questions

	Question	Answer
• Some questions ask for a "yes" or "no" answer.	Is it spring yet? Is the plant growing?	Yes, it is. Yes.
• Some questions ask for more information. • A question can start with **who**, **when**, **where**, **what**, or **how**.	**Who** can tell me about the seasons? **When** will autumn end? **Where** can we go this summer?	The teacher can tell you about the seasons. Autumn will end in November. We can go to the beach this summer.

Read Questions

Read these sentences. Name the sentences that ask questions. How do you know?

Why is this a growing season?
Plants grow tall, but what's the reason?
Plants grow best in summer light,
when days are long and warm and bright.

Write Questions

Write two questions about seasons. Ask a partner your questions.

Writing Project

Write as an Observer

Write a Comparison 

What are the seasons like where you live? Write a few paragraphs to compare or contrast two seasons. Work with your classmates to create a book of seasons.

Study a Model

When you compare, you tell how two things are the same. When you contrast, you tell how they are different. Read Andy's comparison of his two favorite seasons.

My Favorite Seasons

By Andy Halliday

I live near Dallas, Texas. My favorite seasons here are **fall and spring**.

The **topic sentence** tells the two things you are comparing or contrasting.

The temperature during **both** seasons is great. It's usually in the 70s. That's not too hot and not too cold. It's perfect!

The weather during spring is a little **different** from the weather in fall. In spring, we get storms, with lots of wind, thunder, and lightning. Once in a while, there's even a tornado!

Details are organized to show how the seasons are the same and different.

In the fall, we don't get storms or tornadoes. We get football, **though**. That's just as exciting!

Special words help you signal what is the same or different.

Prewrite

1. **Choose a Topic** Which seasons will you write about? Talk with a partner to make your choice.

Language Frames	
Tell Your Ideas	**Respond to Ideas**
My favorite ______ are ______.	Why are ______ and ______ your favorite ______?
The two ______ are alike because they both ______.	What other things are alike?
The ______ are different because ______.	You said ______ and ______ are alike, but I think they're different because ______.

2. **Gather Information** Think of all the ways the two seasons are alike and different. Make notes to gather details.

3. **Get Organized** Put your ideas in a comparison chart.

Comparison Chart

	Fall	Spring
Temperature	in the 70s	in the 70s
Weather	thunderstorms	sunny weather
Sports	football	volleyball

Draft

Use your comparison chart to write your draft.

- Write a topic sentence that tells the two things you are comparing.
- Arrange your details so that the comparison is clear. You can tell about one season first, and then the other. You can also put details about the same things together, like Andy did.

Writing Project, continued

Revise

1. **Read, Retell, Respond** Read your draft aloud to a partner. Your partner listens and then retells the main details. Next, talk about ways to make your writing better.

Language Frames	
Retell	**Make Suggestions**
The ______ you compared are ______ and ______.	I'm still not sure why you say ______ and ______ are alike. Can you add more details?
The ______ are alike because ______.	The order you put the details in doesn't seem to make sense. Try moving ______ to ______.
The ______ are different because ______.	

2. **Make Changes** Think about your draft and your partner's ideas. Then use revision marks to make your changes.

- Do you include enough details? Add more if you need them.

> with lots of wind, thunder, and lightning.
> In spring, we get storms.^

- Make sure the comparison is clear. Check the order of your details.

> The temperature during both seasons is great. It's usually in the 70s. (We get tornadoes in the spring, though.)
> Move this to next paragraph.

Edit and Proofread

Work with a partner to edit and proofread your comparison. Be sure you use the correct end marks for different kinds of sentences. Use revision marks to show your changes.

Punctuation Tip

When you write about temperature, do not use an apostrophe.

70s, not 70's

Present

On Your Own Make a final copy of your comparison. Read it aloud to your class. See if they agree with how you described the seasons.

Presentation Tips	
If you are the speaker...	**If you are the listener...**
Stress comparison words such as *both*, *alike*, and *also*.	Summarize how the two subjects are alike and different.
If your listeners don't agree with your comparison, give more details or examples.	Is it clear how the subjects are alike or different? If not, ask questions.

With a Group Collect names of friends and family members who live in other cities or states. Send them your comparisons. Ask them to write back and tell you how similar or different their own seasons are to yours. Share what you find out.

Talk Together

In this unit, you found lots of answers to the **Big Question**. Now, use your concept map to discuss the **Big Question** with the class.

Concept Map

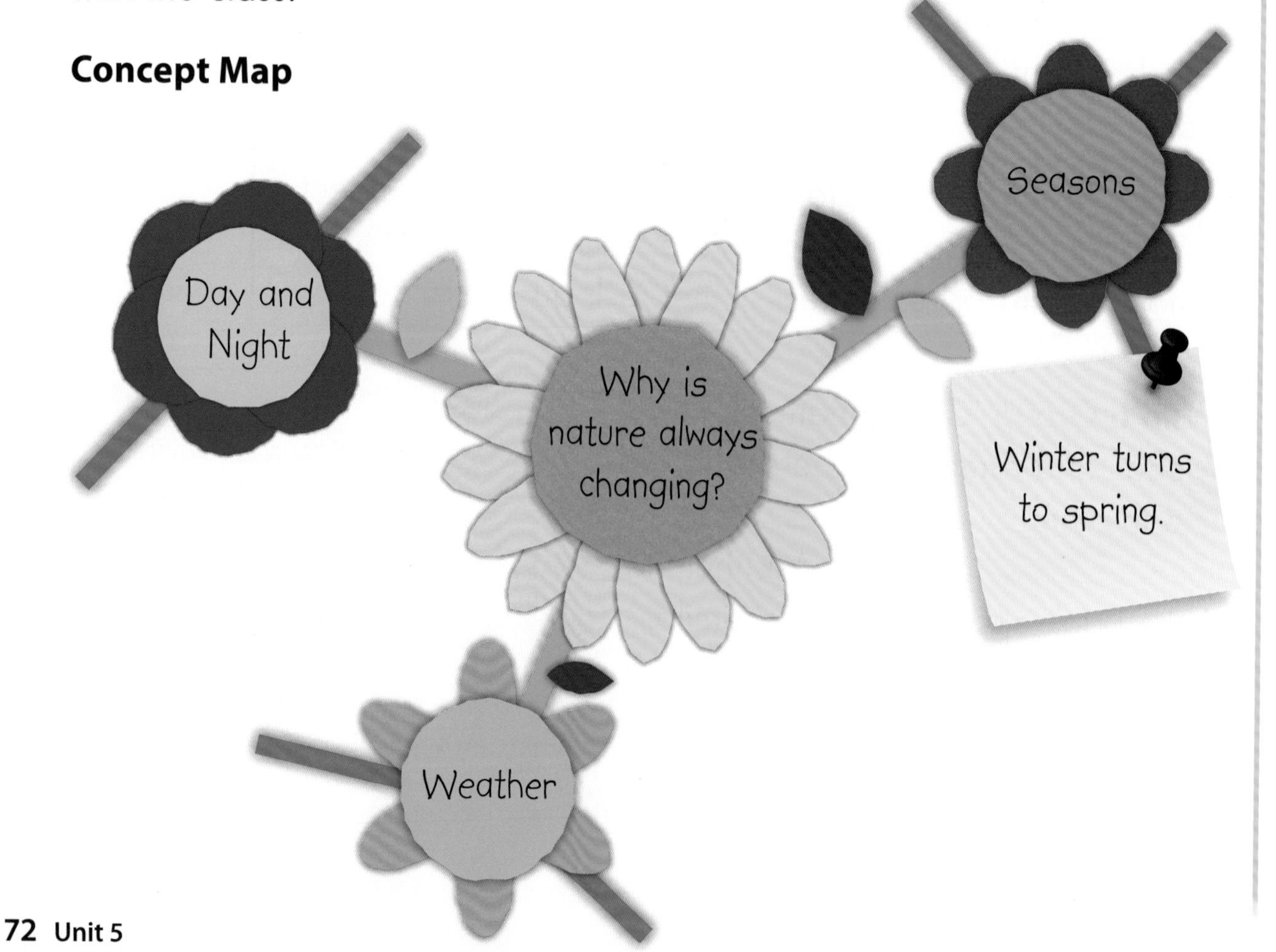

Share Your Ideas

Choose one of these ways to share your ideas about the **Big Question**.

Write It!

Draw a Cartoon

Show what happens during the four seasons. Use one box for each season. Write what happens in each box. Share your cartoon with the class.

It is hot in summer.

Talk About It!

Discuss Nature Topics

On scraps of paper, write ways that nature changes. Put the topics in a box or hat. Take turns choosing topics and discussing them with a partner. Be sure to listen to your partner and speak clearly.

Do It!

Perform a Mime

Work with classmates to create a mime about a way that nature changes. Perform your skit for the class. Have classmates guess what you are miming.

Write It!

Write a Nature Log

Write about changes in nature that you see in the morning, in the middle of day, and at night. Write them in your log. Share with the class.

Unit 6

Better Together

BIG Question Why is it good to work together?

TARRAGONA, SPAIN
A team of castellers joining forces to build a human tower

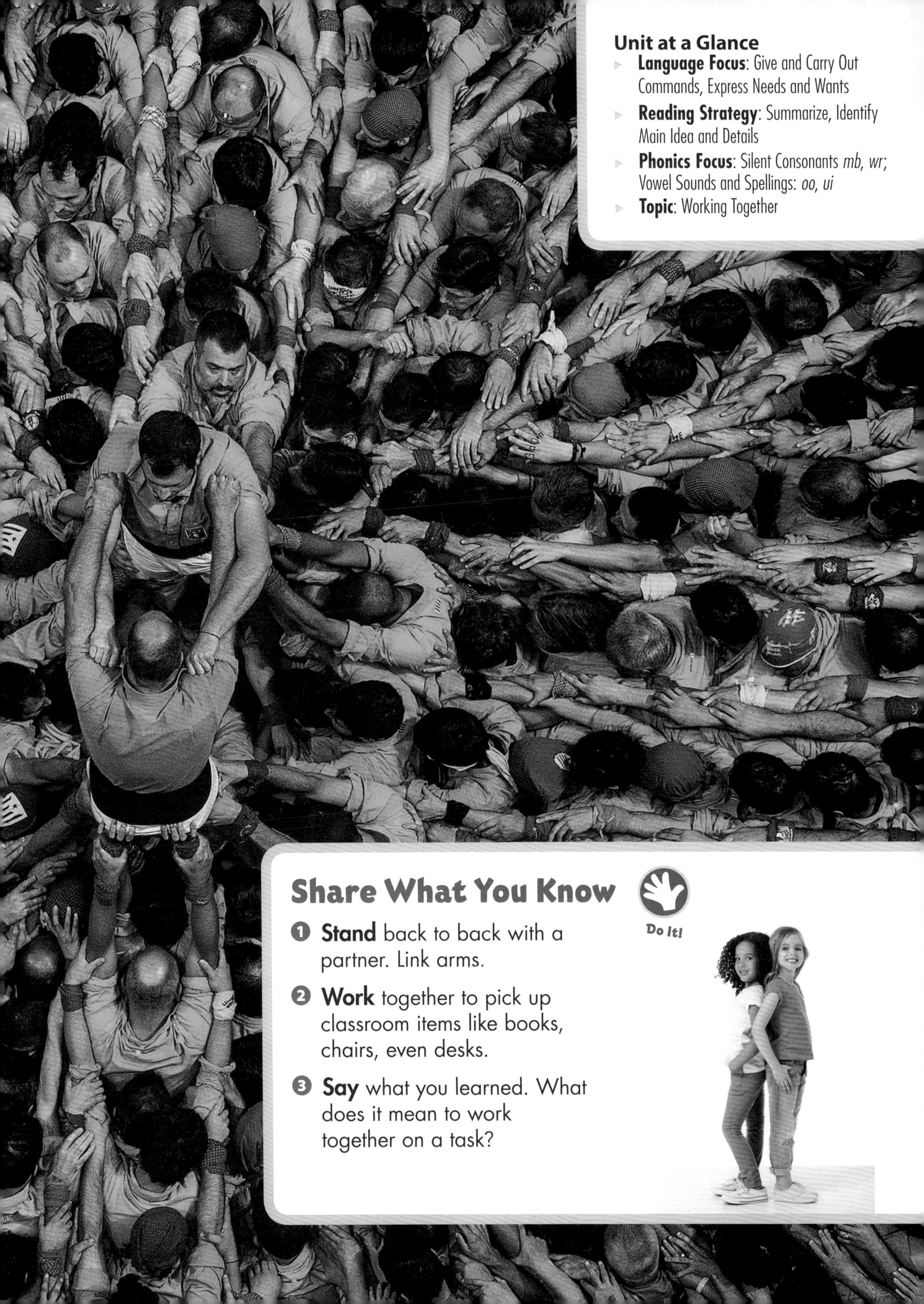

Unit at a Glance

- **Language Focus**: Give and Carry Out Commands, Express Needs and Wants
- **Reading Strategy**: Summarize, Identify Main Idea and Details
- **Phonics Focus**: Silent Consonants *mb, wr*; Vowel Sounds and Spellings: *oo, ui*
- **Topic**: Working Together

Share What You Know

Do It!

1. **Stand** back to back with a partner. Link arms.
2. **Work** together to pick up classroom items like books, chairs, even desks.
3. **Say** what you learned. What does it mean to work together on a task?

PART 1 **Language Focus**

Words to Know
find
take
turn

Give and Carry Out Commands

Listen and read along.

Poem 

Teamwork

Find a trash bag, maybe two.
One for me and one for you.
Take some gloves and put them on.
Pick up trash until it's gone!
Turn and look beneath each tree
And all around until you see
That teamwork helps to get things done
And helps make worktime lots of fun!

Key Words

How does teamwork help our community and **society**?

Team members work **together**.

Sometimes, we work **alone**.

We use **teamwork** to get the job done.

Talk Together

Talk in a group about a class project. When do people choose to work together? When is it good to work alone?

Story Elements

Use a story map to tell about the **characters**, **setting**, and **plot** of a story.

Story Map

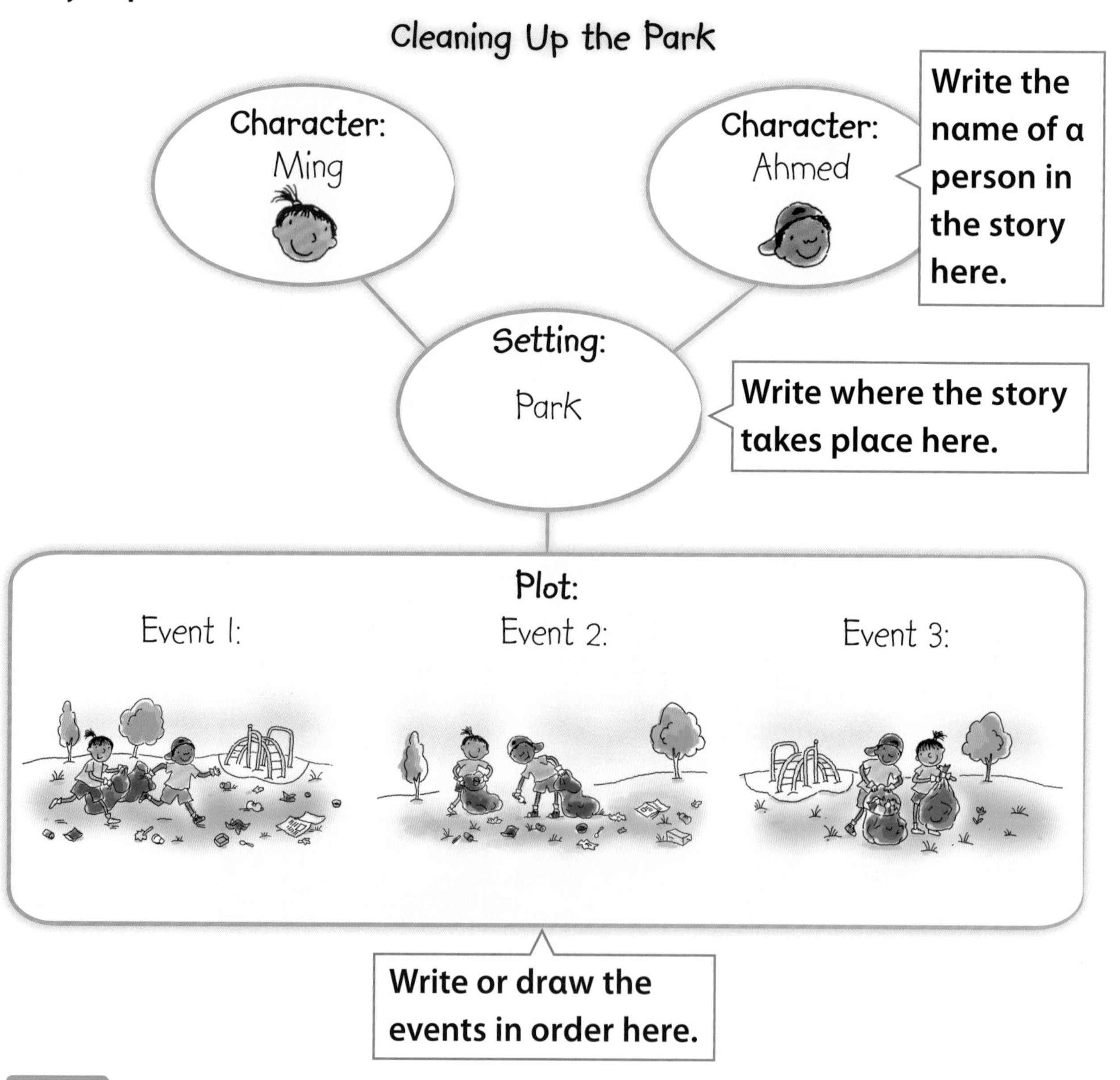

Talk Together

Tell your partner a story about being part of a team. Fill out a story map together.

Academic Vocabulary

More Key Words

add
verb

When you **add** things to a group, you make the group bigger.

cooperate
verb

Two girls **cooperate** with each other to plant trees.

enough
adjective

There is just **enough** milk to fill the glass.

possible
adjective

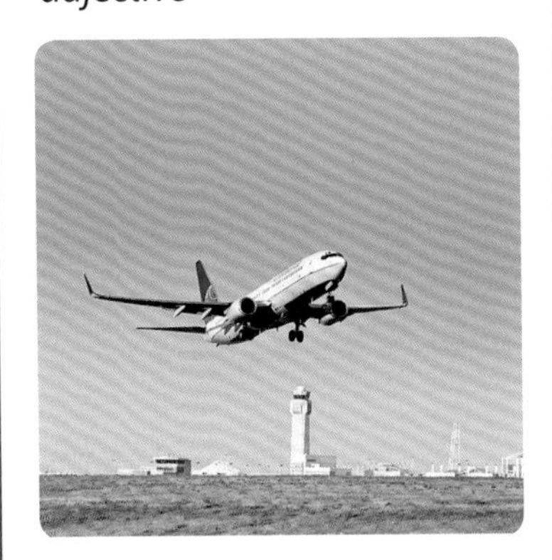

Airplanes make it **possible** for people to fly.

share
verb

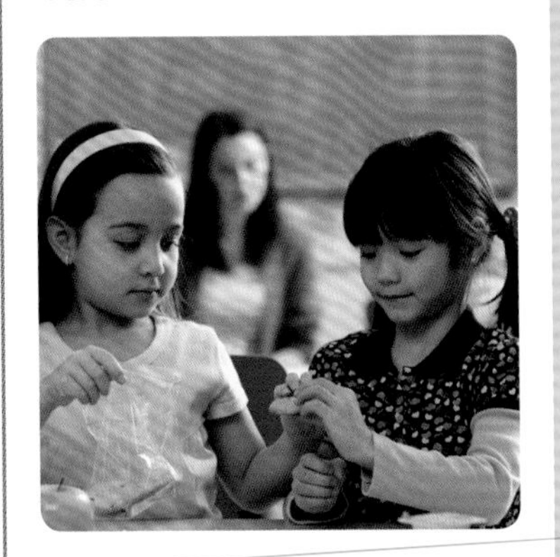

It is nice to **share** food with others. The two girls **share** their lunch.

Talk Together

Make a drawing that shows the meaning for each **Key Word**. Then share your drawings with a partner.

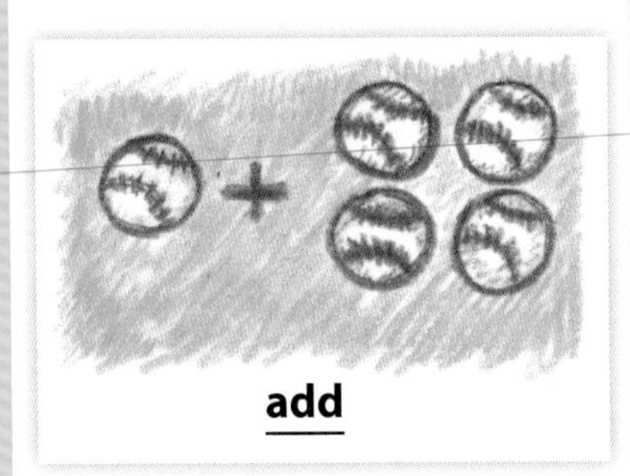

Learn to Summarize

How can you remember important ideas? A good way to do this is to **summarize** information.

Helping People Is Easy

Ming and Ahmed see that the woman needs help.

Ming and Ahmed help her and have fun.

When you **summarize**, you retell the important ideas. Use your own words.

How to Summarize

	**1.** Look at the text and pictures. Look for details.	*I see and read _____.*
	2. Ask yourself: *Which details are the most important?*	The important details are _____.
	3. Tell the important details in your own words.	I say in my own words _____.

Talk Together

Read Ming's description and the sample summary. Then summarize the next part of the text. Use **Language Frames** to tell your partner your summary.

Language Frames

- I see and read ______.
- The important details are ______.
- I say in my own words ______.

Description

Helping Is Fun

Yesterday morning, Ahmed and I were on our way to clean up the park. We saw a woman pushing a crying baby in a stroller. It hardly seemed **possible**, but she was holding two grocery bags, too.

Ahmed said, "Let's try to help."

We walked over to her. "I don't think you have **enough** arms for all that. I'll take the grocery bags," Ahmed said, laughing. "But why don't you rest first?"

"Here are some crackers you can **share** with the baby," the woman said.

I opened the box and offered one to the baby.

"Have some more," I said. The baby began to smile.

Sample Summary

"I see and read that the woman needs help. The important details are she carries a lot, the baby cries, and Ming and Ahmed want to help. I say in my own words that Ming and Ahmed stop to help the woman. Ahmed takes the bags and Ming amuses the baby."

We started to walk. "I have to turn here at the corner," said the woman.

"Don't worry," I said. "We can help you bring your groceries home."

The baby began to laugh. "I think the baby will **cooperate** now," I **added**, laughing.

= A good place to summarize

PART 1 **Phonics Focus**

Silent Consonants: *mb, wr*

lamb

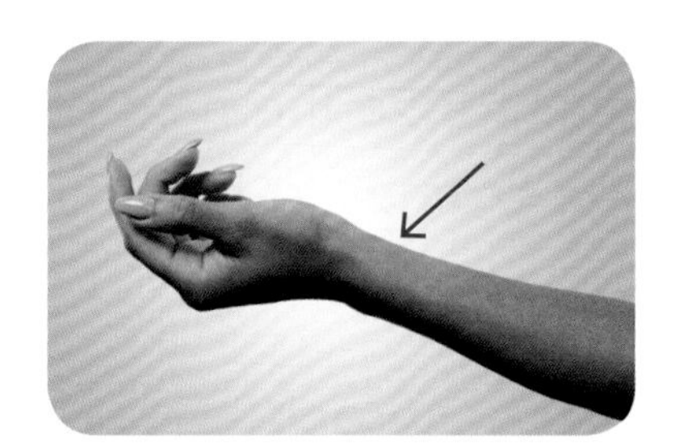
wrist

Listen and Learn

Listen to the picture words. Choose the correct word for each picture.

1. 
brand plum climb

2. 
ranch write waste

3. 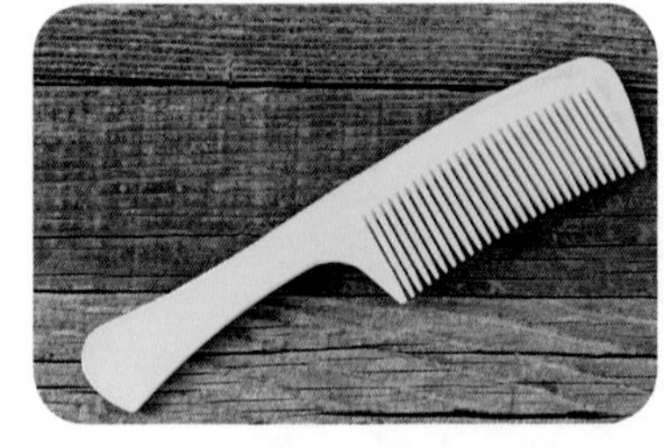
team comb knob

4. 
wren while rest

Use one of the words above to complete the sentence.

I ______ my hair every morning.

Talk Together

Listen and read. Find the words with the silent letter pairs *mb* and *wr*.

Over to You

Zoos Working Together

A day at the zoo is fun. You can see lambs and lions. You can see a monkey on the limb of a tree. You can see a wren on another limb.

Zoos are more than fun places to visit. Zoos work to save animals. They work to keep animals healthy. Zoos can't do this work alone. They turn to other zoos for help. They also turn to people like you and me.

Zoos cooperate with each other. They share animals. This helps the animals have healthy babies.

People can find out about the zoos. They can find out what it takes to help. They can write about what they see. They can study the animals. They can be part of the zoo team.

Work with a partner.
Find the words with *mb* and *wr*. Take turns making new sentences using the words.

Read "Zoos Working Together" with a partner. Practice reading words with silent letters.

Read a Play

Genre

A **play** is a story that can be acted out.
A **script** is the written form of a play.

Parts of a Play

The script shows the **dialogue**, or the words the characters say. **Stage directions** tell them what to do.

stage directions

[GROCER, BUTCHER, *and* BAKER *are talking to* MARIA *and* GRANDPA. *Enter* NEIGHBOR 1 *and* NEIGHBOR 2, *arguing.*]

NEIGHBOR 1: Another poor family, moving into the neighborhood! *Oh, no!*

dialogue for a character

NEIGHBOR 2: Don't rich people ever move?

GROCER: They do, just not to OUR neighborhood.

[*Everyone laughs.*]

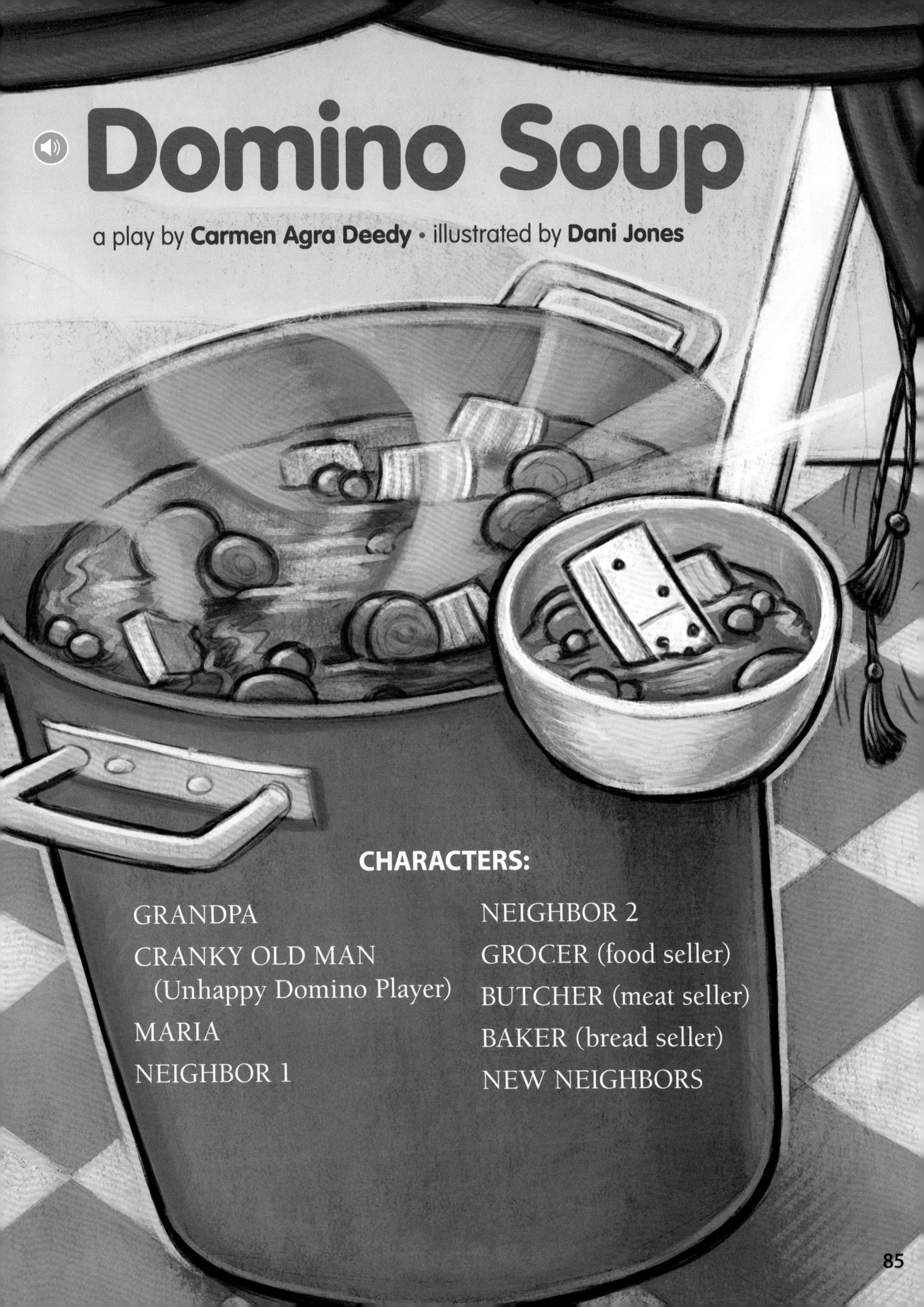

Domino Soup

a play by **Carmen Agra Deedy** • illustrated by **Dani Jones**

CHARACTERS:

GRANDPA
CRANKY OLD MAN
(Unhappy Domino Player)
MARIA
NEIGHBOR 1
NEIGHBOR 2
GROCER (food seller)
BUTCHER (meat seller)
BAKER (bread seller)
NEW NEIGHBORS

▸ Set a Purpose

Grandpa always wins a game of dominoes. Find out how he does it.

ACT ONE

[**SETTING:** *A street corner in **Miami's Little Havana**:* GRANDPA *and* CRANKY OLD MAN *are seated at a table, playing dominoes.*]

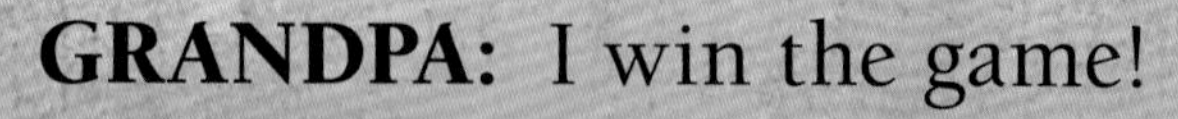

GRANDPA: I win the game!
CRANKY OLD MAN: Again? You always win at dominoes!
GRANDPA: I know. [*smiling*] **It's a gift.**
CRANKY OLD MAN: Bah! [***exits***]

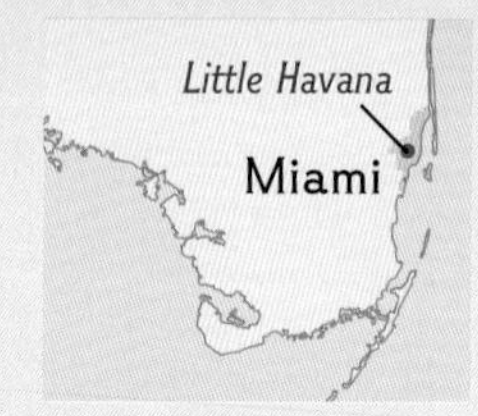

◂ ***Miami's Little Havana*** a neighborhood in Miami, Florida
It's a gift. I am just lucky.
exits leaves

MARIA: How DO you do it, Grandpa?

GRANDPA: I just get the other guys to play the dominoes I need.

MARIA: But how?

GRANDPA: [*chuckles*] I just **make a little suggestion** or two. The trick is to have them think it was THEIR IDEA.

chuckles laughs

make a little suggestion give them an idea

▸ Before You Continue

1. **Character** How does Grandpa always win? What does this tell you about his character?
2. **Setting** Where does Act One take place? Describe the setting.

▸ Predict
What do the neighbors do when a new family moves to the neighborhood?

[GROCER, BUTCHER, *and* BAKER *are talking to* MARIA *and* GRANDPA. *Enter* NEIGHBOR 1 *and* NEIGHBOR 2, ***arguing***.]

NEIGHBOR 1: Another poor family, moving into the neighborhood! Oh, no!

NEIGHBOR 2: Don't rich people ever move?

GROCER: They do, just not to OUR neighborhood.

[*Everyone laughs.*]

arguing talking angrily

MARIA: [*clapping hands*] I know! We could all **share** what we have and make a **welcome dinner**!

[*Laughter stops.*]

BAKER: Me? I sell **barely** **enough** bread to buy more flour!

welcome dinner meal to greet the new family
barely only

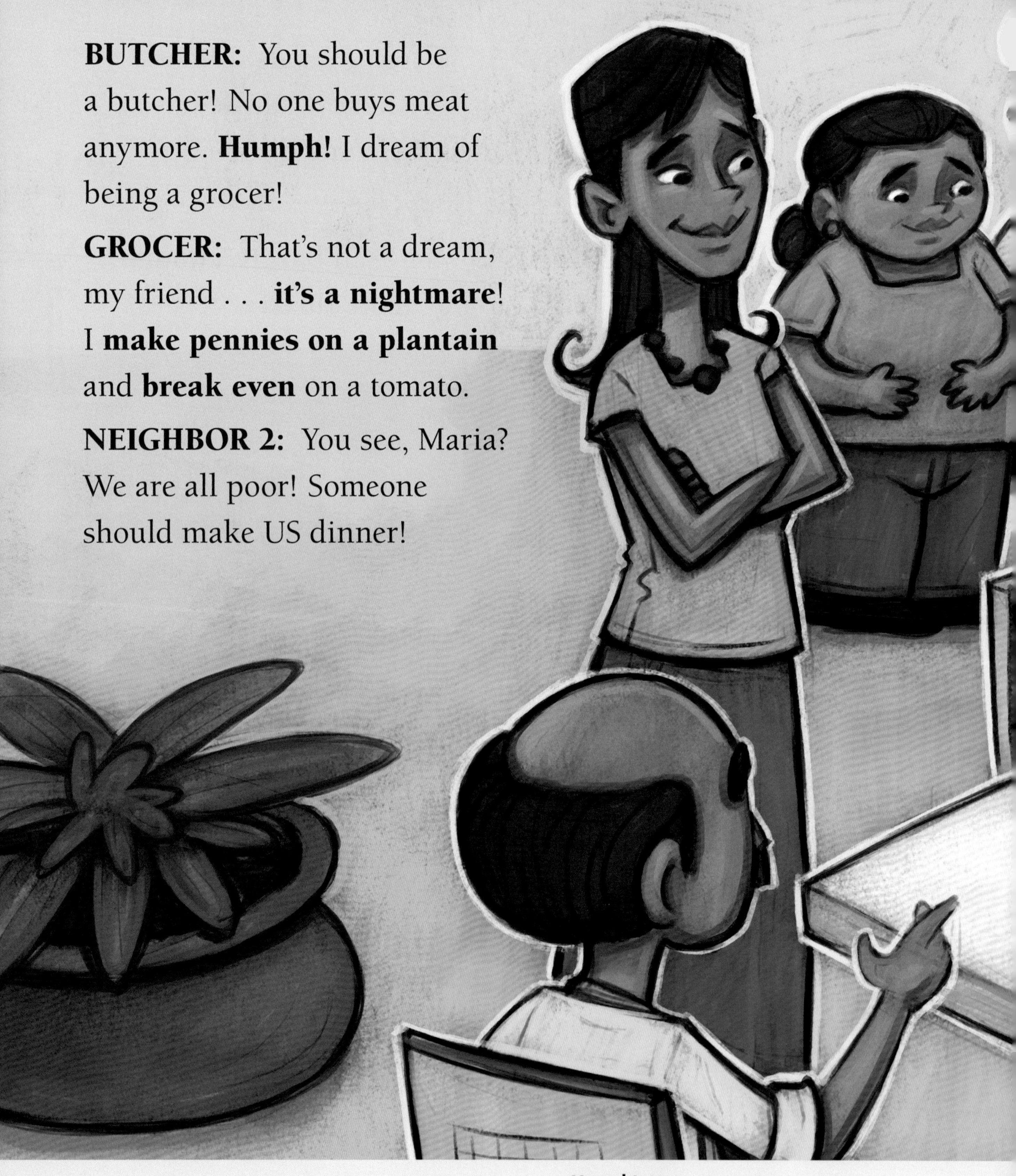

BUTCHER: You should be a butcher! No one buys meat anymore. **Humph!** I dream of being a grocer!

GROCER: That's not a dream, my friend . . . **it's a nightmare**! I **make pennies on a plantain** and **break even** on a tomato.

NEIGHBOR 2: You see, Maria? We are all poor! Someone should make US dinner!

Humph! Ha!
it's a nightmare it is like a bad dream
make pennies on a plantain don't make much money by selling bananas
break even don't make any money

MARIA: But if we all—hmmm. [*rubs chin*] Grandpa, could you **spare** a domino . . . for Domino Soup?

GRANDPA: Only one, my dear?

MARIA: Two would make the soup too strong!

GRANDPA: [*hands over one domino*] Of course.

[*Everyone follows* MARIA *as she hurries* ***offstage***.]

spare give me
offstage off of the stage

Before You Continue

1. **Confirm Prediction** What was your prediction? Was it correct? Explain.
2. **Drama** Find the stage directions on page 89. What happens after Maria tells her idea?

▸ Predict
Maria wants to make Domino Soup. How will she get everyone to work **together**?

ACT TWO

[**SETTING:** *Grandpa's kitchen.*]

BUTCHER: What is Domino Soup?

MARIA: [*drops domino into a pot*] It's a dish my family has made for many years.

EVERYONE: Ahhhhh!

MARIA: [*sniffs*] Mmmm!

NEIGHBOR 1: I don't smell a thing!

NEIGHBOR 2: **Me neither!**

GRANDPA: [***tapping heart***] You must have a big heart to smell Domino Soup.

Me neither! I think the same thing.
tapping heart touching his chest

MARIA: Of course, an onion helps.

GROCER: [*coughs*] I might have an onion. [*exits*]

MARIA: And garlic would **be lovely**—

NEIGHBOR 1: I have garlic! And some potatoes—[*exits*]

NEIGHBOR 2: —and I have carrots! [*exits*]

be lovely make the soup taste good

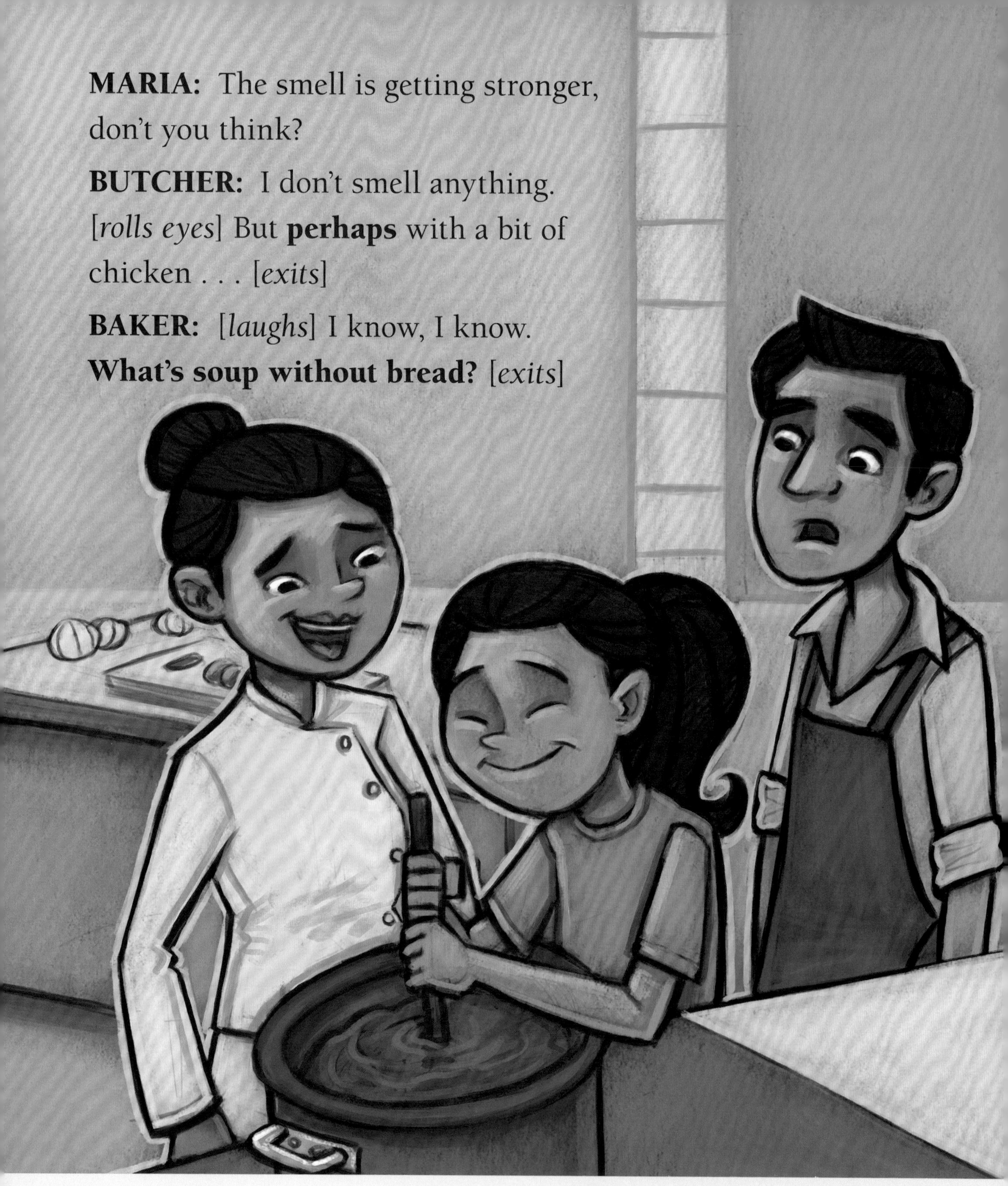

MARIA: The smell is getting stronger, don't you think?

BUTCHER: I don't smell anything. [*rolls eyes*] But **perhaps** with a bit of chicken . . . [*exits*]

BAKER: [*laughs*] I know, I know. **What's soup without bread?** [*exits*]

perhaps maybe

What's soup without bread? Soup tastes better with bread.

[GRANDPA *and* MARIA *are* **alone**.]

GRANDPA: You are a **clever** girl, granddaughter.

MARIA: I have a clever grandfather.

clever smart

Before You Continue

1. **Confirm Prediction** How does Maria get everyone to **cooperate**?
2. **Drama** On page 92, Neighbors 1 and 2 say they can't smell the soup. Who speaks next? What does the person say?

▸ **Predict**
The soup is done. What do you think will happen next?

ACT THREE

[**SETTING:** *Grandpa's busy kitchen.*]

[*Others return and* **add** *to the pot.*]

BAKER: [*bringing bread*] That Domino Soup smells delicious!

[*Everyone agrees.*]

BUTCHER: [*with wonder*] And to think it was made from a domino!

BAKER: You know, this **reminds me of** my favorite soup that my mama used to make. But she called it Thimble Soup . . .

[*A knock at the door* ***interrupts them***.]

reminds me of makes me think about

interrupts them stops everyone from talking

NEW NEIGHBOR: Hello! We—um, just moved in, and we smelled something . . . wonderful.

[*Everyone invites them in.*]

NEW NEIGHBOR: What a **big-hearted** neighborhood!

BUTCHER: [*laughing*] We are, aren't we? Who knew?

big-hearted friendly

BAKER: I hear there's a new family moving in next week.

NEIGHBOR 1: I have a great idea! We should welcome them to the neighborhood with a big **feast**.

NEIGHBOR 2: I'll bring the domino!

[GRANDPA *hugs* MARIA *as* MARIA *winks at the* ***audience***.] ❖

feast meal
audience people watching the play

▶ Before You Continue

1. **Confirm Prediction** Tell a partner what you predicted on page 96. Explain why it was or was not correct.
2. **Summarize** Use your own words to tell what happens in the final scene.

Meet the Author

Carmen Agra Deedy

When Carmen Agra Deedy was a young girl, she loved listening to her family's old stories from Cuba. Now she tells many of those stories.

Soon after learning how to read, Ms. Agra Deedy discovered the town library. The librarian gave her many books to read, and her love of reading began. "No book was safe," she said. "I gobbled them up like potato chips."

▲ **Ms. Agra Deedy says a good book is like a friend.**

Writing Tip

Carmen Agra Deedy knows that good dialogue shows how characters think and feel. Write words for Maria and her grandpa to say next. Remember to show their thoughts and feelings!

PART 1 **Think and Respond**

Talk About It

1. How does the **play** show **dialogue**, or words that the characters say? Give examples.

   The play shows dialogue with _____. One example is _____.

2. Pretend you are Maria. **Give commands** that tell how to make "Domino Soup."

   Please bring me the _____. Then take _____ and _____.
   Last, **add** _____.

3. Why does Grandpa say you need a big heart to smell Domino Soup? What does he want people to do?

   Grandpa _____.

Write About It

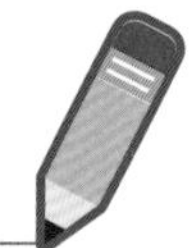

Imagine you are one of the characters in the play. Write a sentence that tells why you think it is important for people to **share** their food. Use **Key Words** in your response.

We should share our food because _____.

Reread and Retell

Story Elements

Make a story map for "Domino Soup."

Story Map

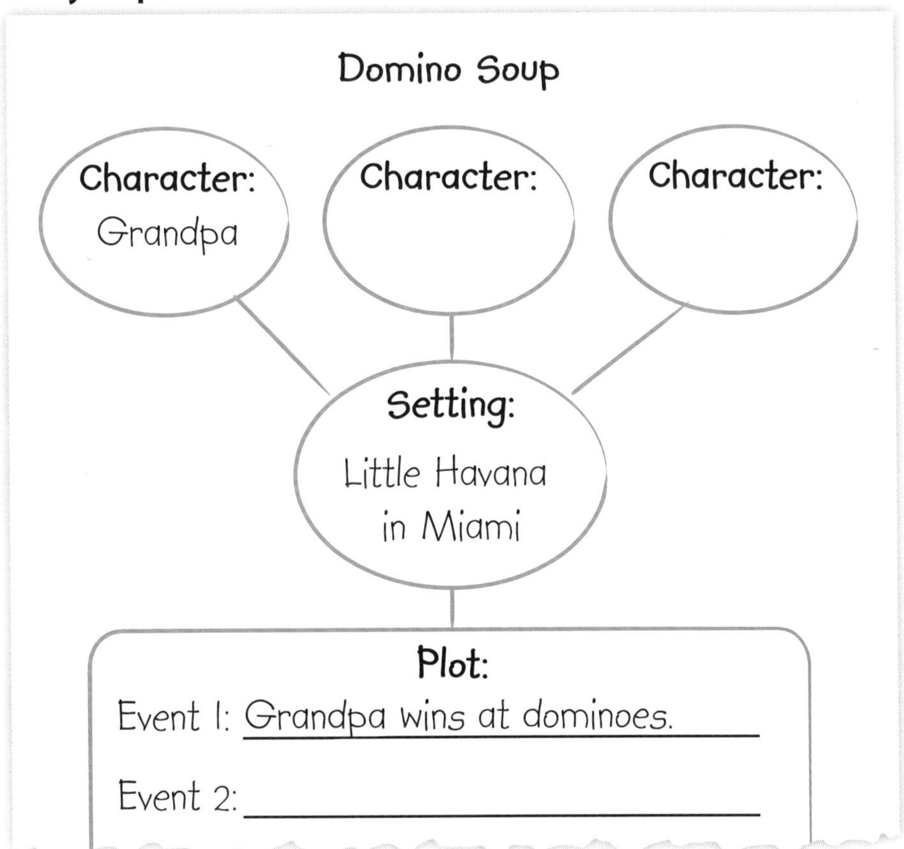

Now use your story map. Tell a partner about the characters, setting, and plot in "Domino Soup."

The play takes place in ______.
The characters are ______.
First ______. Next ______.
Then ______. Finally ______.

Fluency

Practice reading with the correct expression. Rate your reading.

Prefixes

A **prefix** is a word part. You can add a prefix to the beginning of a word. This can change the word's meaning.

The prefix **im-** means "not."

im + **possible** = impossible

It is **impossible** to make soup without a pot.

The prefix **co-** means "together."

co + operate = **cooperate**

We can **cooperate** to make soup.

Try It Together

Read the sentences. Then answer the questions.

The **coworkers** wanted to try the soup right away. But they did not want to be **impolite**. So they waited until the soup was ready.

1. What is a **coworker**? Use the word in a sentence.
2. Polite means "acting in a nice way." What does **impolite** mean?

Making Connections Now read a songwriter's version of the old folk tale "Stone Soup."

Genre A song is like a poem set to music. The words in a song are called **song lyrics**.

Stone Soup

by **John Forster and Tom Chapin**
illustrated by **Sonja Lamut**

In a **threadbare** town at the end of the war
A hungry soldier knocked on a door:
"**Pardon me**, Madam, I need some food . . .
Rum dum diddle-ii food!"

"I'm sorry, sir, but we are hungry, too.
There's no food left
In the whole hungry **village**."

threadbare poor
Pardon me Excuse me
village town

▸ Before You Continue

1. **Setting** How is the song's setting different from the setting in "Domino Soup"?
2. **Explain** Read the first four lines of the song aloud. Tell why the words sound musical.

So the soldier marched to the center of town,

"**Hear ye**! Hear ye! **Gather 'round**!"

He picked up a stone and gave it a kiss.

"Let's make soup out of this!"

"What? Soup from a stone?"

"Sure . . .

All you need is what you've got,

A tasty stone and water in a pot.

Takes some time but feeds a lot.

Stone soup tonight."

"Stone soup? Stone soup?

What is this fellow, a nincompoop?"

Hear ye! Listen, everyone!
Gather 'round! Come close!
What is this fellow, a nincompoop?
Is this man a fool?

But the kids brought stones,

Which he put in the pot.

Boiled the whole thing piping hot.

Then he **hushed the crowd and, solemn-faced**,

Took a rum dum diddle-ii taste.

"Oh, this is **gonna** be good!"

"Please, Sir, please, can we have some?"

"No, not yet. It's not quite done.

It needs a soup bone . . . **for flavor**."

hushed the crowd and, solemn-faced told the people to be quiet, and calmly

gonna going to

for flavor to make it taste good

Before You Continue

1. **Plot** How are the events in this song like the events in "Domino Soup"?
2. **Summarize** Use your own words to tell what happens on pages 104–105.

A little girl **who'd** brought a stone

Said, "We've been saving a big hambone.

Shall I get it?"

"**That'd** be nice."

She was back **in a trice**!

The soldier smiled.

"All you need is what you've got."

He took that bone and threw it in the pot.

Some grown-ups started to see the light.

"Stone soup tonight."

who'd who had

That'd That would

in a trice quickly

Some grown-ups started to see the light. Some adults began to understand what was happening.

Then he took a taste, took a taste:

"Oh, this is gonna be great!"

"Now, Sir, now, can we have some?"

"Not just yet. It's still not done.

It needs . . . a potato and . . . an onion."

The kids jumped up and **off they tore**

And brought the things that he'd asked for,

Not to mention turnip greens,

A carrot and some beans!

off they tore ran away

Not to mention They also brought

Before You Continue

1. **Character** How are the soldier's actions like Maria's actions in "Domino Soup"? How are they different?
2. **Details** What do the kids bring to put in the soup?

The smell of soup began **to float**

Into every nose and throat,

Calling people like a drum,

"Rum dum diddle-ii yum!"

"Stone soup. Stone soup.

We want some of that tasty **goop**."

"No. Not yet. I'm still not through.

It needs one thing from each of you . . .

Whatever you can **spare**."

to float Into every nose and throat to smell wonderful to everyone

goop thick soup

spare **share** with us

So the villagers **scattered to their root cellars**,

Corn cribs and secret nooks

And brought back everything

From an eggplant to a pepperoni.

And that night the whole hungry village

Feasted on soup made out of a stone!

All we need is what we've got,

A tasty stone and water in a pot.

Little things become a lot.

Tiny gifts can fill the pot

When they're **shared** and served up hot.

Stone soup. Stone soup.

Stone soup tonight! ❖

scattered to their root cellars, Corn cribs and secret nooks ran to get food they had hidden

Feasted on Ate

▸ Before You Continue

1. **Clarify** The song says "Little things become a lot." What does this mean?
2. **Plot** How do the people in this song **cooperate** to make the soup? How is this like the events in "Domino Soup"?

Compare Two Versions of the Same Story

How are "Domino Soup" and "Stone Soup" alike? How are they different?

Comparison Chart

	"Domino Soup"	"Stone Soup"
Type of Story	play	song
Characters		
Setting		
Plot		

Write the names of the characters here.

Write details about the setting here.

Write events from the plot here.

Talk Together

Work with two partners. Write a short play about working **together**. Use **Key Words** in the dialogue. Perform your play for the class.

Pronouns

A **pronoun** is a word that can take the place of a noun. When you use a pronoun in a sentence, be sure to use the right one.

Grammar Rules Pronouns

Rule	Example
• For yourself, use **I**.	My name is **Laura**. **I** am eight years old.
• For one man or boy, use **he** or **him**.	**Jorge** is my brother. I sit with **him**.
• For one woman or girl, use **she** or **her**.	My **grandmother** reads. **She** sits on the chair.
• For one place or object, use **it**.	I will give Jack this **book**. Jack wants to read **it**.
• For yourself and another person, use **we** or **us**.	**Jack and I** are best friends. **We** like to play at the park.
• For two or more people, places, or things, use **they** or **them**.	Our **neighbors** are at the park, too. Jack and I wave to **them**.

Read Pronouns

Read these sentences. Find four pronouns. Tell them to a partner.

The boys work on a mural. First they draw a sketch. Then one boy colors it in. He uses bright colors. It is beautiful!

Use Pronouns

Write two sentences about how people in your neighborhood work together. Use at least one pronoun. Share with a partner.

PART 2 Language Focus

Express Needs and Wants

Listen and sing.

Words to Know
good
need
some
want

Song  

Bake Sale

 I **want** a **good** project to work on.

 I think that I have a good plan.

Our library needs **some** more money.

Let's organize help if we can.

Chorus:

 Bake sale, bake sale—

We **need** more books for our library.

 Bake sale, bake sale—

We'll raise lots of money, you'll see.

Tune: "My Bonnie Lies Over the Ocean"

Key Words

How do you complete a **project**?

1 **Organize** ideas.

2 Make a **plan**.

3 **Join** in.

4 Use your **skills**.

5 Work together.

Talk Together

Tell a partner about a project you worked on with other people.

PART 2 **Thinking Map**

Main Idea and Details

The **main idea** is the most important idea in the text. **Details** tell more about this very important idea. Show how the information fits together. Use a main idea diagram.

Main Idea Diagram

Write details from the text here.

Detail

Asami gets a ladder.

Detail

Daniel holds the ladder.

Main Idea

You can work together to reach a goal.

Look at the details to figure out the main idea. Then write it here.

Talk Together

Tell your partner about a time when you worked with someone to reach a goal. Then make a main idea and details diagram.

More Key Words

dream

noun

Her **dream** is to win a medal at the track meet.

education

noun

You go to school to get an **education**.

opportunity

noun

She has an **opportunity** to kick the ball.

result

noun

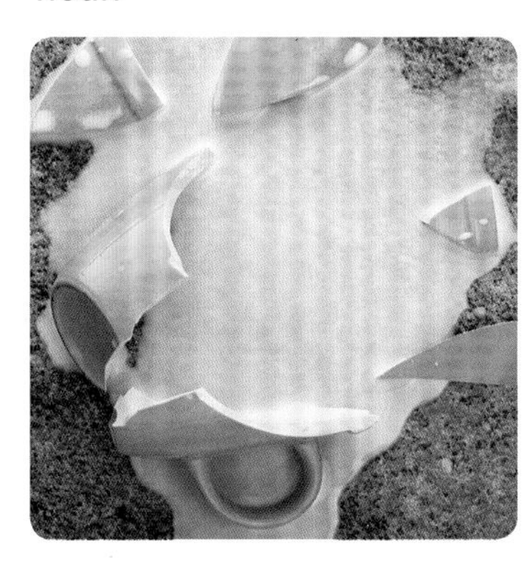

If you trip and drop a cup, the **result** is broken pieces.

success

noun

They win the game. It is a big **success**!

Talk Together

Work with a partner. Use **Key Words** to ask and answer questions.

What opportunity does he have?

He has the opportunity to go to sports camp.

PART 2 **Reading Strategy**

Learn to Identify Main Idea and Details

When you want to understand something, look for what is important about it. Look for important **details**. Put these together to find the most important or **main idea** of the text.

Working Together Gets the Job Done

Carrying a Heavy Load

More Hands to Help

The Job Is Done

Look for clues as you read to find the **details** and the **main idea**.

How to Identify Main Idea and Details

	1. Read the text and look at the pictures.	I read about ____.
	2. Look for details that seem important.	The important details are ____.
	3. Put the details together. Figure out the most important idea.	The main idea is ____.

Talk Together

Read Asami and Daniel's report and the sample. Then use **Language Frames** to state the details and the main idea. Tell your partner about them.

Language Frames

- I read about ______.
- The important details are ______.
- The main idea is ______.

Report

Helping Others

Making a ***Plan***

Our teacher, Ms. Veloso, told us about a homeless shelter nearby. She explained that some families lose their homes. As a **result**, they have to live at the shelter. These people need furniture, and their children want toys. Our class saw an **opportunity** to do some good. We decided to give furniture and toys to the shelter. First, we needed our parents' help.

Sample Main Idea and Details

"I read about the families that live at the shelter.

The important details are that these families need furniture and toys.

The main idea is that the class decides to help these families."

Putting the Plan into Action

We explained the **project** to our parents, and many decided to help. Planning the project gave us a real **education**. Some people had extra chairs and toys to give away. Other people helped load the truck. At the end of the day, we all helped unload the truck at the shelter. Our project was a bigger **success** than we dreamed it would be!

◀ = A good place to identify details and a main idea

PART 2 **Phonics Focus**

Vowel Sounds and Spellings: *oo, ui*

moon

juice

Listen and Learn

Listen to each sentence. Choose the word that best completes the sentence.

1. We went for a swim in the ______.

pool

pile

pail

2. My father wore a ______.

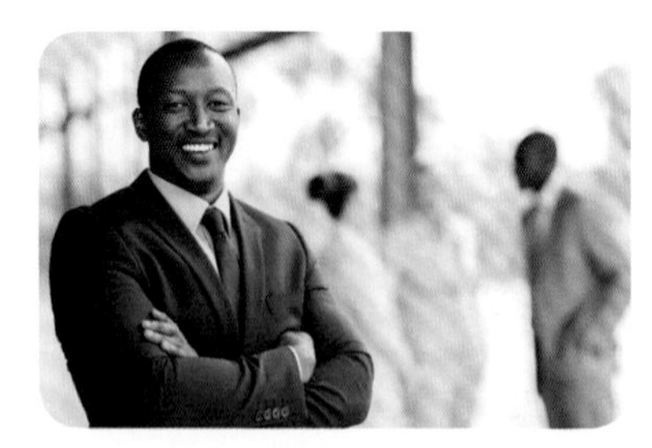

seat

sight

suit

3. A hammer is a useful ______.

tail

tool

tile

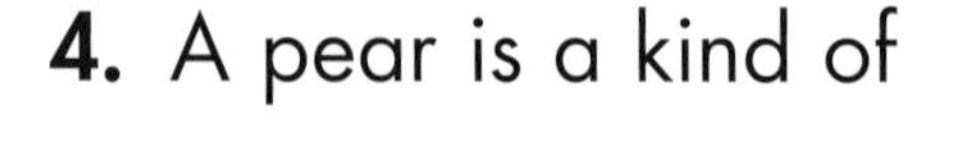

4. A pear is a kind of ______.

fruit

fright

front

Talk Together

Listen and read. Find the words with the vowel sound you hear in the word *moon*.

Over to You

Collecting Water

People need water. Animals need water. Plants need water. Some places have too little water. People want a good way to get water. One way is to collect rainwater. This can be a big project. People join together to build tanks. Some tanks are on roofs. The tanks catch rainwater. The water is stored. Then it can be used when it is needed. Some tanks are built at schools. The students learn how to save water. It becomes part of their education.

Did you know you can reuse water, too? People use water to wash dishes. They use water to wash clothes. They use water to take showers. This water can be saved. It cannot be used for drinking or cooking food. It cannot be used to make juice. It can be used to water plants and fruit trees.

What problems does your school have? What can you and your friends do to help? The result can help everyone.

Work with a partner.

Take turns. Point to a word with the vowel sound you hear in the word *moon*. Your partner reads the word and tells how the vowel sound is spelled.

Read "Collecting Water" with a partner. Practice reading words with the vowel sound you hear in the word *moon*.

Read a Human-Interest Feature

Genre

A **human-interest feature** is nonfiction. It gives facts about people and events of today.

Text Feature

A **map** can show you where things are.

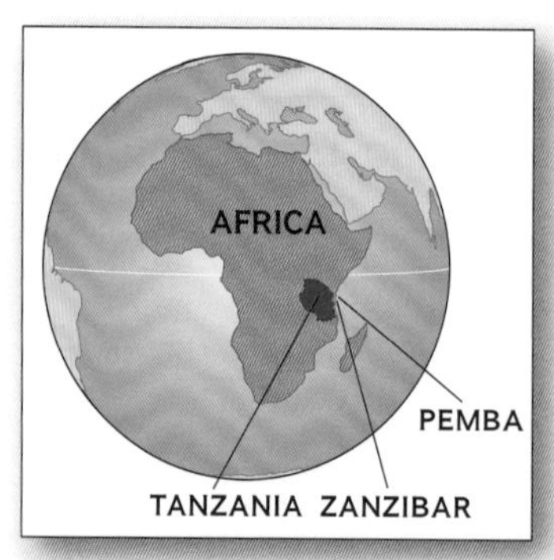

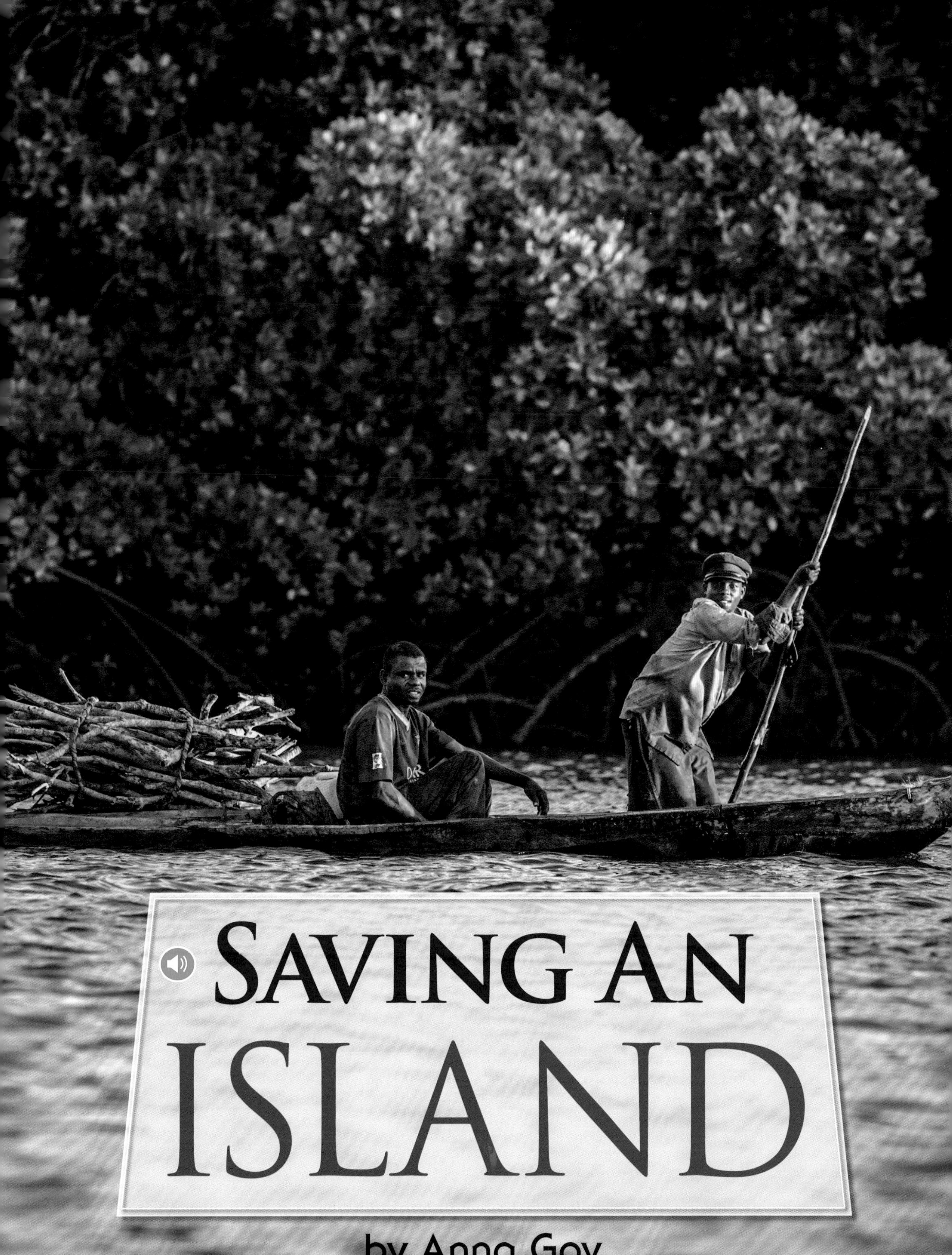

SAVING AN ISLAND

by Anna Goy

Set a Purpose
Find out how a community worked together to save their island.

Pemba Island is a beautiful place. Its Arabic name, Jazīarat Al-Khuḍrah, means "Green Island." The people of Pemba want to keep it that way, but it hasn't always been easy.

▼ Pemba Island is off the coast of Tanzania. It is only 42 miles long and 14 miles wide.

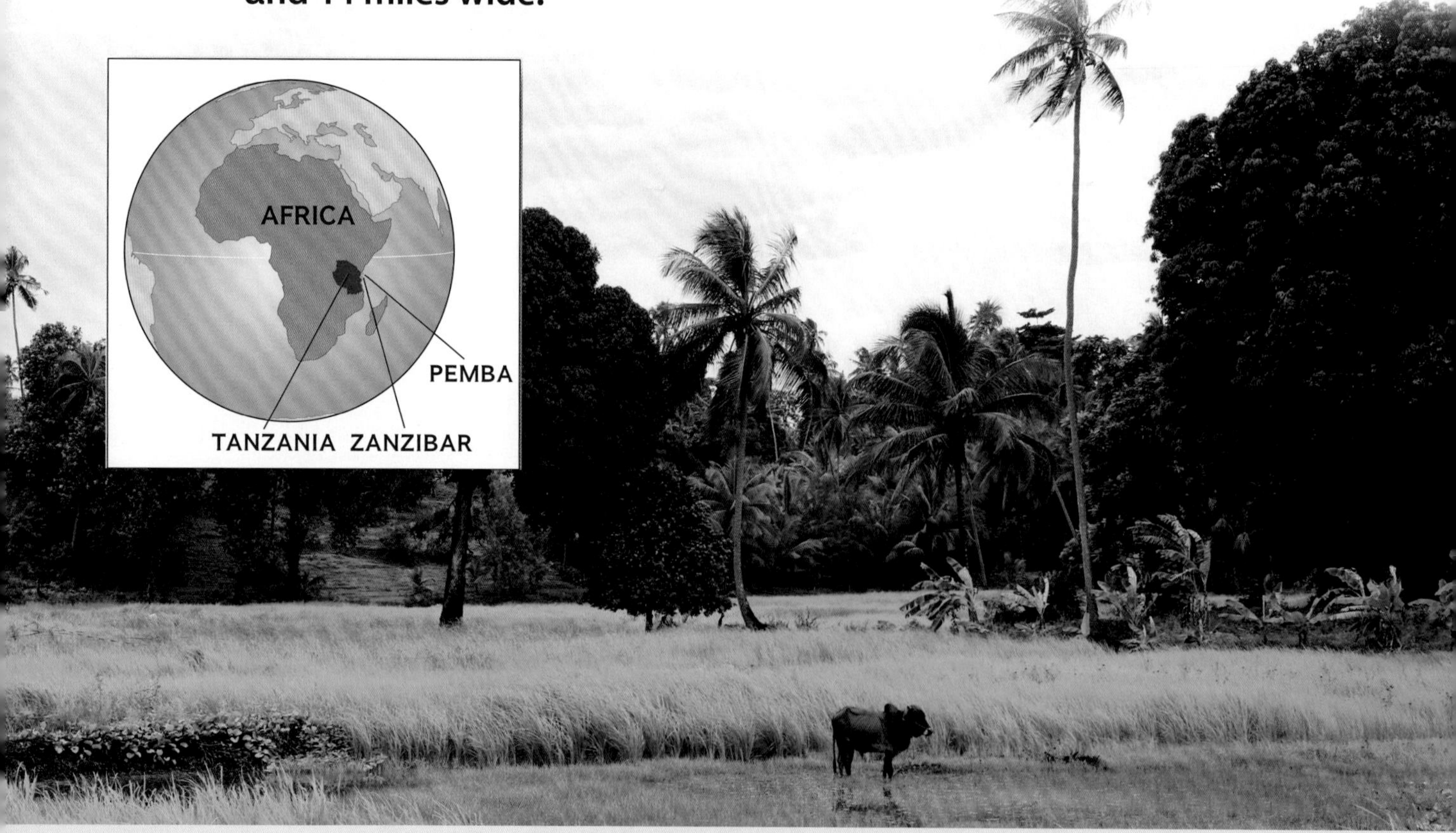

Pemba Island is very **fertile**, and the local people grow many **crops**. **Mangroves** and **lagoons** line the coast. Tourists come to visit its beautiful beaches and see colorful fish in the sea.

fertile good for growing food
crops food that is grown on farms
Mangroves coastal trees ▶
lagoons lakes

▶ Before You Continue

1. **Use Text Features** Look at the map on page 122. Where is Pemba Island located?
2. **Summarize** What have you learned so far about Pemba Island?

Pemba Island is the world's biggest producer of **cloves**. Cloves are used in many countries for cooking. During the **harvest** season, from September to November, you can smell their strong perfume all over the island.

cloves dried flower buds used as a spice
harvest season for collecting crops

The island, however, has many environmental problems. Over the years, its population grew steadily. As a **result**, more and more trees were cut down for **firewood** and to clear land for **farming**.

firewood wood to make a fire
farming growing crops and keeping animals for food

Before You Continue

1. **Make Inferences** Look at the photo on page 124. Why are the cloves on the ground?
2. **Clarify** What was the **result** of the population increase on Pemba Island?

There weren't many trees to protect the land, so rain **washed away** the **soil**. It became more difficult for local people to grow cloves and other crops. They earned less money to support their families.

▼ **A woman selling tomatoes on Pemba Island**

washed away took away

◀ **soil** earth

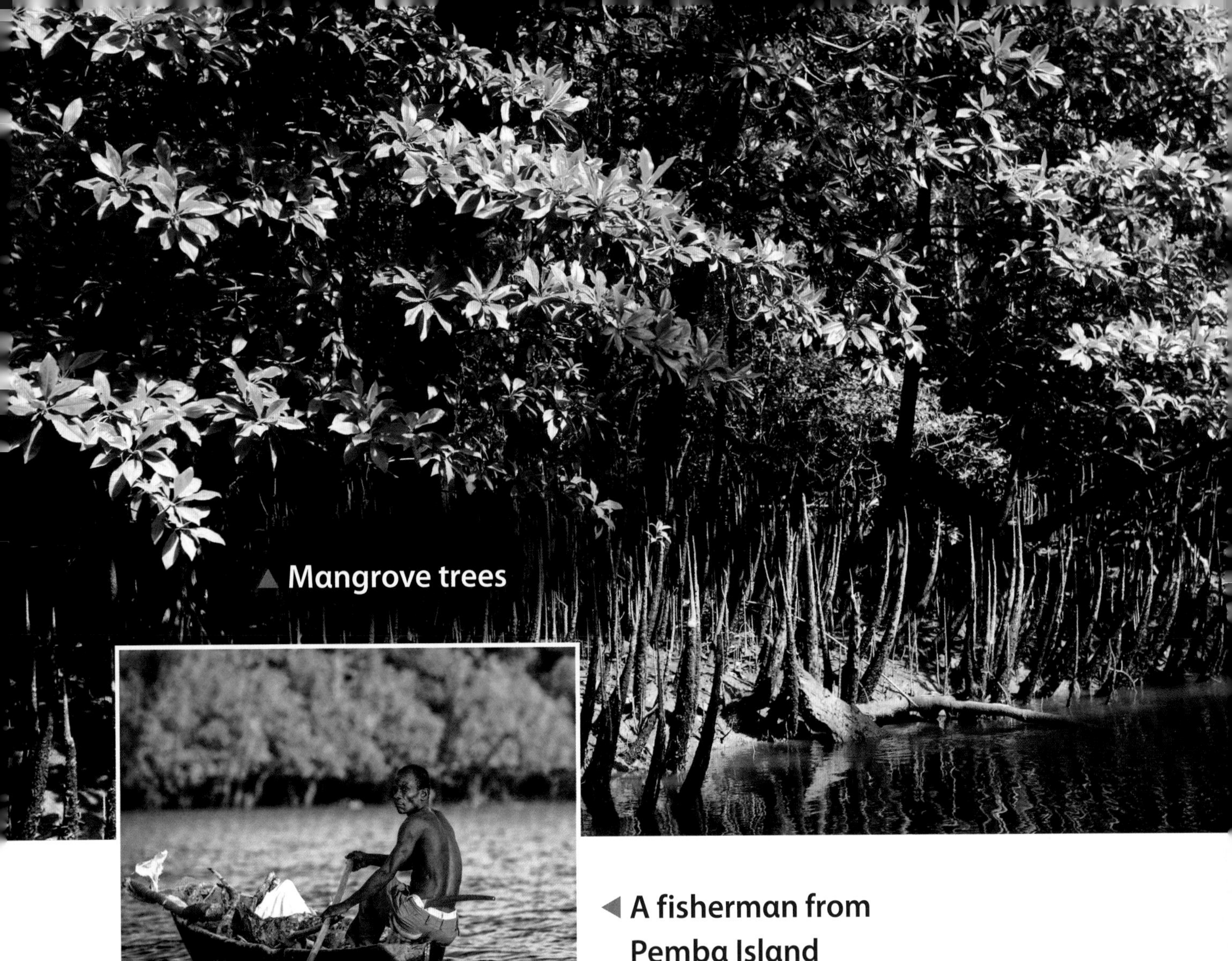

▲ Mangrove trees

◀ A fisherman from Pemba Island

Mangroves on the coast were also cut down. Mangroves **provide** food and shelter for fish. So, there were less fish. This was a big problem for the fishermen. Many people didn't have enough food.

provide give

▶ Before You Continue

1. **Main Idea** Why was cutting down trees a problem for the people of Pemba Island?
2. **Describe** Look at the photos on this page. Describe what you see.

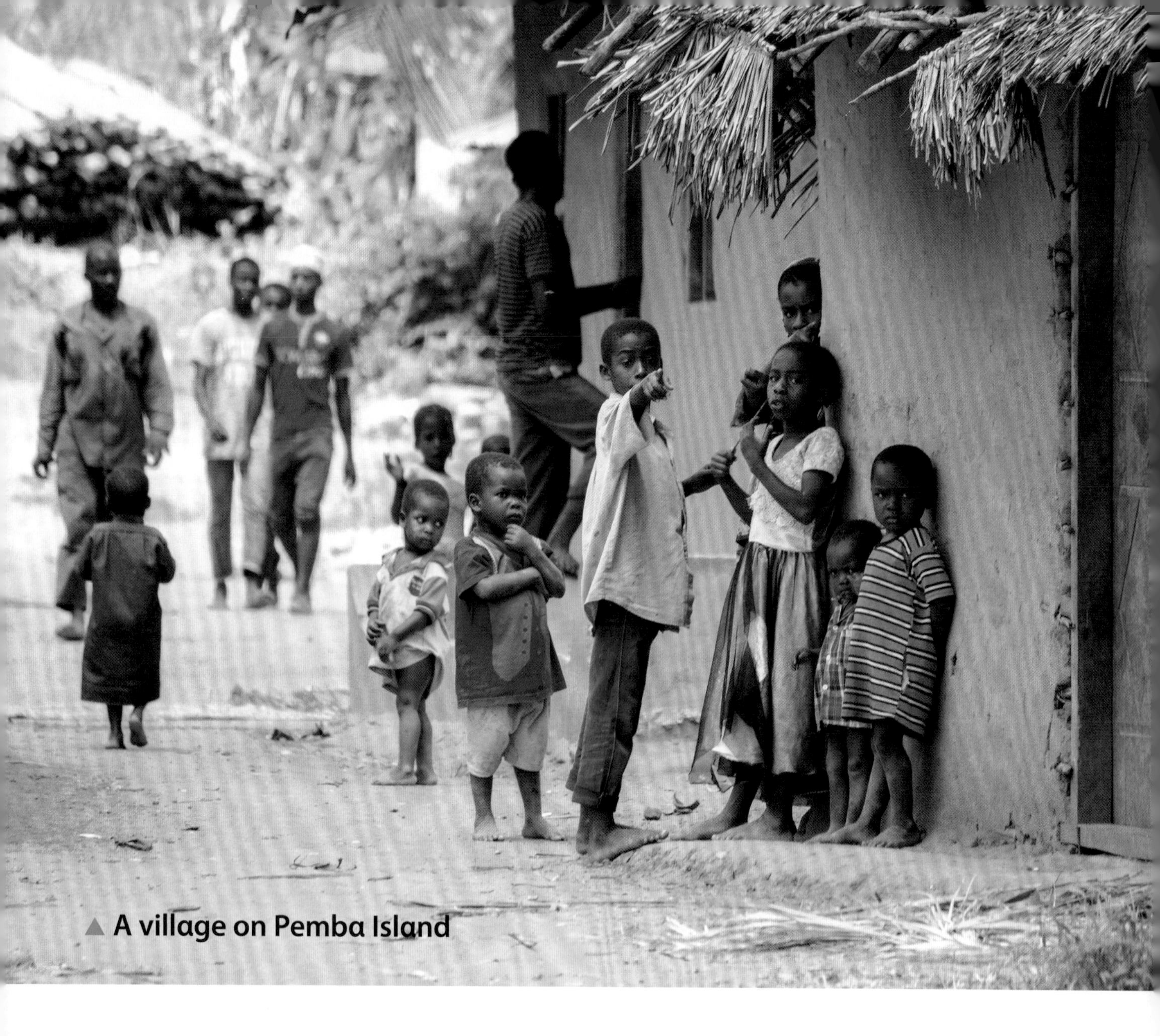
▲ A village on Pemba Island

Community leaders were worried about the island. They started to collect **seeds** and asked the community to help grow them. Many people wanted to **join** in and help. Saving the island would save their future.

◀ **seeds** small part of a plant from which new plants grow

The people of Pemba asked for help from the international community. Different organizations offered their support. Together, they planned many different **projects**. Each project helped grow the forest and protect its **ecology**.

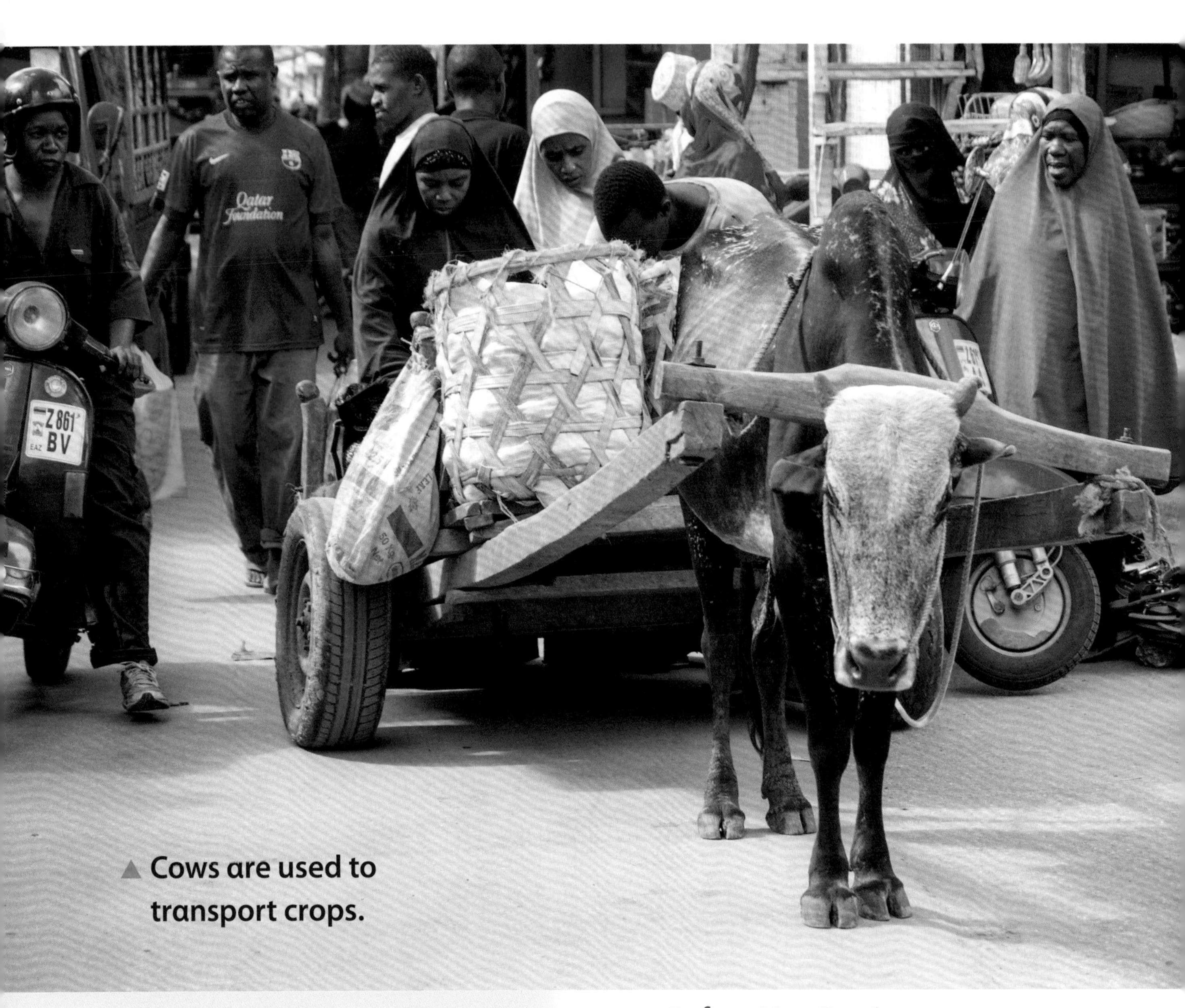

▲ Cows are used to transport crops.

ecology a web of life and natural resources

▶ Before You Continue

1. **Clarify** Why did many people want to **join** the **project** to grow seeds?
2. **Make Inferences** Why do you think the people of Pemba asked for support from the international community?

▲ New plants growing as part of the ecology projects

The community learned how to grow **seedlings**, which they then planted in community land in the forests. They also changed how they grew their crops. The changes protected their land and the soil.

seedlings baby trees

Some members of the community learned a new **skill**. They became **beekeepers**. Bees **pollinated** the plants, helping the **reforestation project**. Beekeepers on the island could also sell the honey from the bees.

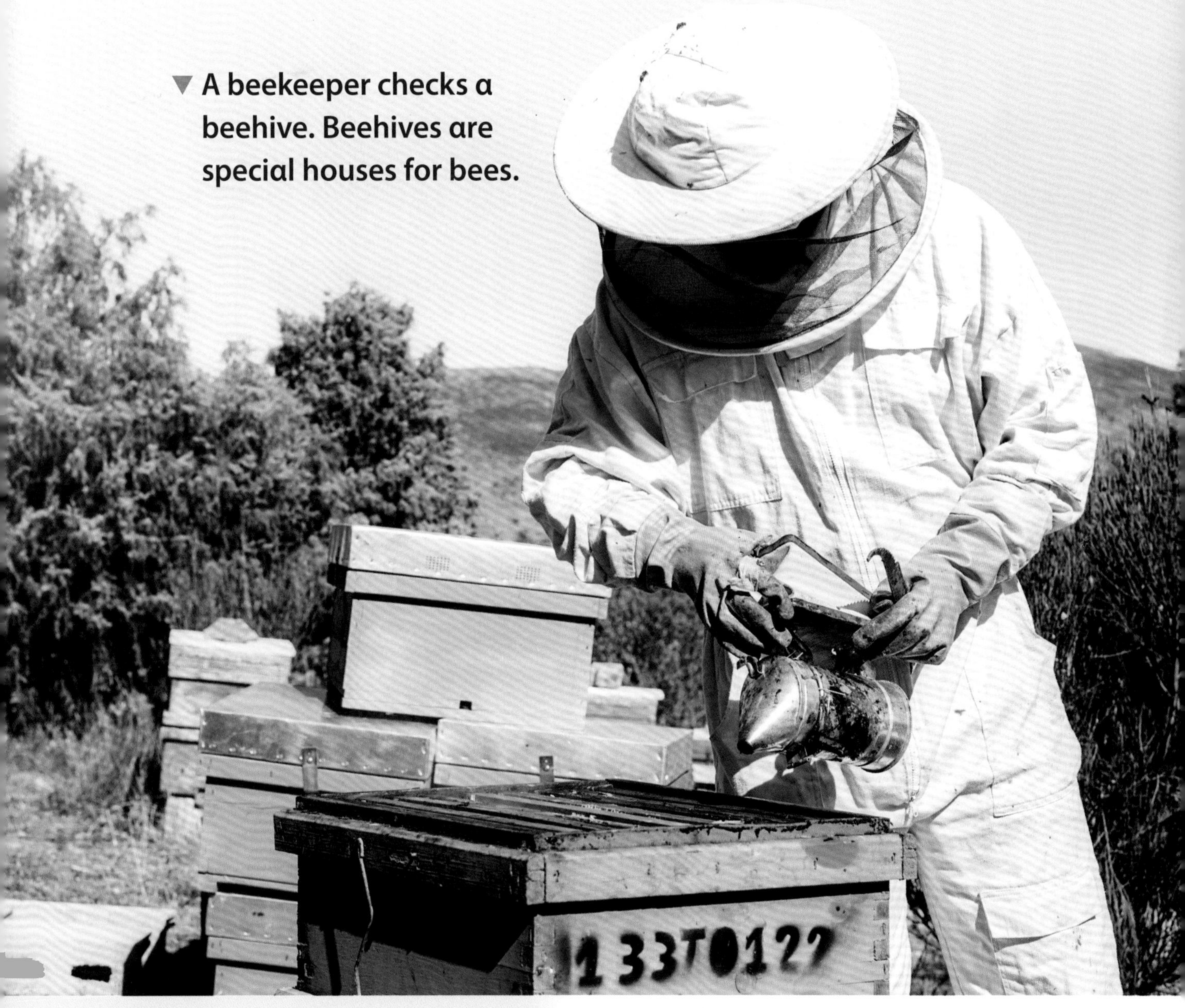

▼ A beekeeper checks a beehive. Beehives are special houses for bees.

beekeepers people who look after bees
pollinated carried pollen (yellow powder) from one plant to another
reforestation planting trees

▸ Before You Continue

1. **Details** How did beekeeping help people in the community?
2. **Summarize** Use one sentence to describe the **projects** on the island.

Over the last 10 years, more than two million trees have been planted on Pemba Island. Many of the trees provide fruit and vegetables. Now there are more trees, and farmers have more crops to sell.

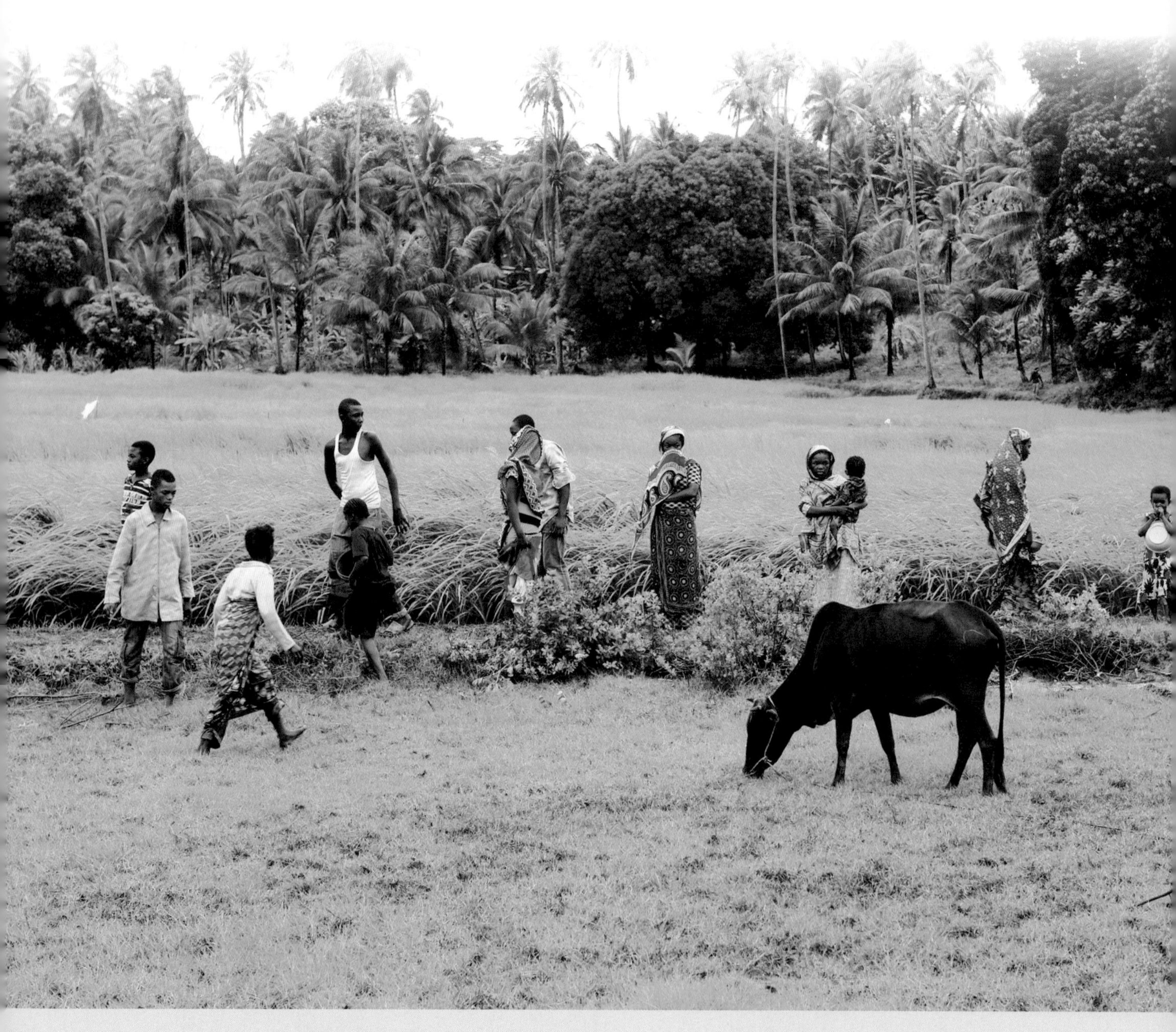

▲ Farmers working on Pemba Island

▲ Children climb a tree on the island.

The people of Pemba Island are **proud of** their **success**. But they know it will take time to see all their **dreams** come true. They continue to work together with one **purpose**: to save their island. ❖

proud of feel good about
purpose objective

Before You Continue

1. **Character** What do we learn about the people of Pemba Island?
2. **Main Idea** Tell the lesson of the story in your own words.

PART 2 **Think and Respond**

Talk About It 

1. What makes this selection a **human-interest feature**?

   It is a human-interest feature because _____.

2. Describe the main reason why the Pemba Island reforestation **project** is a **success**. Tell how you know.

   The main reason is _____. I know because _____.

3. Why do the people of Pemba Island feel such pride in their community?

   The people of Pemba Island are proud of _____. They worked together to _____.

Write About It 

The Pemba Island community **organized** a project to plant trees. Write a sentence. Tell what you think about the Pemba Island reforestation project. Use at least one **Key Word**.

I think the Pemba Island reforestation project is _____ because _____.

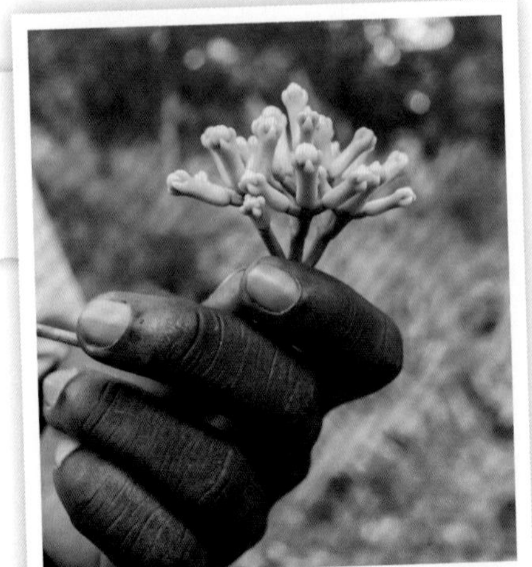

Reread and Summarize

Main Idea

Make a main idea diagram for "Saving an Island." Look for important details in the text. Put them together to figure out the main idea.

Main Idea Diagram

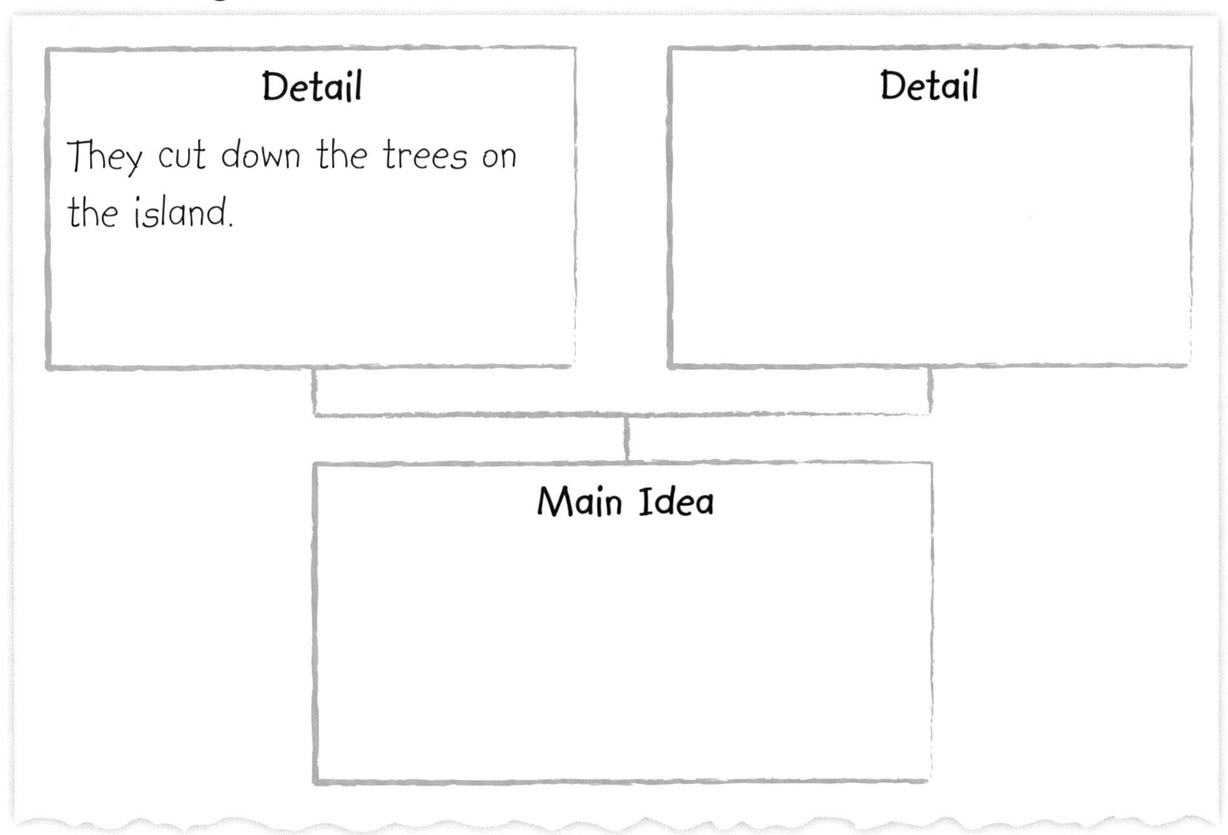

Now use your main idea diagram. Tell your partner about the main idea and details from "Saving an Island."

One detail is ______.
Another detail is ______.
The main idea is ______.

Fluency

Practice reading with the correct phrasing. Rate your reading.

Use Context Clues

If you read a word that you do not know, look at the words around it. These clues from the text, or **context clues**, can help you figure out the meaning of the word.

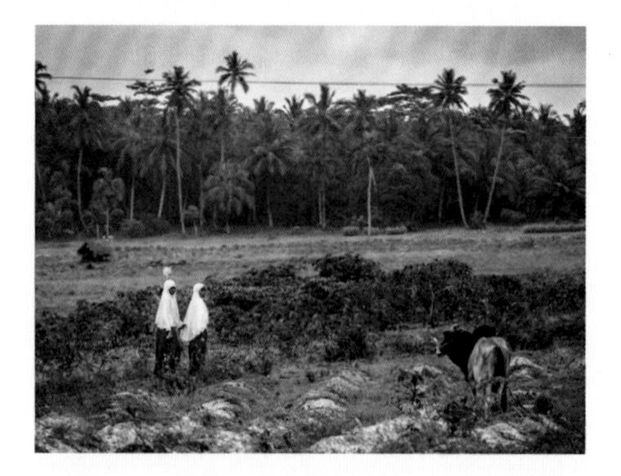

The island, however, has many **environmental problems**. . . As a result, **more and more trees were cut down** for firewood and to clear land for farming.

context clue

The words "more and more trees were cut down" give a clue about the meaning of **environmental problems**.

Try It Together

Read the sentences. Then answer the questions.

My friends and I wanted to start a neighborhood garden. Our neighbors helped us buy the seeds. Everyone joined together to make the garden. Soon, we got the results we wanted: vegetables. Our project was a big **success**!

1. What does **success** mean?
2. What words help you understand the meaning?

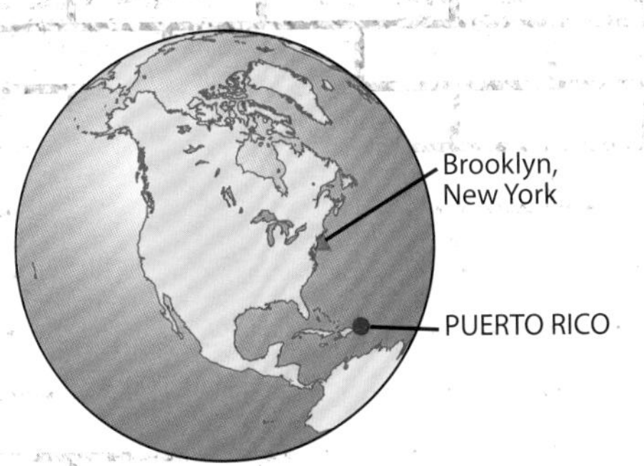

Making Connections Find out how friends work together to make their neighborhood a better place.

Genre A **photo-essay** is nonfiction. It uses photos and words to tell about a topic.

Mi Barrio

by George Ancona

Hi, I'm Marc Anthony. I live in Brooklyn, in a neighborhood called Bushwick. My parents came from Puerto Rico, but I was born here. Most of the people who live here speak Spanish. I go to **P.S.116**.

Mi Barrio My Neighborhood (in Spanish)

P.S.116 Public School 116

Before You Continue

1. **Main Idea** What will this photo-essay be mostly about?
2. **Use Text Features** Look at the map of Earth. Point to the place Marc's parents came from.

There are many murals painted on the walls of the neighborhood. This one was painted by some of the kids in my school.

▼ **Some of Marc's classmates painted this mural on cement walls.**

▲ **Marc and his friend draw at the community center.**

We like to **get together** after school. Some days we go to the community center to draw pictures.

get together meet

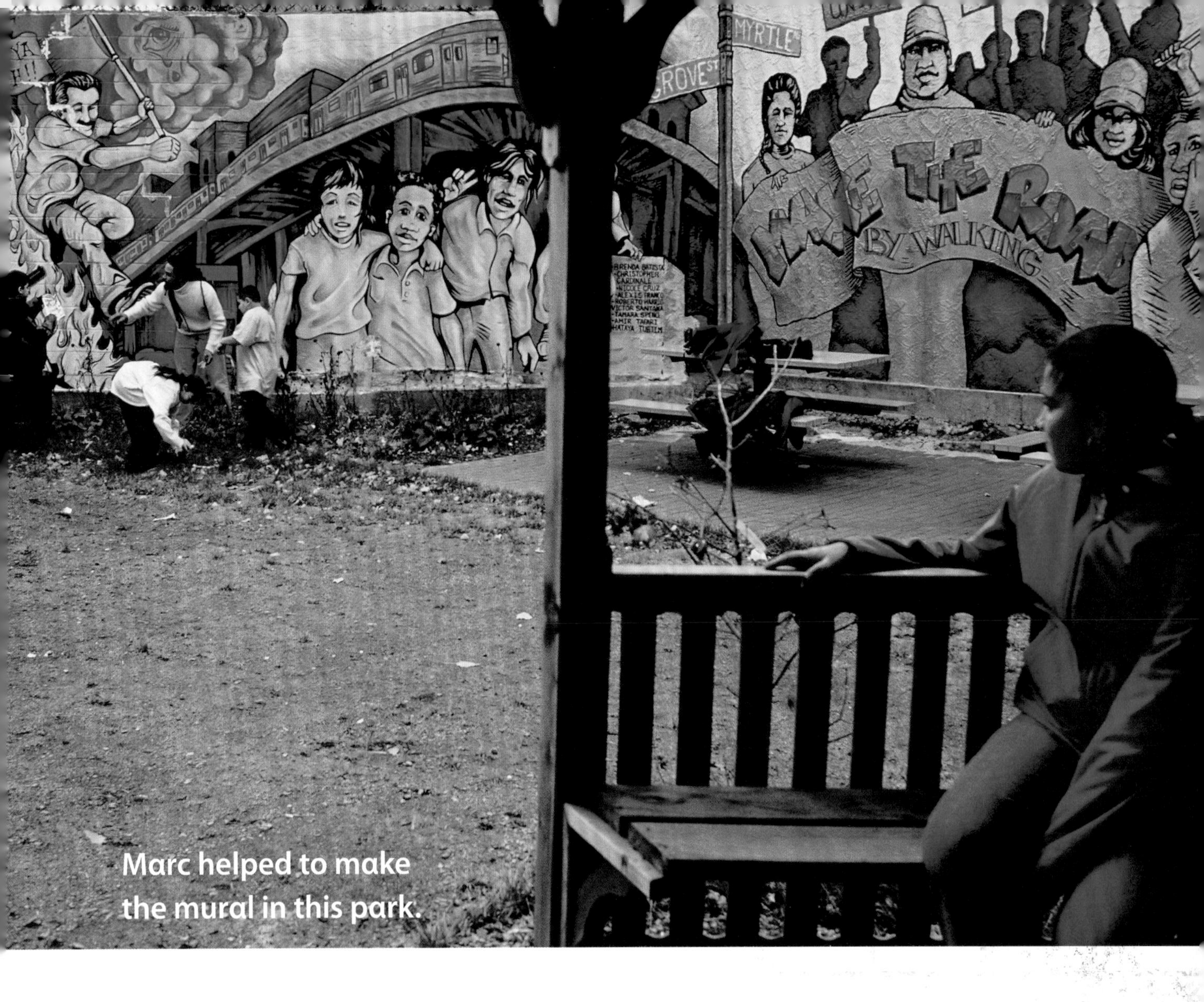

Marc helped to make the mural in this park.

In the summer we help artists paint murals. One of the **projects** we did is a little park with a mural.

Our murals help make our neighborhood beautiful. They make people think about **their culture**. ❖

their culture language, religion, cuisine, social habits, music, and arts of a particular group of people

▶ Before You Continue

1. **Use Visuals** How do the photos help you know what a mural is?
2. **Main Idea/Details** Name two details that support the idea that Marc and his friends like to draw and paint.

More About Murals

- Artists create murals in communities all around the world. They use murals to help them share ideas and tell stories.
- Many murals show characters and places that remind people of their **heritage**.

heritage who they are and where they came from

▲ A colorful mural in the city of San Diego, USA

- Painting murals is nothing new. Artists have painted on walls for **centuries**.
- Murals can be on the inside of buildings or on the outside. When murals are on outside walls, artists must use special paints. Then even if it rains or snows, or if the sun is very hot, the mural will last a long time.

centuries hundreds of years

Before You Continue

1. **Main Idea** Why are community murals important? Use information from the text to explain your answer.
2. **Use Text Features** Look at the caption on this page. Where is the mural?

Compare Texts

"Saving an Island" is a human-interest feature. "Mi Barrio" is a photo-essay. How are the two selections alike and different?

Comparison Chart

	"Saving an Island"	"Mi Barrio"
It is in an urban community.		✔
It is in a rural community.	✔	
The community members help each other.		
The children help their community, too.		
The selection is illustrated with photographs.		
It is a true story.		

Put a check if the statement is true for the selection.

Talk Together

Look at a photograph from one of the selections. Describe it to your partner. Then have your partner describe a photograph to you. Use **Key Words** to talk about how people work together on **projects**.

Possessive Pronouns

A **pronoun** is a word that can take the place of a noun. Some pronouns **tell who owns something**. When you use a pronoun in a sentence, be sure to use the right one.

Grammar Rules Possessive Pronouns	
• For yourself, use **mine**.	• This paintbrush is **mine**.
• For yourself and one or more people, use **ours**.	• The bright blue paint is **ours**.
• When you speak to one or more people, use **yours**.	• The yellow paint is **yours**.
• For one man or boy, use **his**.	• Teresa's painting looks different from **his**.
• For one woman or girl, use **hers**.	• Rob's painting uses the same colors as **hers**.
• For two or more people, places, or things, use **theirs**.	• Our class's paintings are more unusual than **theirs**.

Read Pronouns

Read the passage below. Find the possessive pronouns.

"This is what I painted," said Anna. "Where is yours?"
"Mine is over by the gate," Bobby explains.

Use Pronouns

Write two sentences about a school project. Use a possessive pronoun in each one. Share your sentences with a partner.

Writing Project

Write as a Storyteller

Write a Story

Write a story about people who work together to make something happen. Add your story to a class magazine about cooperation.

Study a Model

Realistic fiction is a story that can happen in real life. Read Cal's story about what happens when friends cooperate.

Kumar's Bath

By Cal Jackson

The **beginning** tells who the **main character** is.

Kumar has been working in the garden again. And now he is all muddy.

"I want you to take a bath," says Kumar's mom. There is one problem. **Kumar's clothes are so muddy that he'll make a mess in the house**!

The reader learns about a **problem** that the characters need to solve.

The **middle** tells what happens next. It has more **details** about the characters and the **setting**.

Kumar calls some of his friends. He tells them all to meet him in his **backyard**. He stands there waiting for them.

Kumar picks up the soap and sponge. His friends aim the hose. Ten minutes later, Kumar and his clothes are all clean. But now everyone is soaking wet!

The **end** tells how the problem is solved.

Prewrite

1. **Choose a Topic** What story will you tell? What happens when people cooperate? Talk with a partner to get ideas.

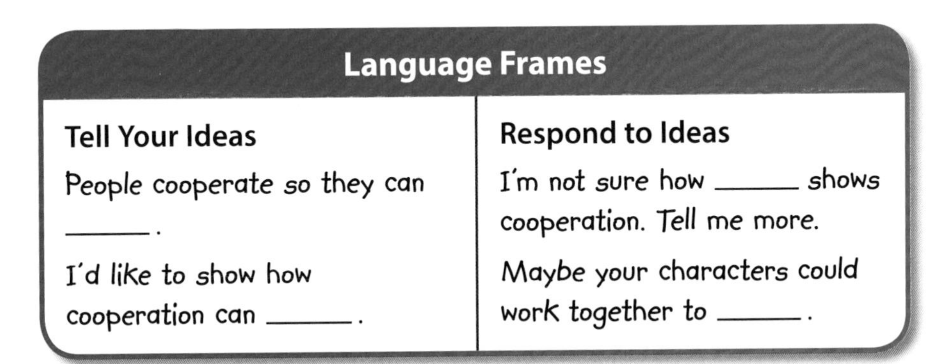

Language Frames	
Tell Your Ideas	**Respond to Ideas**
People cooperate so they can _____.	I'm not sure how _____ shows cooperation. Tell me more.
I'd like to show how cooperation can _____.	Maybe your characters could work together to _____.

2. **Gather Information** Who will your characters be? What problem will they try to solve? What setting will you use? Write down your ideas.
3. **Get Organized** Use a story map to show your story ideas.

Story Map

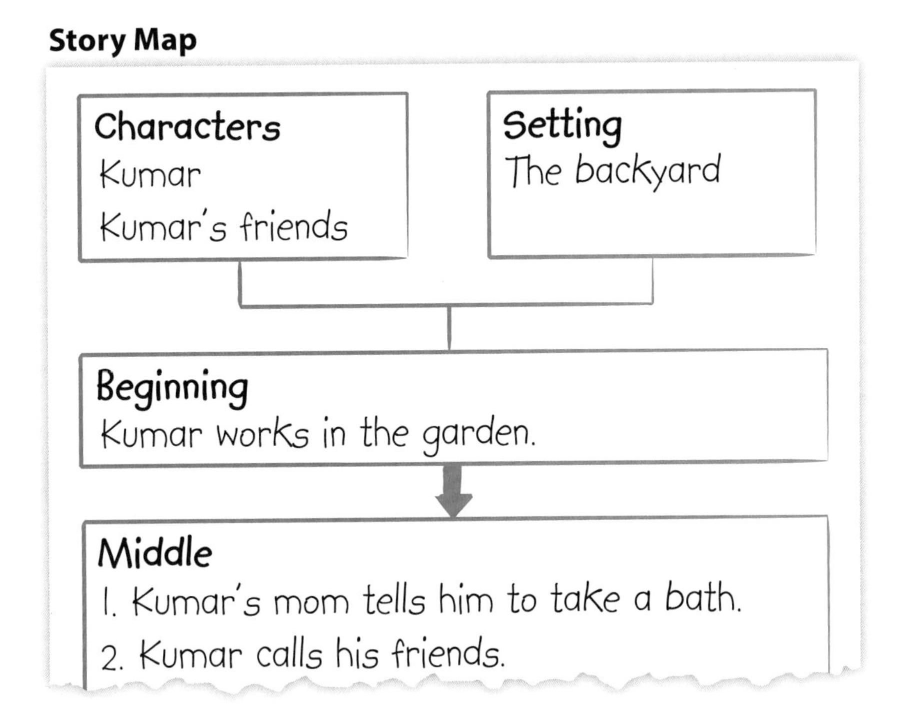

Draft

Make sure your story has a beginning, middle, and end. Use details to tell more about your characters and setting.

Writing Project, continued

Revise

1. **Read, Retell, Respond** Read your draft aloud to a partner. Your partner listens and then retells the story. Next, talk about ways to make your writing better.

Language Frames	
Retell	**Make Suggestions**
The story takes place in/at ______. The main characters are ______.	I can't really picture the setting. Could you add details about ______?
The characters in the story work together to ______.	I didn't understand why ______. Maybe you need to explain that more.
At the end, ______.	

2. **Make Changes** Think about your draft and your partner's ideas. Then use revision marks to make your changes.

- Make sure your readers can picture your characters and setting.

> And now is all muddy.
> Kumar has been working in the garden again.^

- Do you tell every important event? Add any missing details.

> He stands there waiting for them.
> Kumar tells them all to meet him in his backyard.^
> Kumar picks up the soap and sponge.

Edit and Proofread

Work with a partner to edit and proofread your story. Be sure to use the correct form of pronouns. Use revision marks to show your changes.

Present

On Your Own Make a final copy of your story. Read it aloud to your classmates. You can also retell it from memory.

Presentation Tips	
If you are the speaker...	**If you are the listener...**
Use your hands to help your listeners picture what's happening in the story.	Listen for details about character and setting. Try to picture them.
If you are retelling your story, make sure you tell events in order.	Is the speaker a good storyteller? See what you can learn as you watch and listen.

With a Group Publish your stories in a class magazine. Think of a good title. Make copies. Then share the magazine with your friends and family. Show them what cooperation is all about!

Talk Together

In this unit, you found lots of answers to the **Big Question**. Now use your concept map to discuss the **Big Question** with the class.

Concept Map

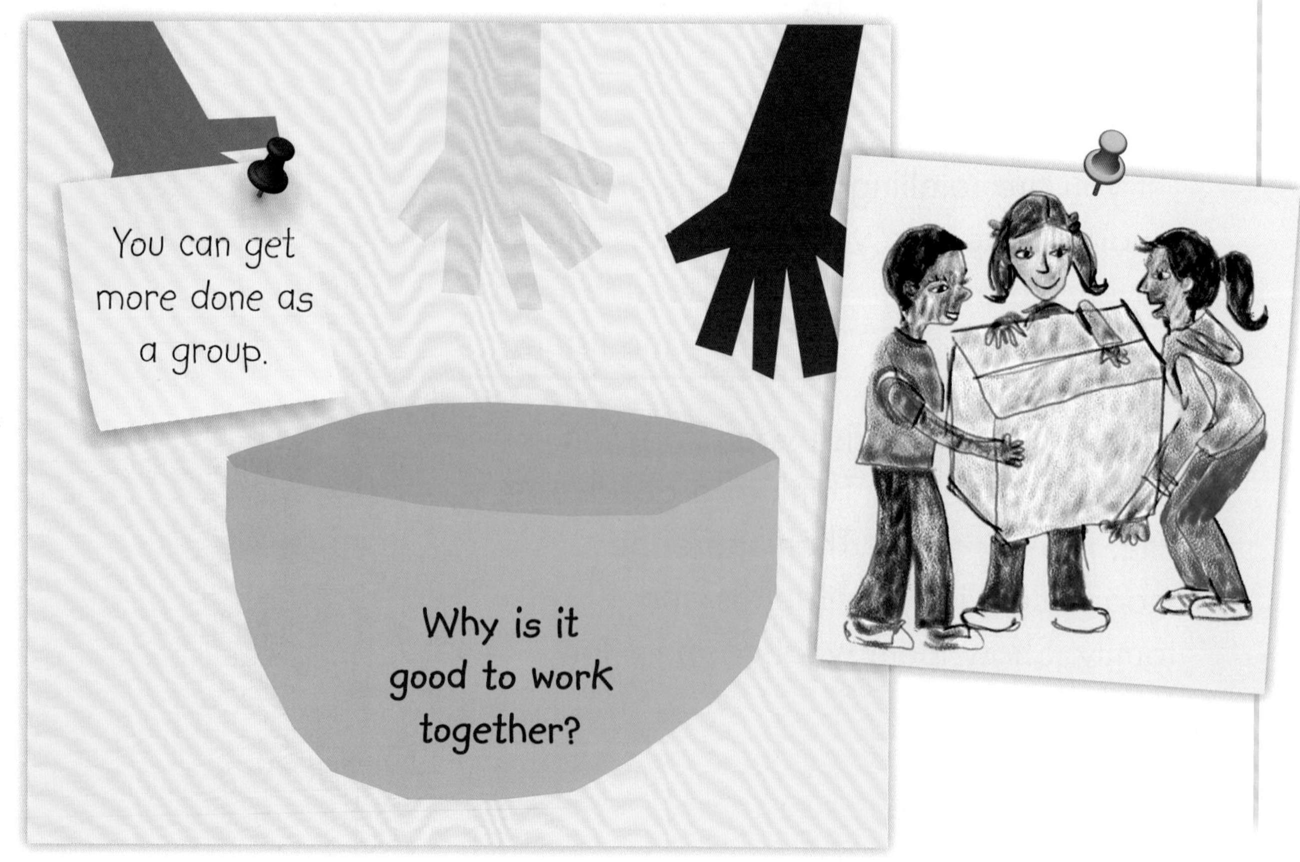

Share Your Ideas

Choose one of these ways to share your ideas about the **Big Question**.

Write It!

Make a Booklet

With a partner, make a booklet about places or groups in your community that help people.

Talk About It!

Storytelling Performance

Work with a partner to tell your own version of "Stone Soup." Act out your version of the story for the class. Speak clearly and with expression. Move your hands and your body as you act out the story.

Do It!

Create a Mural

Work with a group to paint a mural on bulletin board paper. Show what is special about your community. Post the mural in the classroom for all to enjoy.

Write It!

Make a Poster

Pretend you need help to clean the park. Make a poster to ask all your neighbors to help. Make sure your handwriting is legible and that everything is spelled correctly.

Unit 7

Best Buddies

BIG Question

How do living things depend on each other?

MPUMALANGA, SOUTH AFRICA
Red-billed oxpeckers searching for parasites on an impala

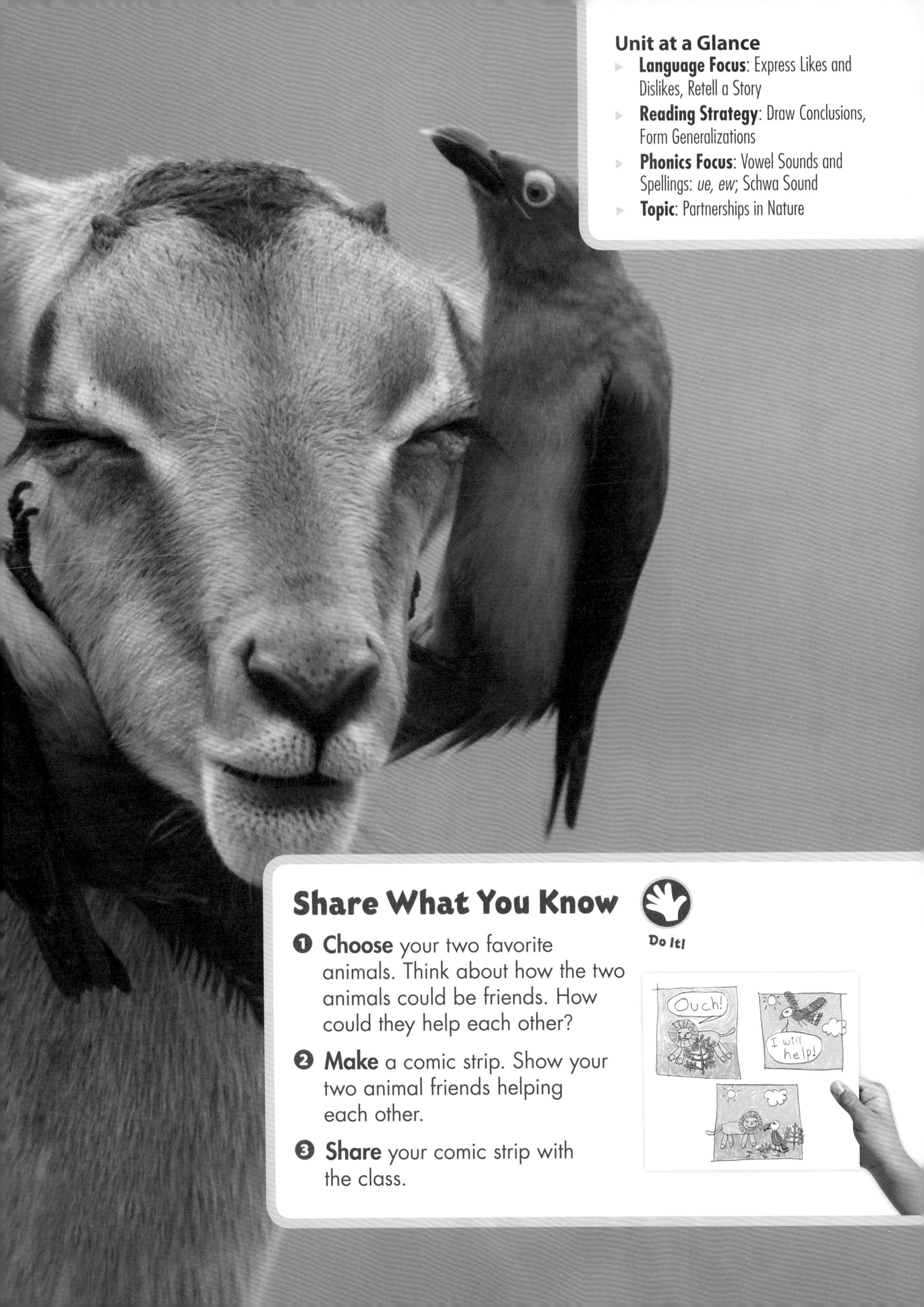

Unit at a Glance

- **Language Focus**: Express Likes and Dislikes, Retell a Story
- **Reading Strategy**: Draw Conclusions, Form Generalizations
- **Phonics Focus**: Vowel Sounds and Spellings: *ue, ew*; Schwa Sound
- **Topic**: Partnerships in Nature

Share What You Know

Do It!

1. **Choose** your two favorite animals. Think about how the two animals could be friends. How could they help each other?
2. **Make** a comic strip. Show your two animal friends helping each other.
3. **Share** your comic strip with the class.

PART 1 **Language Focus**

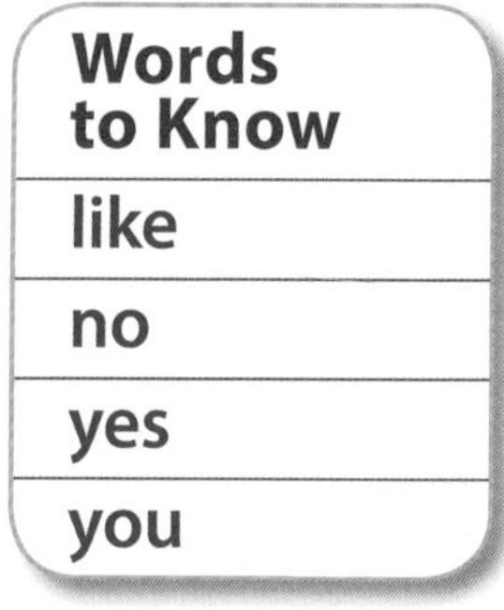

Express Likes and Dislikes

Listen and sing.

Spiders and Wolves

Do **you like** spiders?

Yes, I like helpful spiders.
I like to find their beautiful webs.
They can trap bugs in their sticky webs so
Spiders are members of the food chain.

Do you like gray wolves?

No, I don't like the gray wolves.
They are so strong and often they kill.

But wolves are cousins to
your dog Juno.
They have to kill so they can
survive.

Tune: "Morning Has Broken"

Key Words

Plants have important **roles** in nature. A **chain** can show how they **relate** to animals and each other.

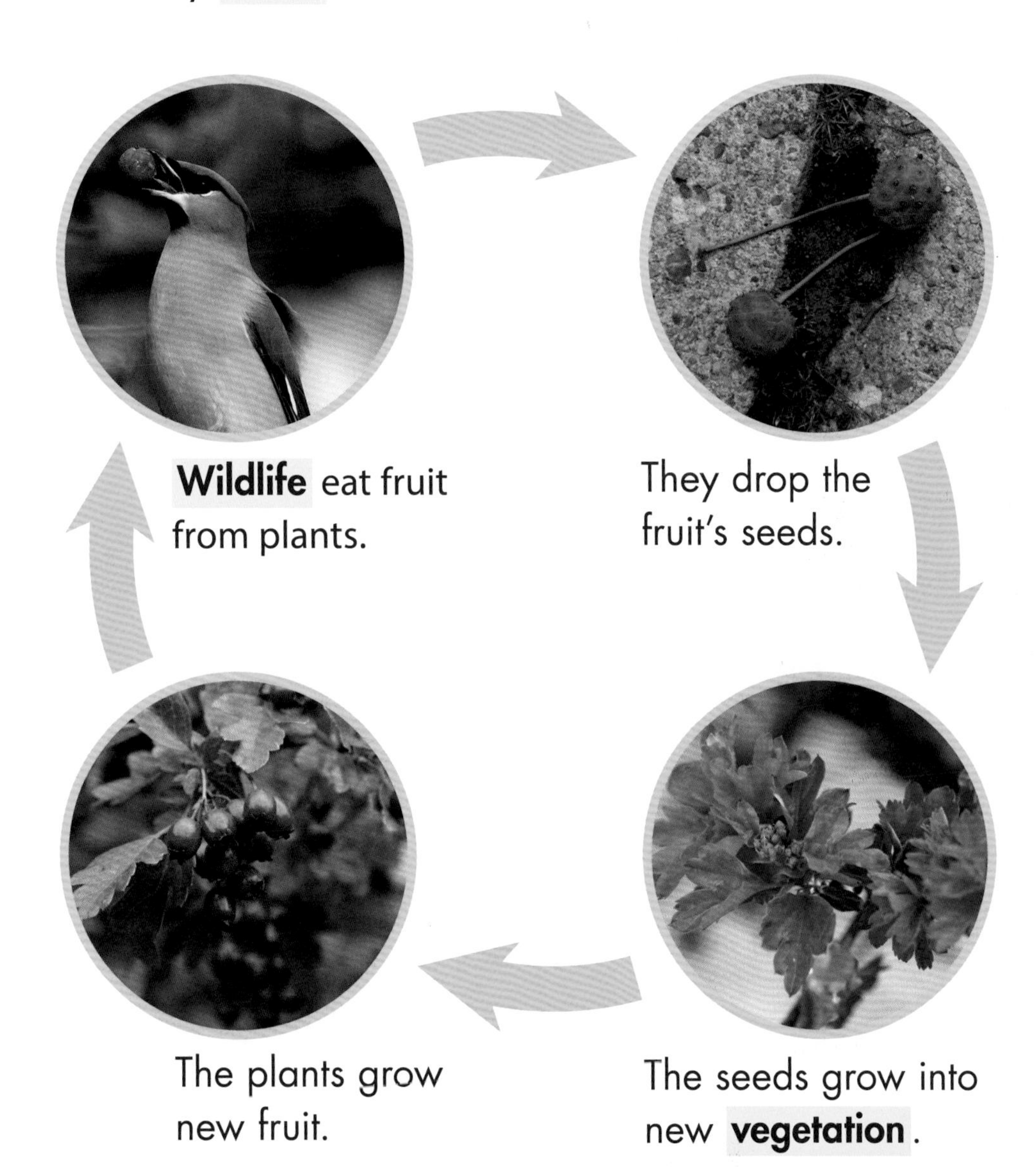

Talk Together

Look at the pictures. How do plants and animals work together in nature?

PART 1 Thinking Map

Characters' Motives

Characters do things in stories. You can figure out why they do these things. You can figure out their **motives**. Use a character map to show what a character does and why.

Character Map

Character	What the Character Does	Why the Character Does It
Sergio 	feeds his dog 	He loves his dog and wants to take good care of her. 

Write the character's name here.

Write what the character does here.

Write why the character acts this way here.

Talk Together

Choose a picture card. Make up a story about the animal on your card. Work with your partner to fill in a character map. Show what the animal does and why.

More Key Words

accept
verb

Her mother **accepts** the flowers and a hug.

connect
verb

He **connects** the wires to make the computer work.

important
adjective

Firefighters have an **important** job.

necessary
adjective

A seatbelt is **necessary** to stay safe in a car.

others
noun

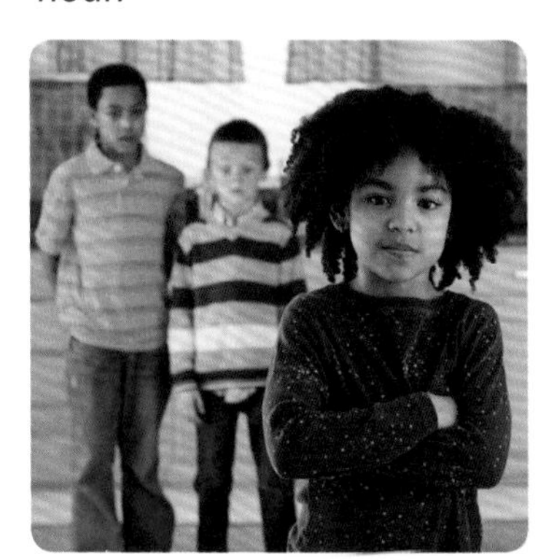

Casey stands away from the **others**.

Talk Together

Write a sentence for each **Key Word**. Take turns reading your sentences with a partner.

Parents have an important job.

It is important for neighbors to work together.

PART 1 **Reading Strategy**

Learn to Draw Conclusions

Look at the pictures. What do you see that you think is **important**? Think about how these pictures go with one another. Then **draw a conclusion**, or decide what you think the pictures are about.

Conclusion: Squirrels and trees are good for each other.

When you read, you **draw conclusions**, too.

How to Draw Conclusions

👁	**1.** Notice an important idea in the text.	*I read ____.*
👁	**2.** Look for another idea that you think is important.	*I also read ____.*
🧩	**3.** Put the ideas together. Draw a conclusion about the text.	*I conclude ____.*

Language Frames

- I read ______.
- I also read ______.
- I conclude ______.

Talk Together

Read Joshua's description. Read the sample and draw your own conclusions. Then use **Language Frames** to tell a partner about them.

Description

The Oak Tree and the Squirrel

It is easy to **accept** the idea that trees are **important** to squirrels. Do you know that squirrels are also important to oak trees? You probably know that oak trees provide a place for squirrels to run, play, nest, and live. The trees also have acorns. Acorns are one of the foods that squirrels like best. In fact, acorns let squirrels help regrow oak trees. Trees, acorns, and squirrels are linked together in a **chain**.

Squirrels know that there may be no food once winter comes. So it's **necessary** to collect acorns and nuts during autumn. Then, the squirrels bury the food they find. During the winter, squirrels uncover and eat some of the acorns. **Others** are misplaced. They stay in the ground.

Sample Conclusion

"I read that there may be no food when winter comes.

I also read that in autumn squirrels bury acorns they find.

I conclude that those acorns help squirrels survive the winter."

In the spring, shoots of a small oak tree may grow. Does a squirrel that **connects** with an acorn help to build a tree? Yes, and one day, squirrels may have a new place to build a nice, large nest.

= A good place to draw a conclusion

PART 1 **Phonics Focus**

Vowel Sounds and Spellings: *ue, ew*

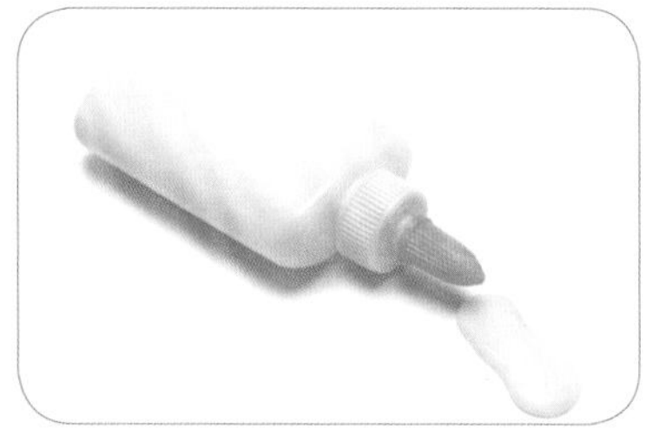
glue

screw

Listen and Learn

Listen to each picture word. Choose the pictures with the vowel sound you hear in the word *moon*.

1. **ue**

2. **ew**

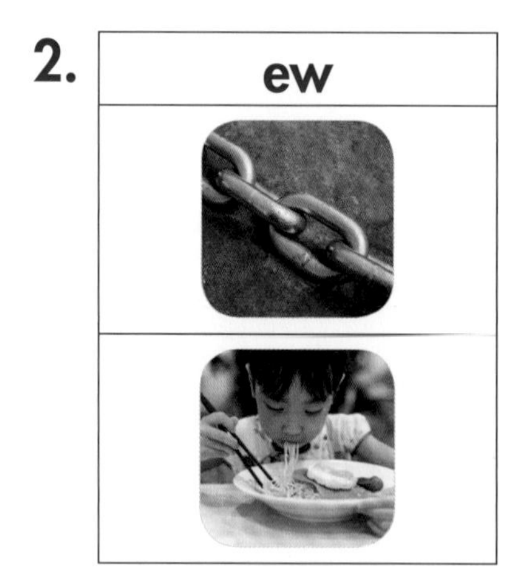

3. **ue**

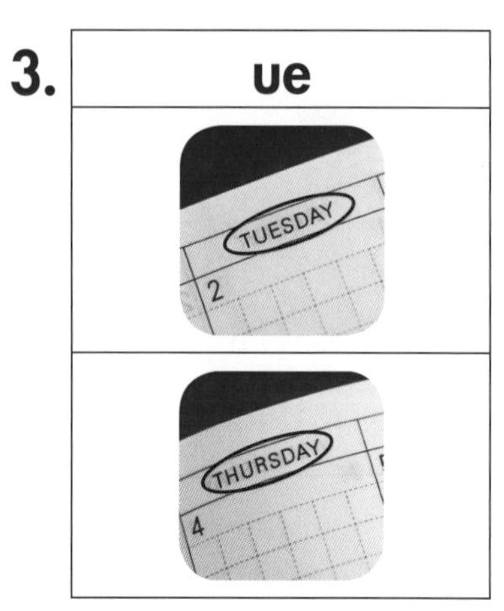

4. **ew**

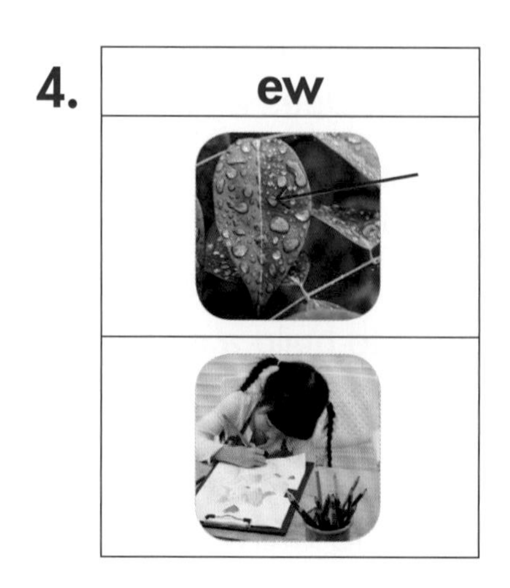

Talk Together

Listen and read. Find the words with the sound you hear in the word *moon* spelled *ue* and *ew.*

Over to You

Nature's Chain

We are all connected to wildlife. How? Here is one way. The rivers and oceans near you may be getting warmer. This is partly due to the actions of people. Yes, it is true.

Here is an example. You really like orca whales. You go on a whale-watching trip. The day is bright. The waters are blue. The boat is new. On the trip, you don't see any whales. The boat crew tells you that there are fewer orcas now. The whales eat salmon. The water is too warm for salmon. The salmon are dying. There's not enough salmon for orcas to eat. Soon, there could be no orcas.

People are part of nature's chain. Pollution makes the waters warm. The warm waters kill the salmon. The whales have nothing to eat. It is important for people to accept their role in nature's chain. Then they can do what is necessary to protect the environment.

Work with a partner.

Find the words with the vowel sound you hear in the word *moon* spelled *ue* and *ew.* Take turns making sentences using the words.

Read "Nature's Chain" with a partner. Practice reading words with *ue* and *ew.*

Read a Folk Tale

Genre

A **folk tale** is a story that has been told for many years. Many of the same folk tales are told around the world. This folk tale is told in Indonesia, India, and Congo.

Characters and Setting

The characters in this story are animals.

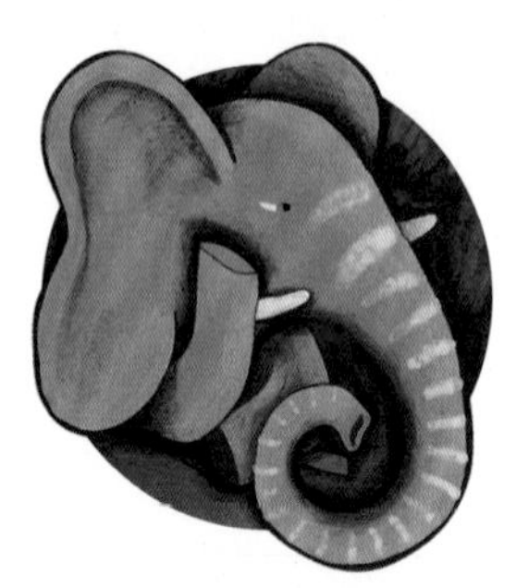

Elephant

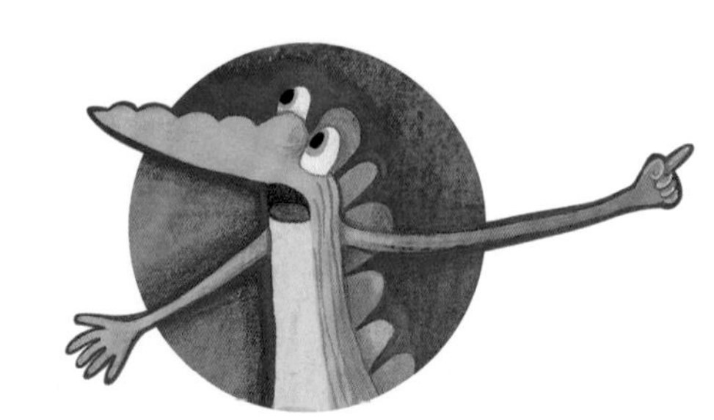

Gecko

This story happens at night in Bali, Indonesia. That's the setting.

ASIA
BALI
AUSTRALIA

Go to Sleep, Gecko!

Retold by **Margaret Read MacDonald**

illustrated by **Geraldo Valério**

▸ **Set a Purpose**
Gecko cannot go to sleep! Find out why.

One night, Elephant **was awakened by** a loud noise right under his window.

"GECK-o! GECK-o! GECK-o!"

"Gecko, what are you doing here? It is the middle of the night. Go home and go to bed."

was awakened by woke up because he heard

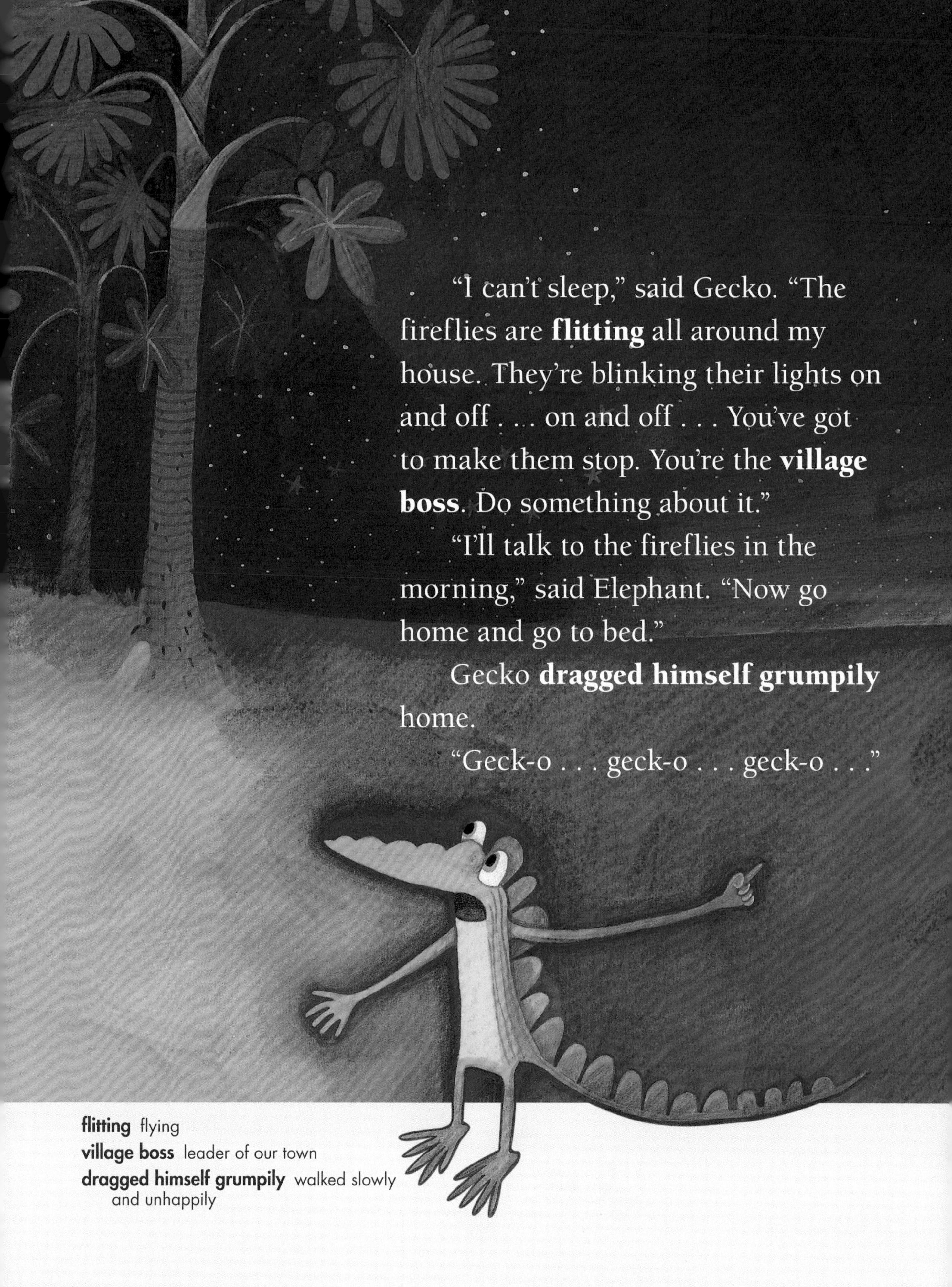

"I can't sleep," said Gecko. "The fireflies are **flitting** all around my house. They're blinking their lights on and off . . . on and off . . . You've got to make them stop. You're the **village boss**. Do something about it."

"I'll talk to the fireflies in the morning," said Elephant. "Now go home and go to bed."

Gecko **dragged himself grumpily** home.

"Geck-o . . . geck-o . . . geck-o . . ."

flitting flying
village boss leader of our town
dragged himself grumpily walked slowly and unhappily

Next morning, Elephant called the fireflies.

"Is it true that you have been **flashing** your lights on and off . . . on and off . . . all night long? Have you been keeping Gecko awake?"

flashing blinking

"Oh, yes," said the fireflies. "We have to blink our lights on and off all night. Rain washes out holes in the road. Without our lights, someone would step in a hole!"

"Why, that is very **thoughtful** of you," said Elephant. "Just keep on doing what you've been doing. You can go home now."

So the fireflies went home.

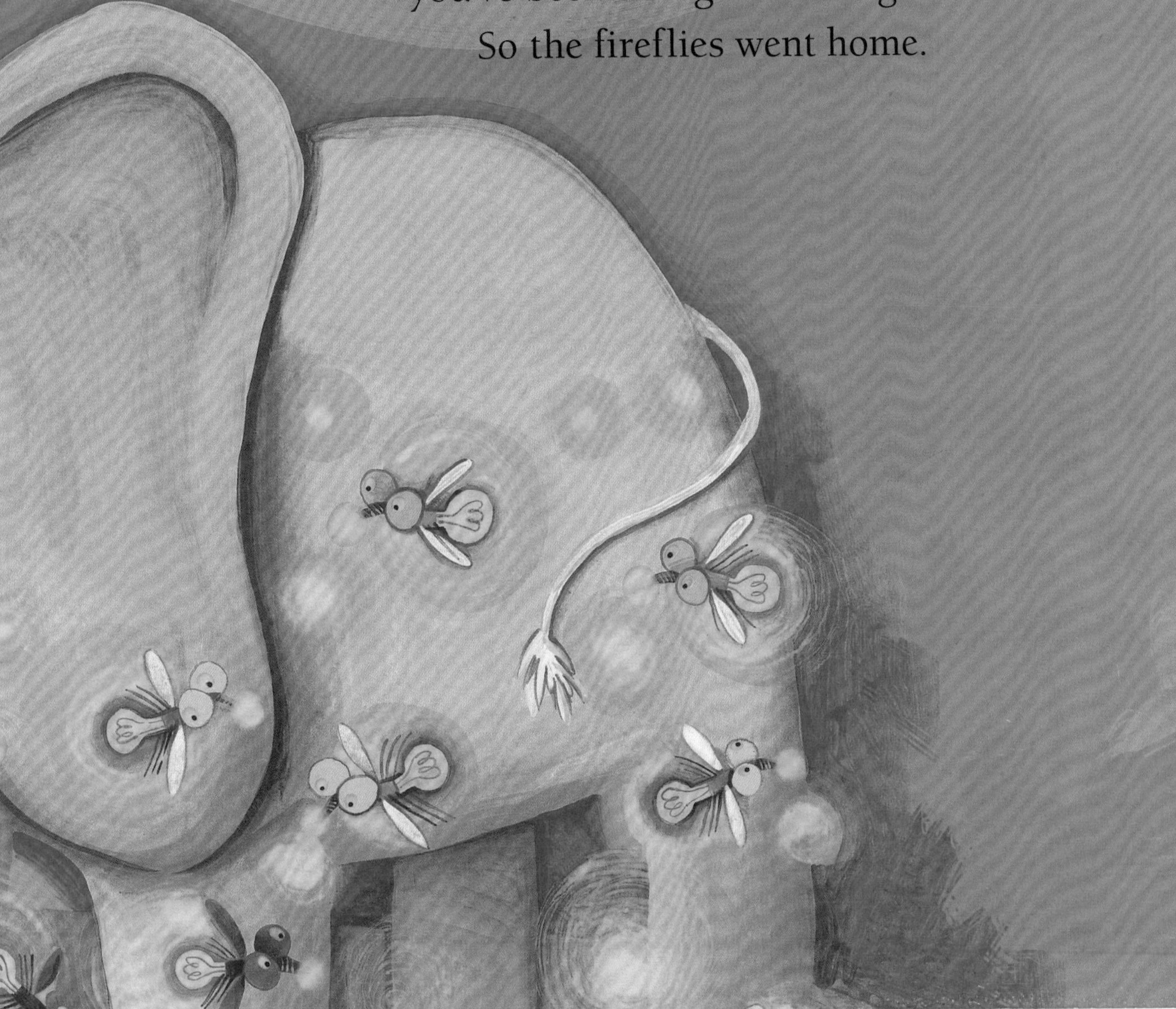

thoughtful nice; kind

Before You Continue

1. **Cause/Effect** Why can't Gecko go to sleep?
2. **Setting** Look at the pictures on pages 162–163. What can you tell about the setting of the story?

Predict
Will Elephant find a way to help Gecko go to sleep?

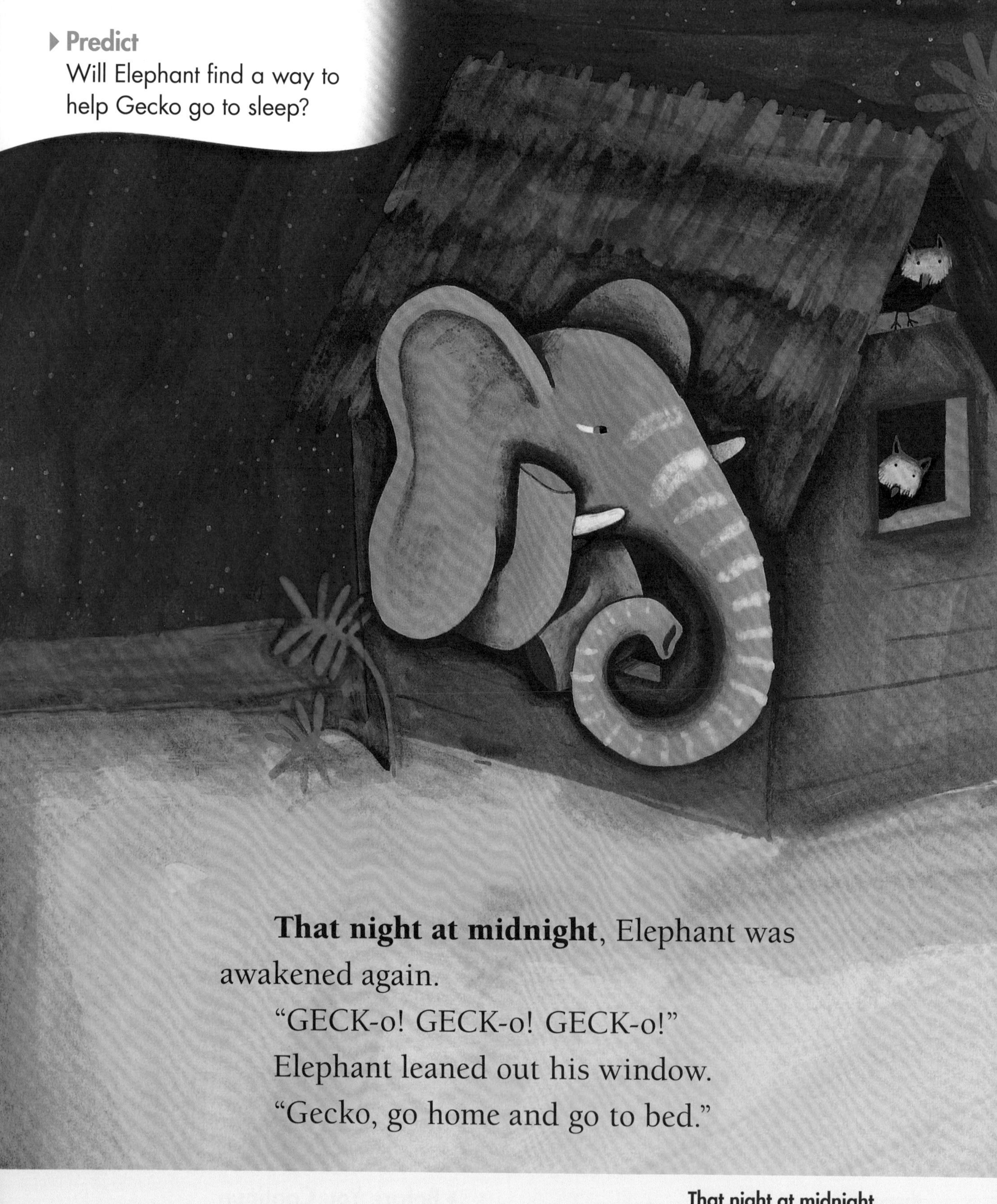

That night at midnight, Elephant was awakened again.

"GECK-o! GECK-o! GECK-o!"

Elephant leaned out his window.

"Gecko, go home and go to bed."

That night at midnight
In the middle of the night

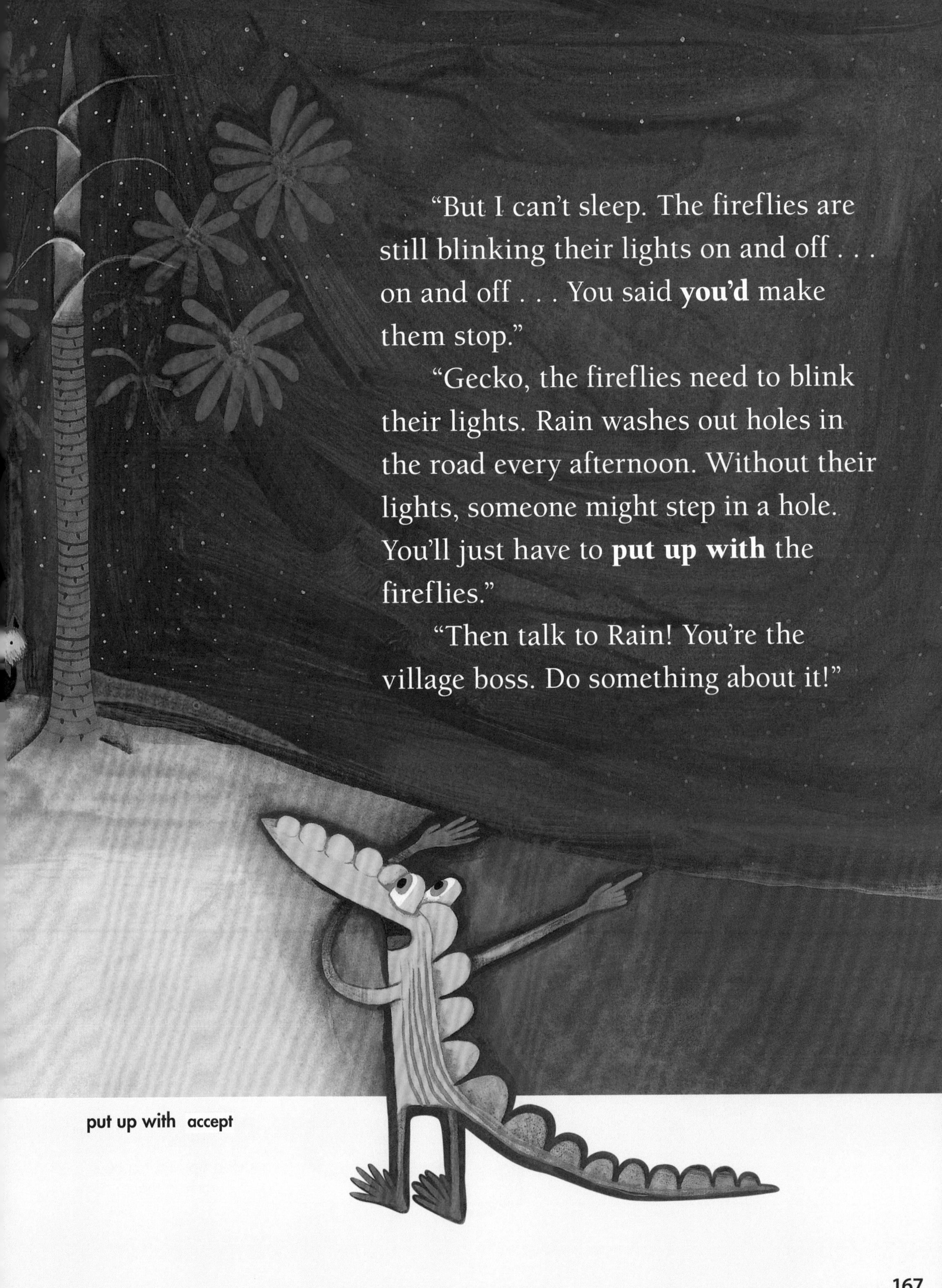

"But I can't sleep. The fireflies are still blinking their lights on and off . . . on and off . . . You said **you'd** make them stop."

"Gecko, the fireflies need to blink their lights. Rain washes out holes in the road every afternoon. Without their lights, someone might step in a hole. You'll just have to **put up with** the fireflies."

"Then talk to Rain! You're the village boss. Do something about it!"

put up with accept

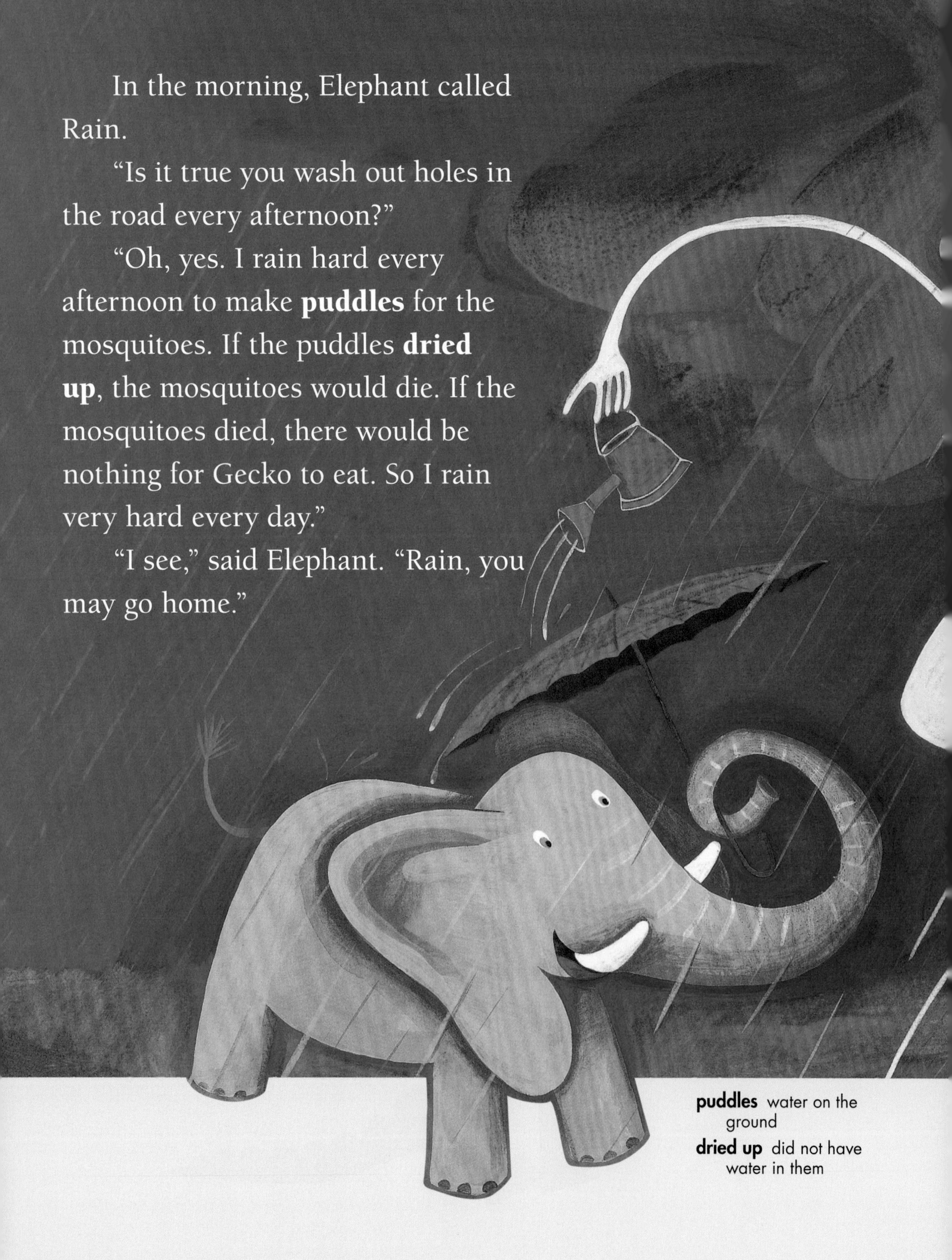

In the morning, Elephant called Rain.

"Is it true you wash out holes in the road every afternoon?"

"Oh, yes. I rain hard every afternoon to make **puddles** for the mosquitoes. If the puddles **dried up**, the mosquitoes would die. If the mosquitoes died, there would be nothing for Gecko to eat. So I rain very hard every day."

"I see," said Elephant. "Rain, you may go home."

puddles water on the ground

dried up did not have water in them

Before You Continue

1. **Confirm Prediction** Think about your prediction. Has Elephant helped Gecko go to sleep? Explain.
2. **Character's Motive** Why does Rain make puddles in the road every afternoon?

▶ **Predict**
Will Gecko ever learn to **accept** the fireflies?

That night at midnight, Elephant was awakened yet again.

"GECK-o! GECK-o! GECK-o!"

He leaned out his window. "Gecko, go home and go to bed!"

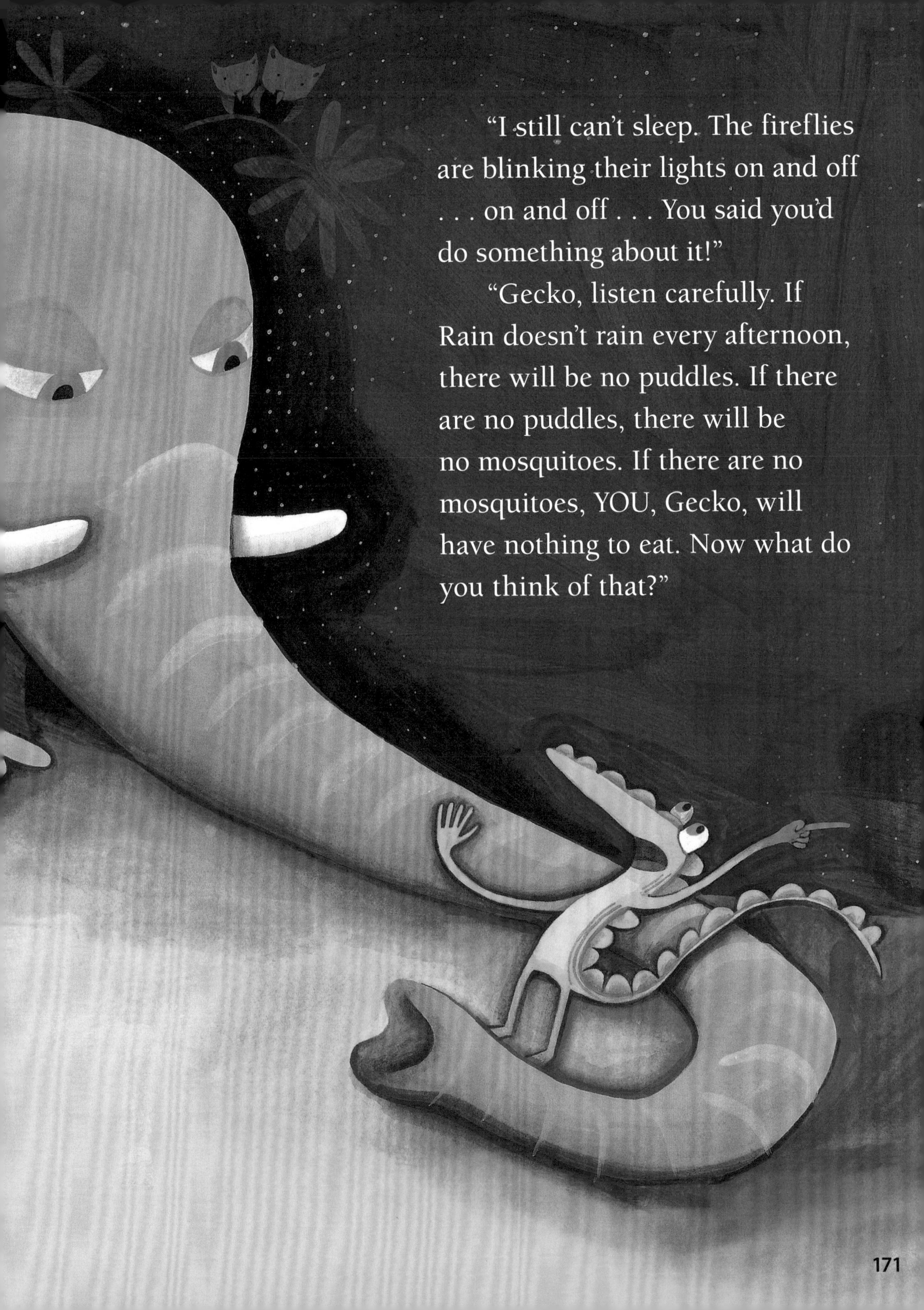

"I still can't sleep. The fireflies are blinking their lights on and off . . . on and off . . . You said you'd do something about it!"

"Gecko, listen carefully. If Rain doesn't rain every afternoon, there will be no puddles. If there are no puddles, there will be no mosquitoes. If there are no mosquitoes, YOU, Gecko, will have nothing to eat. Now what do you think of that?"

Gecko thought.

If Elephant told Rain to stop raining, there would be no holes and puddles in the road. If there were no holes and puddles in the road, the fireflies would stop flashing their lights . . . but Gecko would have nothing to eat!

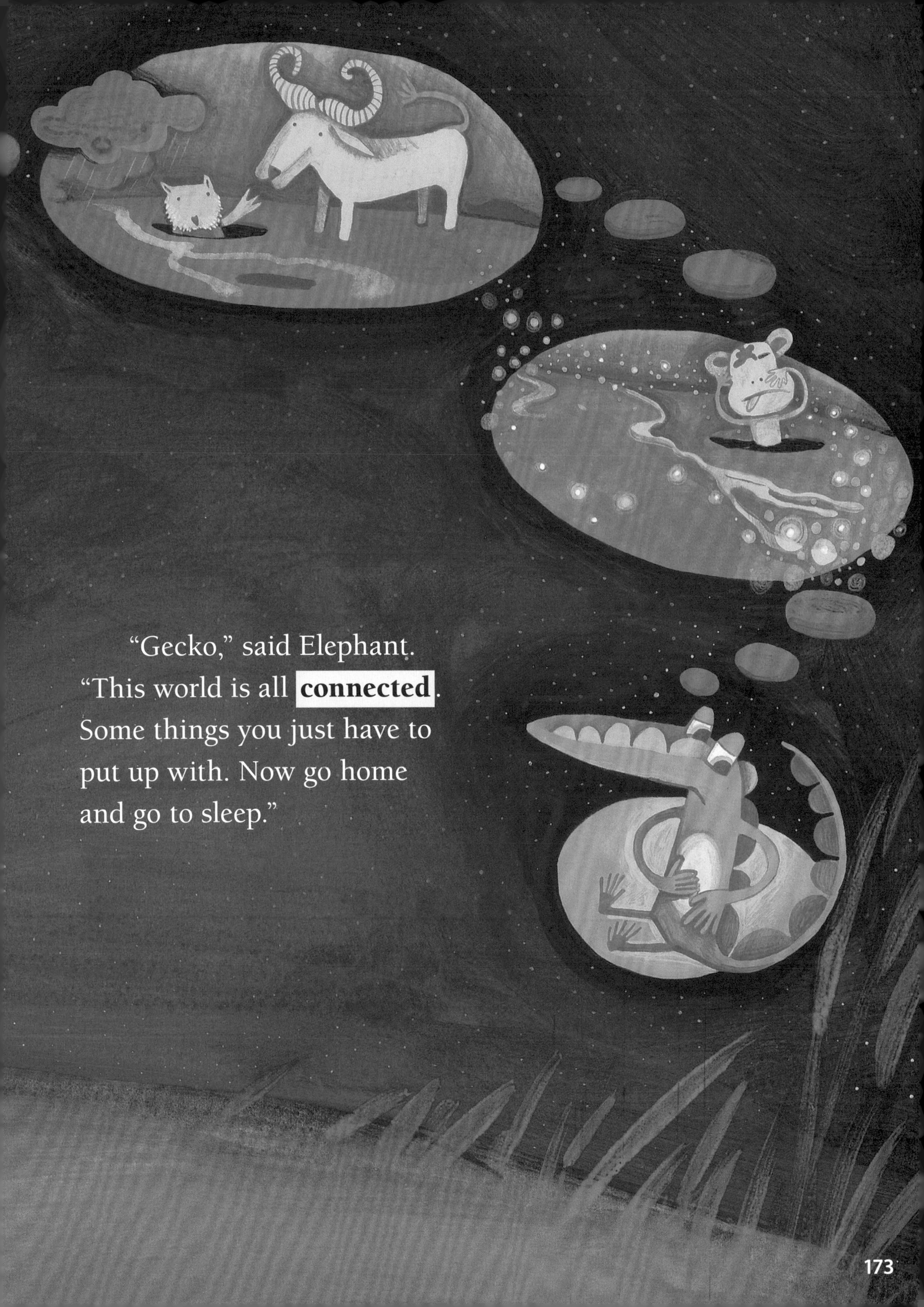

“Gecko,” said Elephant. “This world is all **connected**. Some things you just have to put up with. Now go home and go to sleep.”

So Gecko went home. Gecko closed his eyes and went to sleep. Outside the fireflies blinked on and off . . . on and off . . .

Some things you just have to put up with. ❖

Before You Continue

1. **Confirm Prediction** Does Gecko **accept** the **role** of the fireflies? Explain.
2. **Draw Conclusions** Think about how Elephant treats Gecko. What does this show about Elephant's character?

AWARD WINNER

Meet the Illustrator

Geraldo Valério

Geraldo Valério loves art. When he was a boy growing up in Brazil, he liked to draw. At first he used colored pencils and pens. Then when he was ten years old, he began painting.

Now, it is Mr. Valério's job to illustrate children's books. He reads the stories and then paints pictures for them. "Most of all, I love playing with colors while painting the illustrations," he said.

Drawing Tip

Find places in the story where Mr. Valério's illustrations help you see and feel what the words say. Then make your own drawing. Try to show something that the author describes.

PART 1 **Think and Respond**

Talk About It 

1. How do you know this selection is a **folk tale**?

It is a folk tale because ______________________________.

2. In the end, Gecko had to choose between getting rid of the fireflies and eating. What did he choose? Do you agree? Explain.

Gecko chose ______________________________.

I agree/disagree because ______________________________.

3. What **lesson** does Gecko learn about the way things **connect**?

Gecko learns ______________________________.

Write About It 

Work with a partner. Write a short letter to your favorite character from the folk tale. Tell him what you think about his actions in the story. Use **Key Words** in your letter.

May 12, 20__

Dear _____,

I like/don't like the way _____. I agree/disagree that _____.

Yours truly,

<your name>

Characters' Motives

What do the characters do in "Go to Sleep, Gecko!"? Why? Make a character map.

Character Map

Character	What the Character Does	Why the Character Does It
Gecko	He complains about the fireflies.	He can't sleep.

Now use your character map. Tell a partner about your favorite character in "Go to Sleep, Gecko!"

My favorite character is ______. This character ______ because ______.

Fluency

Practice reading with correct expression. Rate your reading.

PART 1 **Word Work**

Use a Dictionary

You can **use a dictionary** to find out what a word means. The words in the dictionary are in alphabetical order. Find the word **accept** in the dictionary.

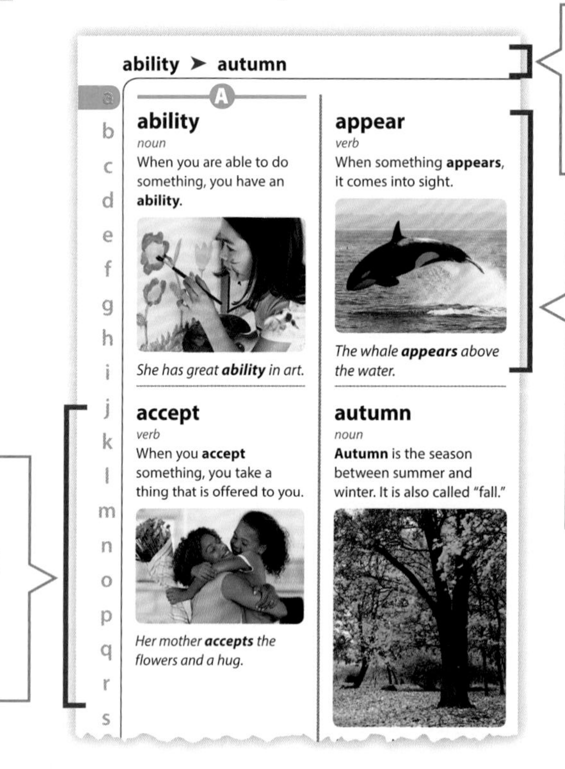

ability ➤ autumn

A

ability
noun
When you are able to do something, you have an **ability**.

*She has great **ability** in art.*

appear
verb
When something **appears**, it comes into sight.

*The whale **appears** above the water.*

accept
verb
When you **accept** something, you take a thing that is offered to you.

*Her mother **accepts** the flowers and a hug.*

autumn
noun
Autumn is the season between summer and winter. It is also called "fall."

a b c d e f g h i j k l m n o p q r s

Look at the **guide words** to find the right page.

The entry for **appear** comes after **accept** and before **autumn**.

This **entry** tells about the word **accept**.

Try It Together

Read the sentences. Then answer the questions.

At the end of the story, Gecko learns how everything in nature is connected to everything else. It's an **important** lesson. He learns that even the fireflies are playing a **necessary** role when they blink. Accepting that helps Gecko go to sleep!

1. Look in a dictionary for the word **important**. Write the definition of the word.

2. Write a sentence with the word **necessary**. Use a dictionary if necessary.

Making Connections Now read about other living things in nature and how they **connect** to one another.

Genre A **profile** tells about a person and what the person does.

Enric Sala
Marine Ecologist

by Kristin Cozort

Enric Sala has always wondered about things that live in the ocean. When he was young, he loved to swim. He liked to watch all kinds of animals and plants through his mask. He wanted to be an **underwater explorer**.

Today, Mr. Sala is a marine ecologist. He studies how underwater plants and animals **relate** to each other. He learns how they need each other to stay alive.

underwater explorer person who looks for new things in the ocean

Before You Continue

1. **Draw Conclusions** How do you think Mr. Sala feels about underwater **wildlife**? How do you know?
2. **Make Connections** How can you **connect** Mr. Sala's job today with what he did when he was young?

Underwater Cities

Mr. Sala studies coral reefs in the Pacific Ocean. A coral reef is like an underwater city. Thousands of plants and animals live there. They **compete for** food and space. Coral reefs are beautiful. They are also easily harmed.

▲ Many different kinds of **vegetation** and animals live in a coral reef.

compete for try to be the first to find

Reefs and Humans

Mr. Sala also studies how people's actions can change coral reefs. Sometimes people **pollute the water or overfish**. That changes the way all the living things **connect** to one another.

Coral reefs can become **damaged**. Then, many animals must find new homes. Some animals just disappear. Mr. Sala wants to **prevent this**.

▼ This reef is damaged. Many animals can't find food here.

pollute the water or overfish make the water dirty or kill too many fish for food
damaged hurt
prevent this keep the animals' homes safe

Before You Continue

1. **Ask Questions** You ask yourself, "What is it that Mr. Sala wants to prevent?" What can you do to find the answer?
2. **Make Inferences** How does Mr. Sala feel about the coral reefs? How do you know?

All Parts Matter

Mr. Sala believes that all living things in a coral reef should be kept safe. "Underwater **ecosystems** are like airplanes," Mr. Sala says. "They need all of their parts to **function**. Who wants to travel on a plane knowing five or ten parts are missing?"

"To take better care of marine **habitats**, we first have to study them. It's the only way to understand **the full impact humans have on** these places," Mr. Sala says. ❖

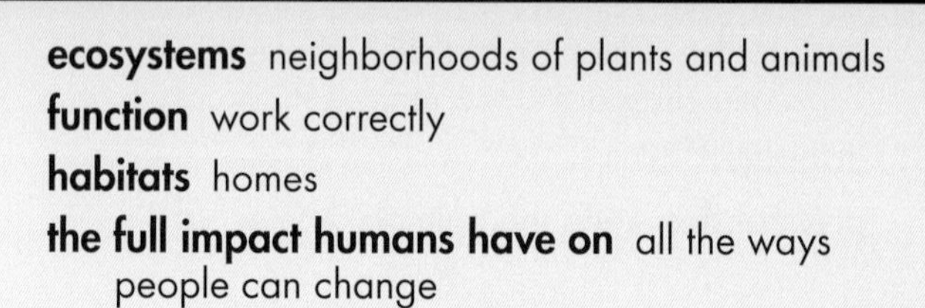

ecosystems neighborhoods of plants and animals
function work correctly
habitats homes
the full impact humans have on all the ways people can change

Enric Sala swims with a green turtle. They are at Dirty Rock off Coco's Island in Costa Rica.

Before You Continue

1. **Draw Conclusions** What is **necessary** to help preserve life in the ocean?
2. **Topic/Main Idea** What is the topic of this selection? What is the main idea?

Compare Genres

"Go to Sleep, Gecko!" is a folk tale and "Enric Sala: Marine Ecologist" is a profile. How are they the same? How are they different?

Folk Tale

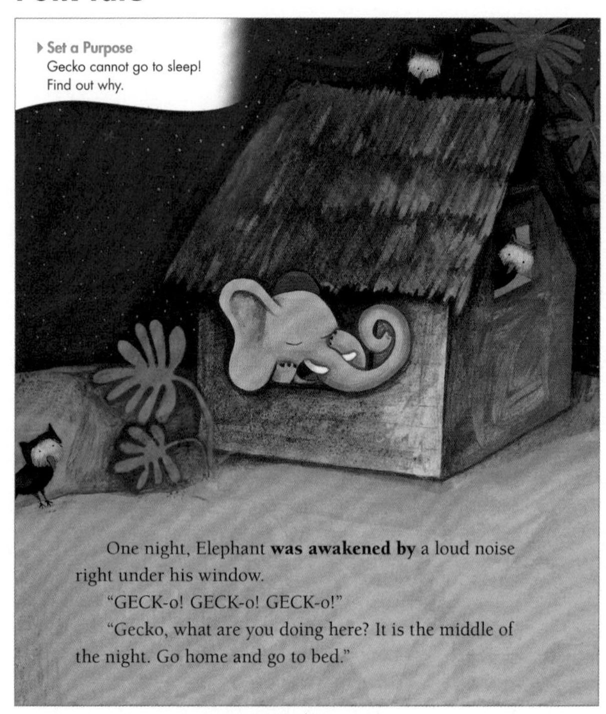

a story with animal characters

Profile

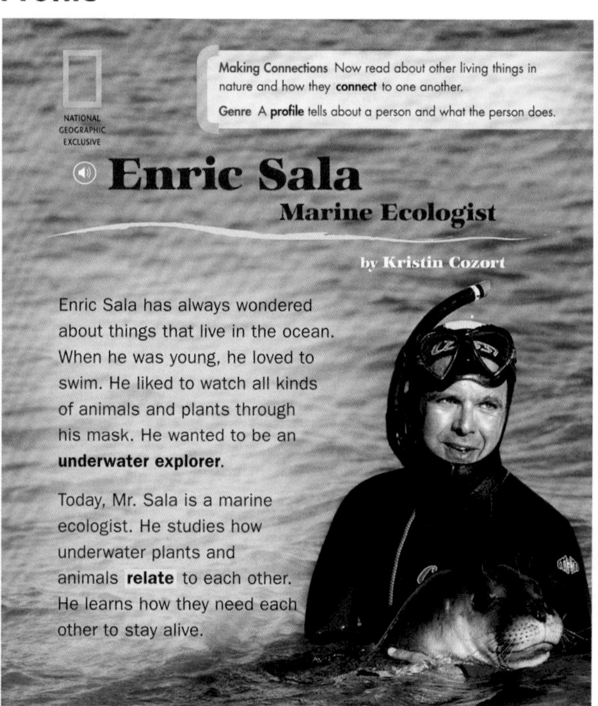

tells about a person and what the person does

Talk Together

Look at the pictures in the folk tale with your partner. Take turns telling how the characters depend on each other. Use **Key Words**.

Past-Tense Verbs

All action verbs show when the action happens. **Past-tense verbs** show that the action happened in the past.

Grammar Rules **Past Tense Verbs**

Regular Past Tense	Add **-ed** to the end of many verbs to show an action in the past.	**Examples:** walk + **-ed** = walk**ed** jump + **-ed** = jump**ed**
Irregular Past Tense	Some verbs have special forms to show past tense. You have to remember the forms.	**Example:** begin → began say → said

Read Past-Tense Verbs

Read these sentences from "Go to Sleep, Gecko!" Identify one irregular past-tense verb and one regular past-tense verb.

> Elephant leaned out his window. "Gecko, go to bed."
>
> "But I can't sleep. The fireflies are still blinking their lights on and off... on and off... You said you'd make them stop."

Use Past-Tense Verbs 

Write two sentences about how animals help one another. Use at least one regular and one irregular past-tense verb. Share your sentences with a partner.

Retell a Story

Listen to the poem and read along.

Words to Know
after
before
when
while

Partners

Poem 

Before this small bird flies onto its back,
The rhino's too itchy to play.
After the bird eats the bugs on its hide,
The rhino is feeling okay.

When this little bird helps a rhino,
It eats many bugs off its back.
While the rhino enjoys a good cleaning
The little bird has a good snack.

Science Vocabulary

Key Words

How do animals **respond** to other **species**?

Some animals are **partners**. They help each other.

Some animals are **enemies**. They **threaten** each other.

Talk Together

Why do you think some animals are partners and others are enemies?

Topic and Main Idea

The **topic** is what a selection is mostly about. The **main idea** is the most important idea about the topic. Look at these pictures.

Topic and Main Idea Chart

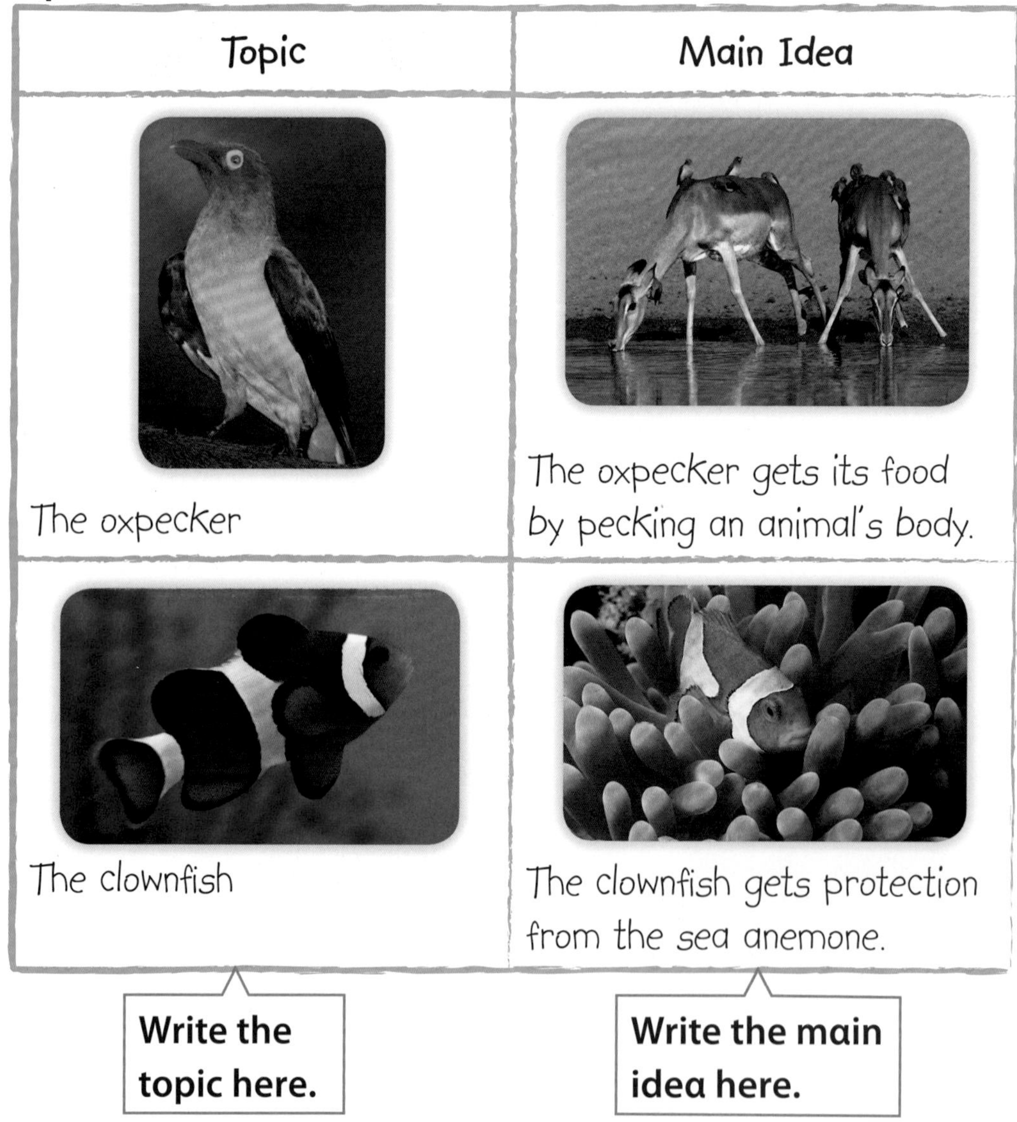

Talk Together

Read a nonfiction text with a partner. Work together to find the topic and main idea. Then write the information in a chart.

More Key Words

ability
noun

She has great **ability** in art.

danger
noun

If you walk too close to the edge, you are in **danger** of falling.

difficult
adjective

It can be **difficult** to learn some new things.

unusual
adjective

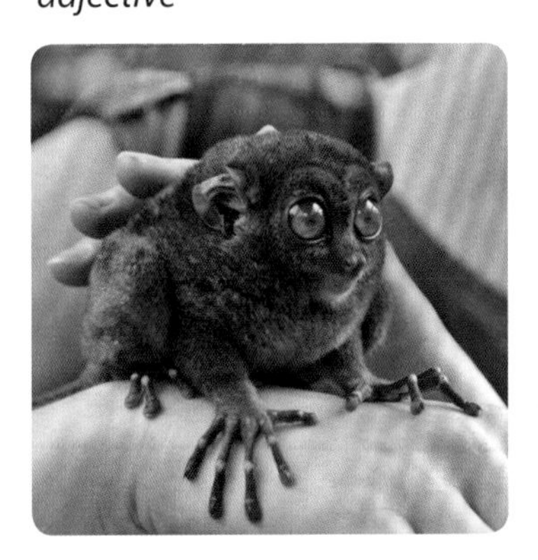

This tiny animal is very **unusual**.

useful
adjective

Tools are **useful** for fixing broken things.

Talk Together

Make a Word Map for each **Key Word**. Then compare your maps with a partner's.

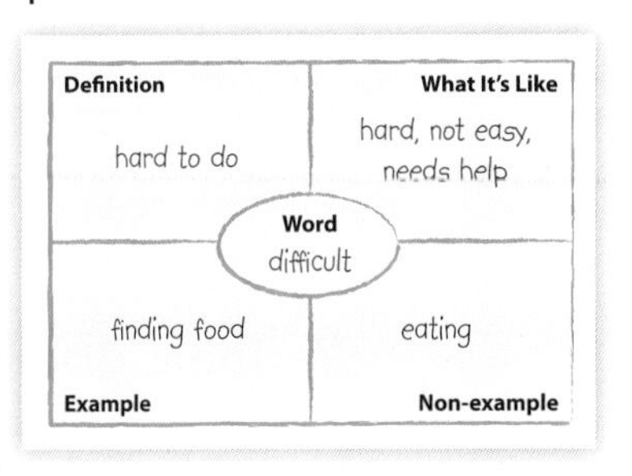

Learn to Form Generalizations

Look at the pictures. What kind of relationship do the ants and flower have? Can you think of other things that have this kind of relationship? If so, then you can form a **generalization**.

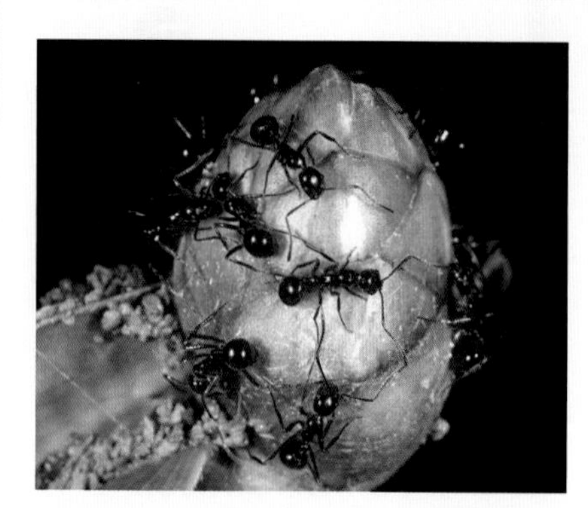

The ants keep other bugs away from the flower.

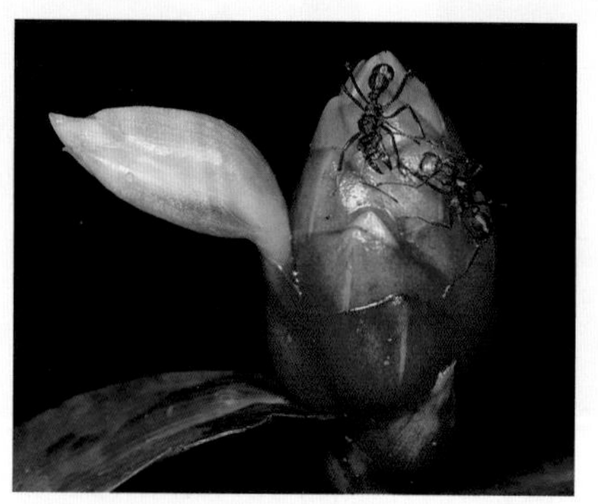

The flower makes food that the ants like.

A generalization is a statement that has to do with many situations. When you read, you **form generalizations**, too.

How to Form Generalizations

1. Think about the important ideas in the text.

I read ______.

2. Think about how they go together. How are they like things you know from your own life?

I know ______.

3. Make a statement that seems true for both the text and what you know. Use words like *some, many, most,* or *all.*

Most of the time, it is true that ______.

Language Frames

- I read ______.
- I know ______.
- Most of the time, it is true that ______.

Talk Together

Read Graciela's and Emily's blog entry. Read the sample and form your own generalizations. Then use **Language Frames** to tell a partner about them.

Blog Entry

https://eltngl.com/reachhigherseries

Read 'n Share Blog

Today's Posts | Calendar | Announcements | News | Search REGISTER | SIGN IN

June 16, 2019

This Week's Selection: **Graciela & Emily: The Science Blog**

June 16, 2019

Before today, we had never even heard of the trap-jaw ant or the costus flower. Both of these **unusual species** live in the rainforest. Do you want to know what makes them special? They are great **partners**.

While we were researching our science report, this is what we found out. When the trap-jaw ant visits a costus, it gets a good meal by sucking nectar from the flower. Yum.

But how is the ant **useful** to the flower? The trap-jaw ant has a special **ability**. Its bite is full of **danger**, since it has a very large jaw that it can open and shut very fast. That means it can injure other small creatures. If we got bit, we would feel a painful sting. Ouch!

If another insect wanders too close, the trap-jaw ant **responds** by biting it. Then that insect will not do any damage to the flower. We could all use such a good partner!

Sample Generalization

"I read that the trap-jaw ant and costus flowers are great partners.

I know of other plants and animals that are partners, like trees and squirrels.

Most of the time, it is true that partners in nature help each other somehow."

= A good place to form a generalization

PART 2 **Phonics Focus**

Schwa Sound

salad

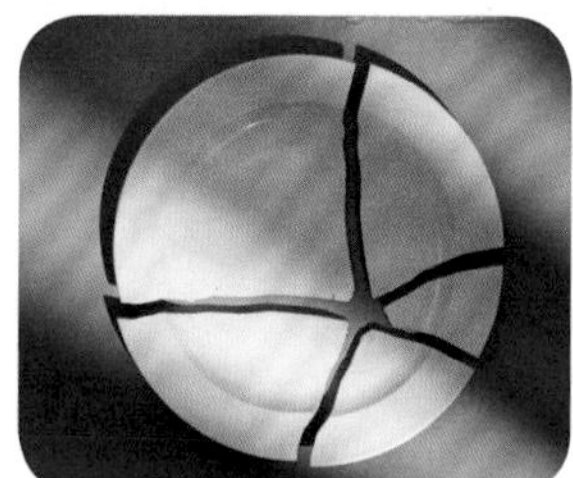

broken

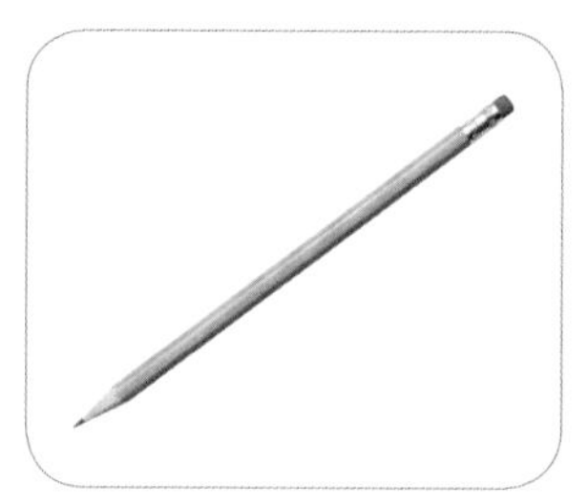

pencil

carrot

Listen and Learn

Listen to each word. Then sort the words by the spelling of the schwa sound.

onion	again	token	reason
cousin	habit	ago	silent

a	**e**	**i**	**o**
______	______	______	______
______	______	______	______

Choose two words from above. Write your own sentences with the words.

Talk Together

Listen and read. Find the words with the schwa sound.

Over to You

Animals Helping Each Other

Animals can help each other. Sheep and llamas are one example. Sheep cannot protect themselves. Predators threaten sheep. Some farmers keep llamas with their sheep. The llamas protect the sheep. The llamas fight when predators attack. They kick. They spit. They even scream. They fight hard. They make the enemies run away.

Birds help zebras. They also help rhinos. Ticks are small bugs. They bite zebras. They bite rhinos. Birds eat the ticks. The birds get a free meal.

These animal partners might seem unusual. But they depend on each other. They are happy to help each other.

Work with a partner.
Find words with the schwa sound. Sort the words according to how each schwa sound is spelled.

Read "Animals Helping Each Other" with a partner. Practice reading words with the schwa sound.

Read a Science Article

Genre

A **science article** gives facts about a topic.

Text Features

Look for **headings**. They tell you what each section, or part, of the article is about.

Keeping Clean

heading

Some animals help others stay clean. Cleaner shrimps do that. They live in the sea at cleaning stations.

Odd Couples

by Amy Sarver

Set a Purpose
Find out about some **unusual** ways that animals work together.

Pairing Up in the Wild

Animals in the wild have a **difficult** life. They need to find food, stay healthy, and hide from **danger**.

To make life easier, some animals pair up. The two kinds of animals may be very different. Yet these **odd couples** live together. This is called a symbiotic relationship. Each animal helps the other. Let's see how this works.

Keeping Clean

Some animals help others stay clean. Cleaner shrimps do that. They live in the sea at **cleaning stations**.

To get clean, a dirty fish stops by. A shrimp climbs onto the fish. The shrimp has tiny **claws**. The claws pick dead skin and **pests** off the fish. The hungry shrimp eats what it picks. The fish gets cleaned.

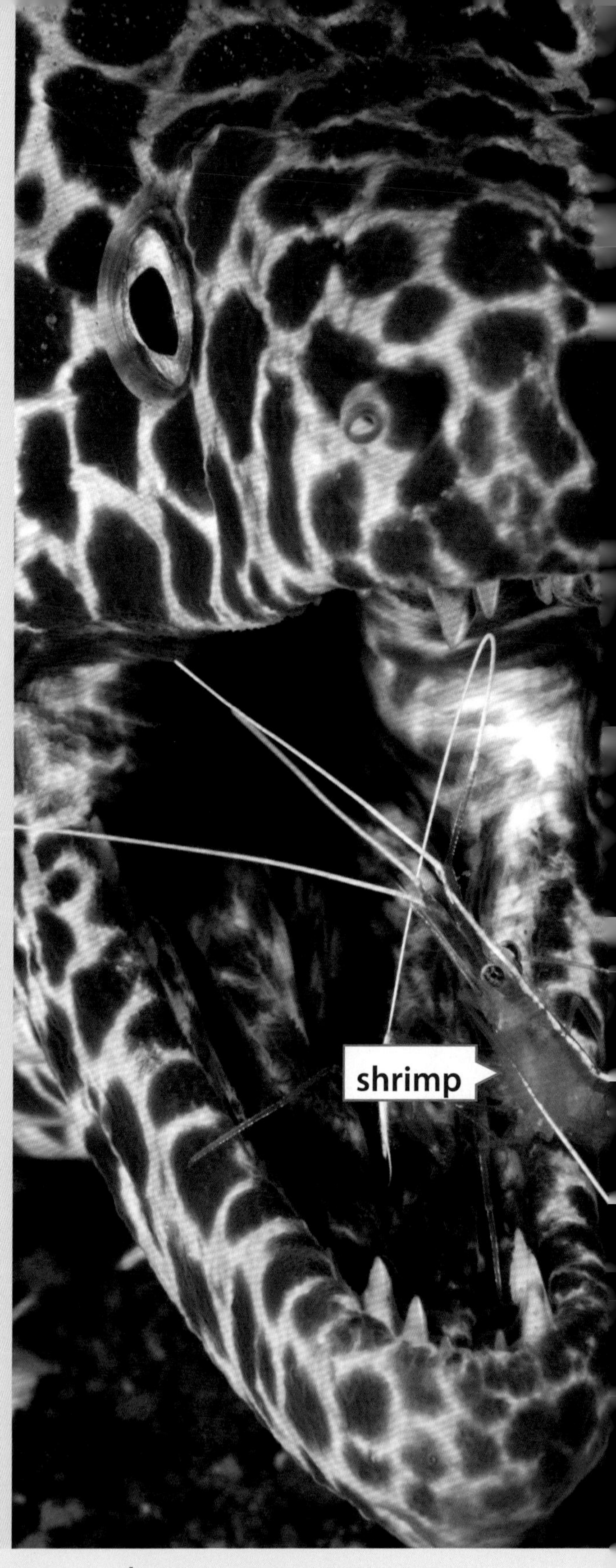

A cleaner shrimp cleans a moray eel's mouth. ▶

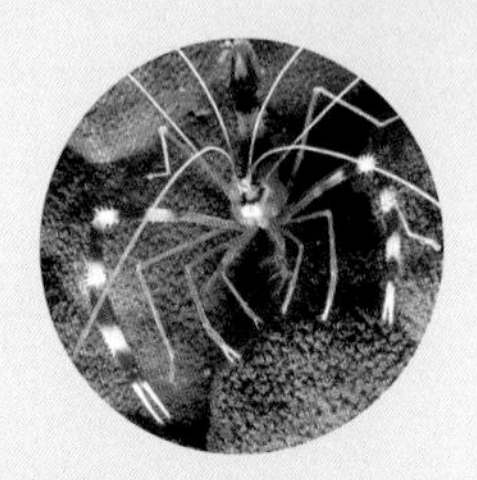

cleaning stations places where many animals come to get clean

◀ **claws** sharp nails on its toes

pests harmful bugs

Shrimps are not the only cleaners. So are plovers. These brave birds clean crocodile teeth. **Crocs** cannot do that themselves.

Plovers eat tiny animals stuck to a croc's teeth. **It's a good trade.** Birds get food. Crocs get clean teeth.

Crocs Crocodiles

It's a good trade. This is good for both the plover and the crocodile.

Before You Continue

1. **Use Text Features** Is "Keeping Clean" a good heading for pages 198–199? Explain.
2. **Generalize** What general point can you make about some animals, based on what cleaner shrimps and plovers do?

Riding Along

Like plovers, oxpeckers are birds. They ride on giraffes, **rhinos**, and other big **buddies**.

The big animals don't mind. Why not? Well, the birds eat bugs. That's good for the big animals. **In return**, the birds get plenty of food. It's a perfect **pairing**!

▲ One big buddy for an oxpecker bird is an antelope.

rhinos rhinoceroses
buddies friends
In return As a trade
pairing way to be **partners**

remora

Some remora fish get a ride from a shark!

Sea animals also work together. Some fish ride on other sea animals. The remora is a fish that **attaches** itself to sharks. It sticks to the shark's body. The shark gives the fish a ride. In return, the fish eats **the shark's leftover food**.

attaches sticks
the shark's leftover food the food the shark has not eaten

Before You Continue

1. **Problem/Solution** How do antelopes and sharks solve a problem for their animal buddies?
2. **Compare** How are the oxpecker and remora the same? How are they different?

Finding Food

Some animals like the same food. Both the honeyguide bird and the ratel love honey. So they **team up**.

The bird finds a **beehive**. Then the ratel uses sharp claws to tear it open. Both animals get **a sweet treat**.

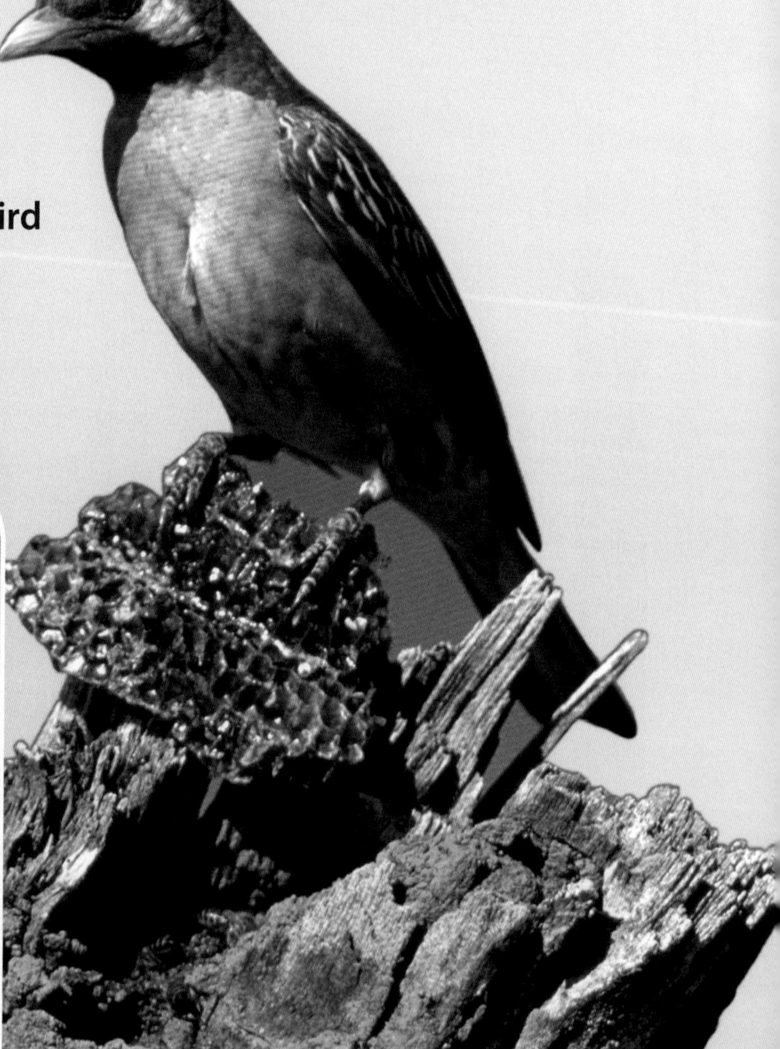

This honeyguide bird finds a beehive. ▶

▲ The ratel is also called a honey badger.

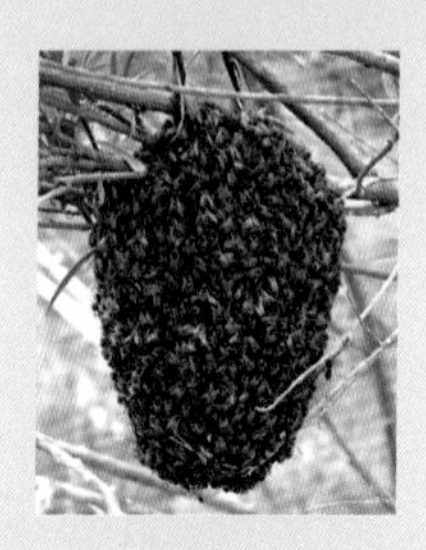

team up work together

◀ **beehive** place where bees live and make honey

a sweet treat something good to eat

Coyotes and badgers also team up as hunting **partners**. Both like to catch small animals such as ground squirrels.

When the squirrel is above the ground, the coyote runs fast and catches it. Sometimes the squirrel **darts** into a hole. That's when the badger uses its long claws to dig under the ground and catch it.

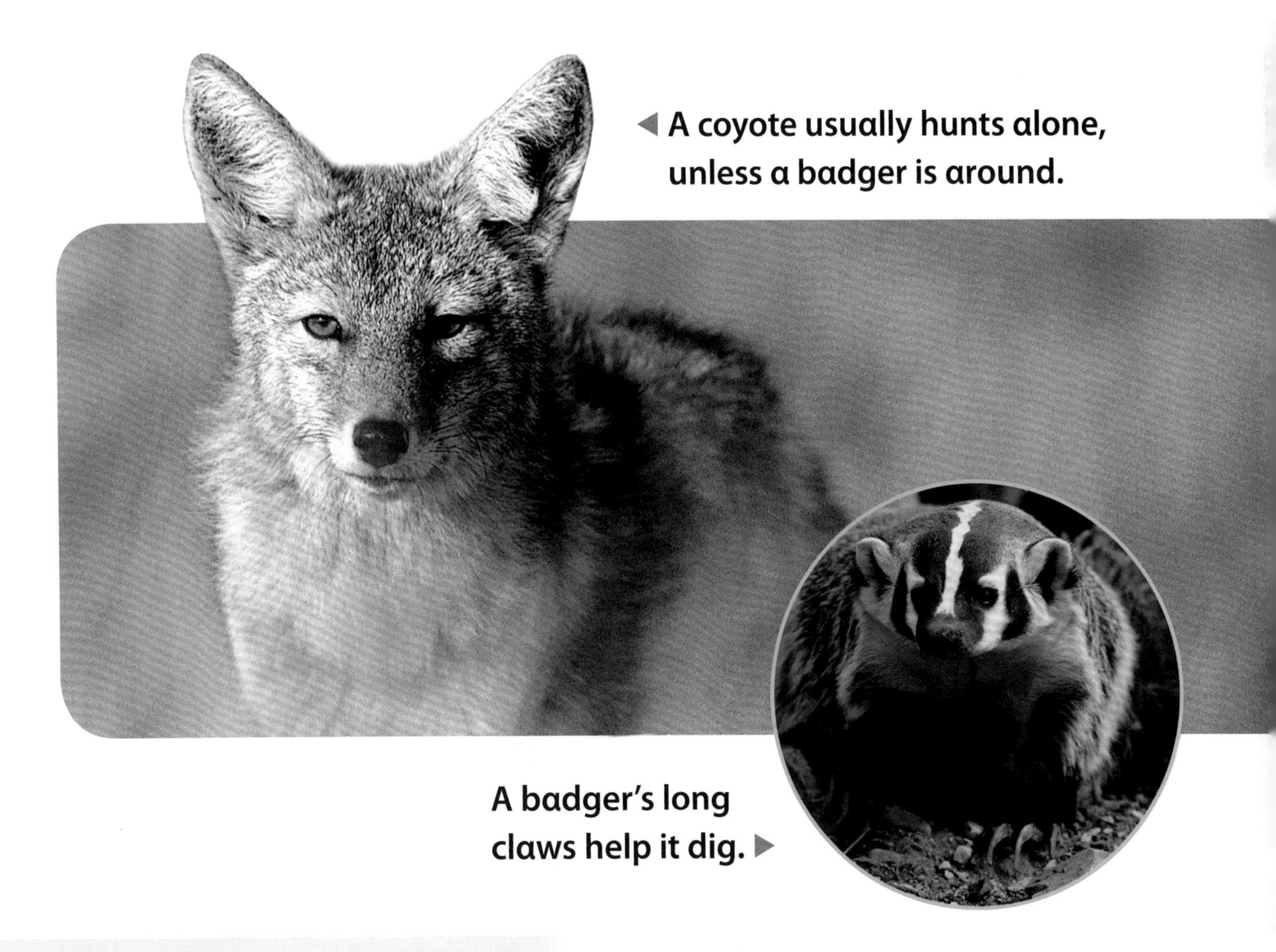

◀ A coyote usually hunts alone, unless a badger is around.

A badger's long claws help it dig. ▶

darts runs quickly

▶ Before You Continue

1. **Generalize** What general point can you make about some animals, based on what you read about ratels and other badgers?
2. **Explain** How do coyotes and badgers work together to get food?

Keeping Safe

The sea anemone and the clownfish make a great underwater team. Sea anemones have tentacles that catch fish and sting them.

Most fish stay away from the tentacles, but the clownfish hides in them. The tentacles don't sting the clownfish. Its body has a thick **layer of mucus** that protects the clownfish from stings.

▲ A clownfish hides from its **enemies** in a sea anemone.

layer of mucus slippery covering
enemies fish that want to eat it

How does the clownfish help the anemone? It helps the anemone get food. The clownfish is colorful. Hungry fish can **spot it** easily.

Sometimes a hungry fish chases a clownfish into the anemone. Then the anemone stings the fish and eats it.

▼ **An anemone eats a shrimp.**

spot it see it

Before You Continue

1. **Explain** How do the clownfish and the sea anemone make an **unusual** team?
2. **Generalize** What general point can you make about how some creatures get food, based on the sea anemone?

Helping Each Other Live

All animals try to survive. For some, that means living with or near other kinds of animals.

At first, these odd couples may seem strange, but look again.

These **partners** help one another find food, get clean, and stay safe. Each animal helps the other **get the most out of life**. ❖

▲ A shrimp helps this fish stay clean.

Remoras get plenty of food from a shark.

An oxpecker helps keep pests off an impala.

get the most out of life live happily and safely

Before You Continue

1. **Generalize** How does living together help animal **partners** get the most out of life? Use examples from the text.
2. **Main Idea** What is the main idea of "Odd Couples"? Tell a partner.

Talk About It

1. What facts did you learn from the **science article**? Read the facts aloud and then answer.

   I learned ________________.

2. What is a symbiotic relationship? Use your own words to explain.

   A symbiotic relationship is ________________.

3. Think about the different animals in "Odd Couples." What do they tell you about size? Is it important in animal **partners**? Explain.

   The size of the animals is/is not ________________.

Write About It

Write two questions about the animal pairs in the selection. Use at least one **Key Word**. Trade papers with a partner. Write answers to your partner's questions.

Question: *What does the _____ do? Why?*

Answer: *The _____ does _____ because _____.*

Topic and Main Idea

Make a topic and main idea chart for "Odd Couples." Add details to the chart. Use them to figure out the topic of the selection.

Topic and Main Idea Chart

Topic:	Main Idea: Animal partnerships help both animals survive.

Details: Cleaner shrimp keep other fish clean.
Details:

Now use your topic and main idea chart. Tell your partner about "Odd Couples."

One detail is ______. Another detail is ______. The selection is mostly about ______.

Fluency

Practice reading with correct intonation. Rate your reading.

Use Context Clues

If you read a word that you do not know, look at all the words around it. These clues from the text, or **context clues**, can help you figure out the meaning of the word.

Cleaner shrimp have the **ability** to clean a dirty fish. They **can pick off tiny pieces of food** from the fish.

context clues

The words "can pick off tiny pieces of food" give clues about the meaning of **ability**.

Try It Together

Read these sentences. Look for context clues to tell what the words **species** and **pattern** mean.

There are over 17,000 species of butterflies in the world. These groups of butterflies all have different patterns and designs on their wings.

Making Connections Read about two more of nature's amazing **partners**.

Genre A **science article** can tell how things in nature work.

Working Together

by **Lori Wilkinson**

There are many interesting **partnerships** in nature. One **unique pair** is the honeybee and the flower. Each does a job the other cannot do on its own. Honeybees and flowers need each other to **thrive**.

partnerships teams
unique pair special team
thrive live and grow

Before You Continue

1. **Set Purpose** What do you already know from this page about bees and flowers? Why will you read the article?
2. **Clarify** Find words that tell what a partnership is. Then say it in your own words.

Honeybees Need Flowers

Honeybees get their food from flowers. Flowers make a sweet juice called nectar. Bees drink the nectar. They fly to their hives. There they turn the nectar into honey for their babies to eat.

Flowers also make pollen. Pollen helps new flowers grow. But for a honeybee, pollen is good food. It has all the **vitamins, minerals, and protein** a bee needs.

pollen

▲ A honeybee collects nectar and pollen from a flower.

vitamins, minerals, and protein healthy things

▲ A bee takes pollen from one flower to another.

Flowers Need Honeybees

Plants need honeybees to help them make more plants. When a bee sits on a flower, some pollen sticks to it. When the bee flies to other flowers, it spreads the pollen around. Without the honeybee, **fewer** new flowers would grow! ❖

fewer not many

▶ Before You Continue

1. **Topic/Main Idea** What is the topic of this article? What is the main idea?
2. **Generalize** What general point can you make about how some insects help plants, based on what you learned about honeybees?

Compare Topics and Main Ideas

"Odd Couples" and "Working Together" both have **topics** and **main ideas**. How are these ideas the same? How are they different? Work with a partner to complete the chart.

Comparison Chart

Title	Topic	Main Idea
"Odd Couples"		
"Working Together"		

The topic is what the selection is mostly about. Write the topic here.

The main idea is the most important message. Write the main idea here.

Talk Together

Talk with a partner. Name some pairs of animals. Use **Key Words** to tell how the animal **partners** help each other.

Future Tense

Future-tense verbs tell what will happen in the future. There are two ways to make a verb tell about the future.

Grammar Rules **Future Tense**

Future Tense with *will:*	Sample Sentences:
will hunt	The badger **will hunt** later.
will eat	The ratel **will eat** honey.
Future Tense with *(be) going to*:	**Sample Sentences:**
am going to visit	I **am going to visit** the aquarium.
is going to be	It **is going to be** fun.
are going to see	We **are going to see** clownfish.

Read Future Tense Verbs

Read these sentences with a partner. Find three verbs that show what will happen in the future.

Sea animals will help each other. Some fish are going to ride on other sea animals. The remora is one fish that will attach itself to a shark

Use Future Tense Verbs 

Look at the photograph of the giraffe. Write two sentences telling what you think the giraffe is about to do. Use future tense verbs.

Writing Project

Write as a Researcher

Write a Science Report 

Write a report about a partnership in nature. You will publish your report in a classroom science magazine.

Study a Model

When you write a report, you gather information from different places. You organize the information and share it with others.

Open House

By Amy Lin

Hermit crabs and sea anemones sometimes work as partners. They make a very strange pair.

A **hermit crab** has a **soft body**. It **needs protection**. So it **lives in shells** it picks up from the ocean floor.

A **sea anemone** is an animal that looks like a plant. It **sticks on rocks or coral**. When it's hungry, it **has to wait for smaller animals to float by**. Then it **stings them** with its poison tentacles and eats them.

Sometimes, a **crab and an anemone team up**. A **crab will pick up an anemone** and put it on its shell. The **anemone gets to eat** the crab's leftover food. The **crab is protected** by the anemone's tentacles. Both win!

The first paragraph presents the **topic** of the report.

Facts and **details** support the main idea in each paragraph.

The report is well organized. Each paragraph has a different **main idea**.

Prewrite

1. **Choose a Topic** What will your report be about? Get ideas from books and websites. Talk about those ideas with a partner.

Language Frames

Tell Your Ideas	Respond to Ideas
I know about ______ and ______.	______ sounds interesting. I'd like to read about that!
I once saw a show about ______. I could write about that.	What do ______ and ______ do?
I'd like to learn more about ______.	Tell me more about ______.

2. **Gather Information** What do you want to find out? Write questions. Find the answers in books or on the Internet. Talk to someone who knows about the topic.

3. **Get Organized** Use a main idea and details chart to help you organize your information.

Topic, Main Idea, and Details Chart

Topic: Hermit crabs and sea anemones work as partners.	
Main Idea 1: Hermit crab needs protection	Details: Soft body Lives in shells to protect itself
Main Idea 2:	Details:

Draft

Use your chart and notes to write your draft. Begin by telling about the topic. Write about each main idea in a new paragraph. Add facts and details. Include a picture if you can.

Revise

1. **Read, Retell, Respond** Read your draft aloud to a partner. Your partner listens and then retells the main points. Next, talk about ways to make your writing better.

Language Frames

Retell	Make Suggestions
Your report is about ____.	I didn't understand ____.
The main ideas I heard are ____.	Can you say it in a different way?
Some interesting facts and details are ____.	Can you add more details about ____?

2. **Make Changes** Think about your draft and your partner's ideas. Use revision marks to make your changes.
   - Did you explain each idea clearly? Add details if you need to.

   It needs protection. So
   A hermit crab has a soft body. ^It lives in shells it picks up from the ocean floor.

   - Put your details in an order that makes sense.

   them
   When it's hungry, it stings ^~~smaller animals~~ with its poison tentacles and eats them. it has to wait for smaller animals to float by. Then

Spelling Tip

Remember that some verbs, like *dig*, have irregular past tense forms. Spell them correctly.

Edit and Proofread

Work with a partner to edit and proofread your report. Pay special attention to verb tense. Use revision marks to show your changes.

Present

On Your Own Make a final copy of your report. Present it out loud to your class. Invite your listeners to ask questions.

Presentation Tips	
If you are the speaker...	**If you are the listener...**
Speak clearly. Pronounce all words correctly.	Think about what you should be learning from the report.
If your listeners have questions, answer them with more details from your notes.	Listen for the main ideas and the details that support them.

With a Group Collect all of the reports. Publish them in a magazine called "Nature's Partners." Make copies of the magazine and share them with another class.

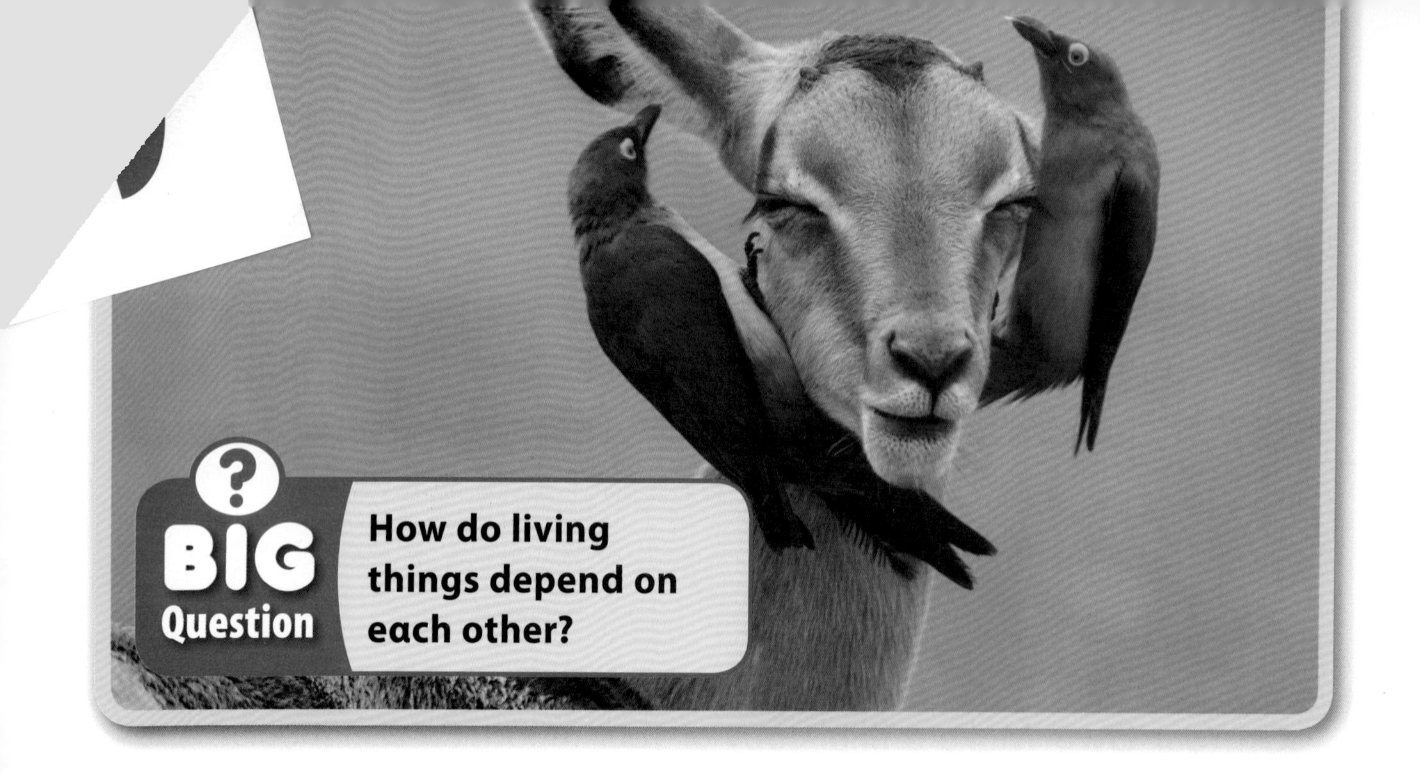

Talk Together

In this unit, you found lots of answers to the **Big Question**. Now, use your concept map to discuss the **Big Question** with the class.

Concept Map

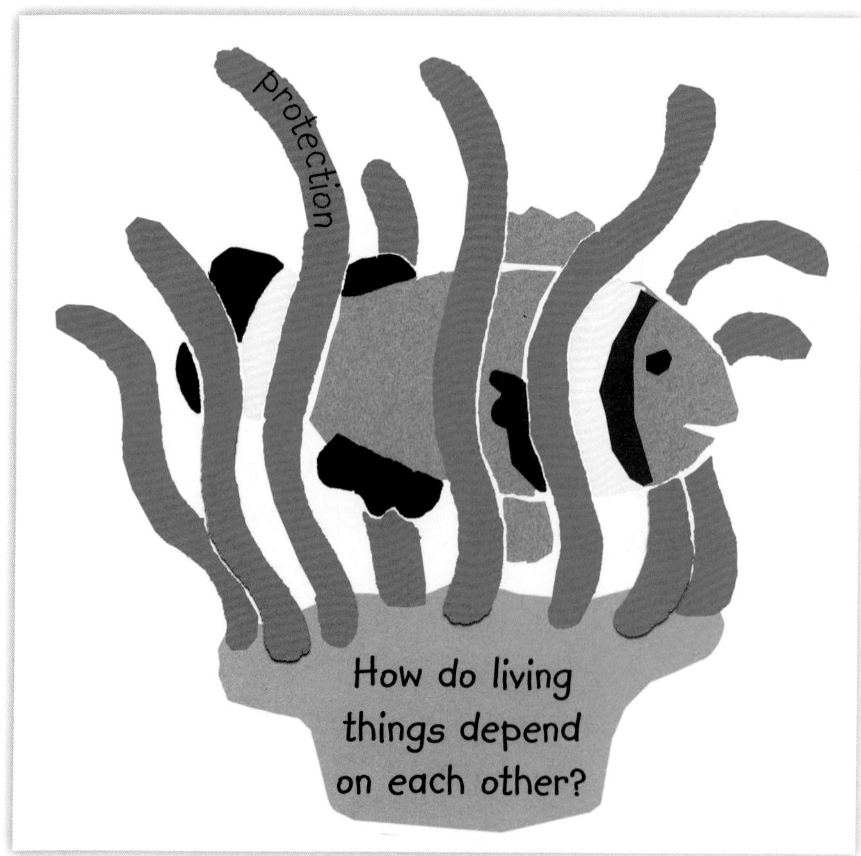

Share Your Ideas

Choose one of these ways to share your ideas about the **Big Question**.

Write It!

Write a Song

Work with a partner to write a song about how living things depend on each other. Prepare to sing the song for your class. Teach the song to your classmates so they can sing along.

Talk About It!

Give a Radio Report

Work with a partner to write a report about a partnership in nature. Record your report. Remember to keep your voice natural and speak slowly and clearly. Then play the report for the class.

Do It!

Perform a Puppet Show

Create paper bag puppets of different animals that help each other. Then write dialogue for a skit about the animals.

Write It!

Make a Booklet

Make a booklet that asks people to protect coral reefs and the animals that live there.

8

Our World

BIG Question

What does the world mean to you?

INTERNATIONAL SPACE STATION
An astronaut in space taking a photograph of Earth

Unit at a Glance

- **Language Focus**: Make a Request, Express Intentions
- **Reading Strategy**: Review
- **Phonics Focus**: Suffixes: *-ly, -ness; -ful, -less*
- **Topic**: The World We Live In

Share What You Know

Do It!

1. **Make** a quilt square that tells about you, your family, or your culture.
2. **Put** all the squares together to make a class quilt.
3. **Tell** the class about your square. What does the quilt say about your country and its culture?

My square tells about my family.

PART 1 **Language Focus**

Words to Know
may
please
we
will

Make a Request

Listen and sing.

Independence Days

Song  

A Mexican tradition is Independence Day.
It's on September 16. That's when **we** celebrate.
There's dancing and there's music, and good food to eat.

May I help you make some?

Yes, thank you. That's sweet.

The U.S. also has an Independence Day.
July Fourth is a time for picnics and parades.

Please tell me what **will** happen on July the Fourth.

We'll go to see some fireworks,
And we'll play some sports.

Tune: "Corre, Niño"

Key Words

What do the pictures tell you about **cultures** in different countries?

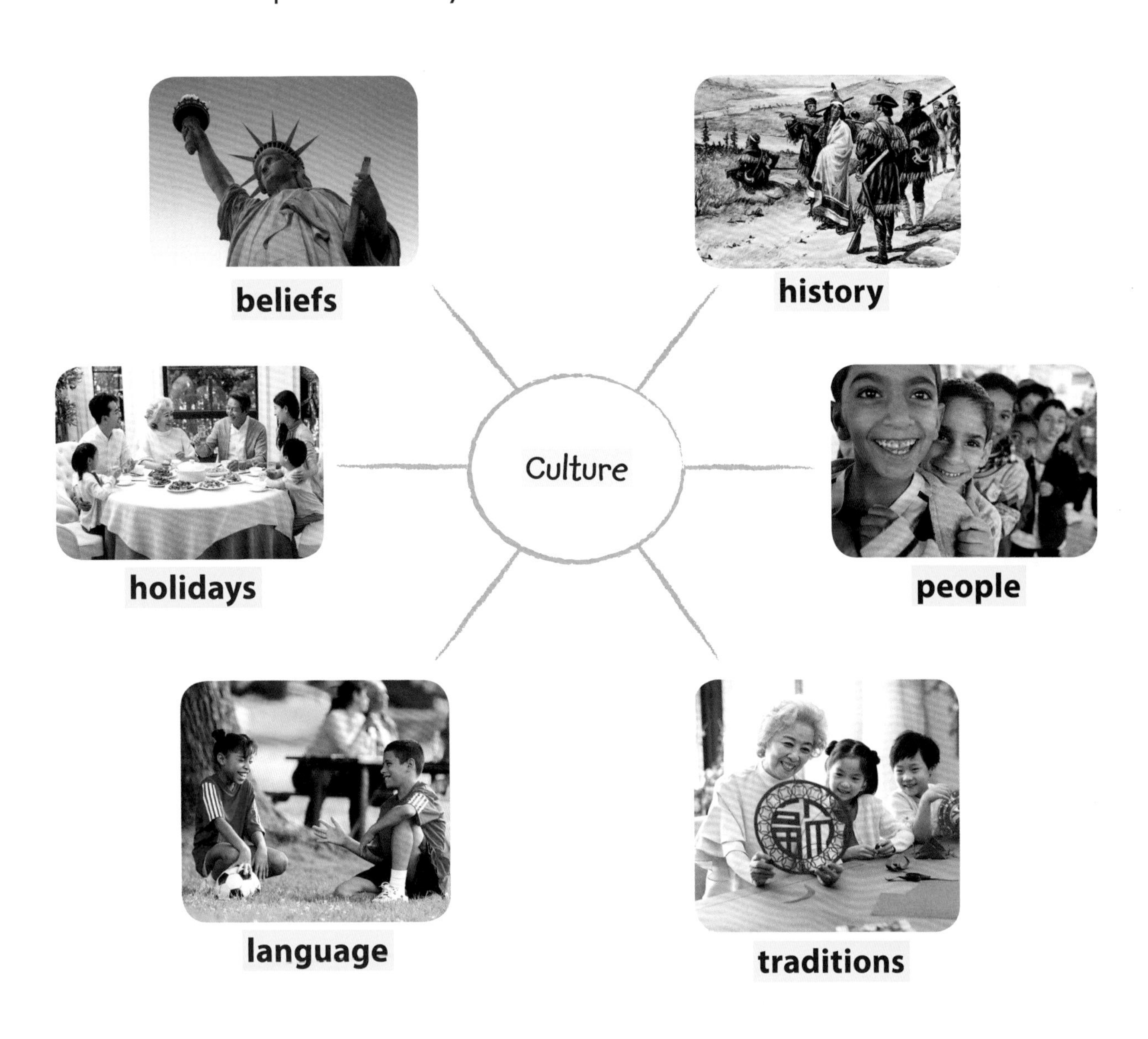

Talk Together

What other things are part of your country's culture? Which parts are most important to you?

Character's Feelings

A character is a person in a story. A **character has feelings.** Use a character map to name the feelings. Then tell why the character has those feelings.

Character Map

Character	How the Character Feels	Why the Character Feels This Way
Gisele	Gisele is curious.	Gisele wants to find out more about the Taj Mahal and who built it.
David	David is happy.	David likes to see his mom happy.

Write the name of the character here.

Describe how the character feels here.

Explain why the character feels that way here.

Talk Together

Tell your partner about a story that you like. Talk about the main character's feelings. Then, fill in a character map.

Academic Vocabulary

More Key Words

alike
adjective

These dogs look **alike**.

celebrate
verb

Many people **celebrate** holidays by watching fireworks.

difference
noun

One apple is red. That is the **difference**.

expect
verb

I **expect** the clouds will turn into rain today.

variety
noun

I have a **variety** of crayons. They are many colors.

Talk Together

Make a study card using each **Key Word**. Write the word on the front. Write the meaning and a sentence on the back. Use the cards to quiz your partner.

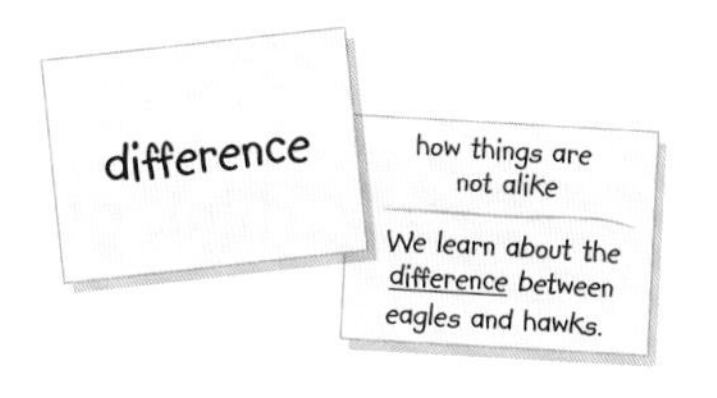

Choose Reading Strategies

Good readers use reading strategies. You can use more than one strategy. It is important to know what strategies to use and when to use them. As you read:

- Think about the strategies. Each one is a different tool. It can help you understand what you read.

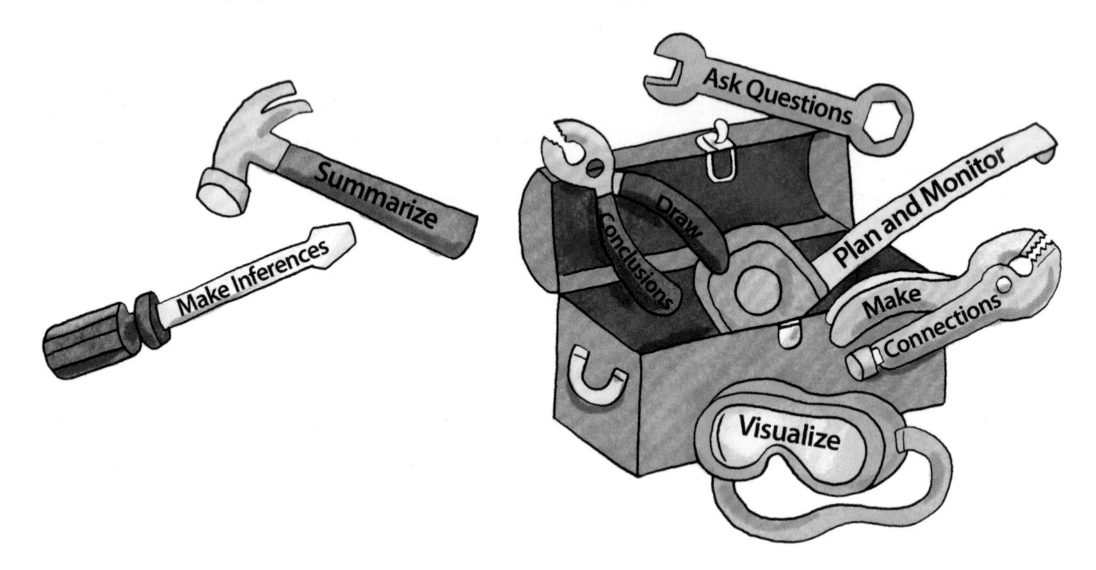

When you read, choose a reading strategy to help you understand.

How to Choose a Reading Strategy

	1. Think about what you want to understand.	I want to know _____.
	2. Figure out which strategy will help you understand what you read.	I can _____.
	3. Think about how the strategy helps you.	This strategy helps me _____.

Talk Together

Practice using at least two reading strategies.

Reading Strategies

- Plan and Monitor
- Make Inferences
- Ask Questions
- Make Connections
- Visualize
- Draw Conclusions
- Summarize

Description

A World Celebration

I live in Dubai, in the United Arab Emirates. My favorite **holiday** is World Book Day. It's a **tradition** that started in the United Kingdom. It is now **celebrated** in more than 100 countries around the world. We celebrate the books we love and their authors. It helps me remember how much I enjoy reading, although I like to play computer games, too!

On World Book Day, all the children in my school dress up as their favorite character from a book. This year, I'm going to get dressed as Willy Wonka from *Charlie and the Chocolate Factory*. I **expect** we will see a **variety** of different costumes.

At school, we are going to have a parade. Then there will be a prize for the best costume. It's a really enjoyable day. It also has an important message: reading is fun!

PART 1 **Phonics Focus**

Suffixes: *-ly*, *-ness*

slowly

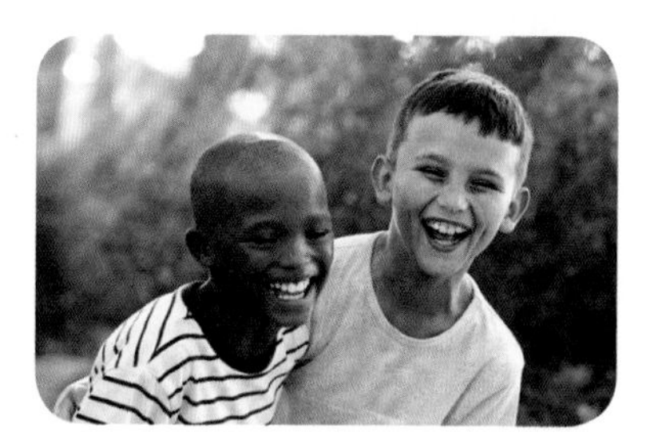

happiness

Listen and Learn

Listen to the picture words for the suffix *-ly* or *-ness*. Choose the same suffix from the box to complete each word.

ly	ness

1. 

There was sad______ in her voice.

2. 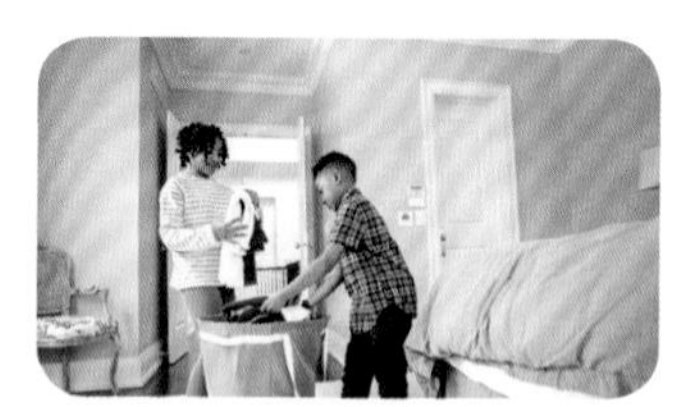

They cleaned the room quick______.

3. 

The bright______ of the sun hurt their eyes.

4. 

Hold the baby chick careful______.

Talk Together

Listen and read. Find the words with the suffixes *-ly* and *-ness*.

Over to You

An American Holiday

The Fourth of July is an American holiday. We celebrate freedom on this day. We declared our independence from Great Britain on July 4, 1776. We happily celebrate this day every year. Most people have the day off. That is fun. People proudly walk in parades. Bands play. Flags wave. People watch. We have picnics. We have parties in the parks. We eat fun foods. People give speeches. Listeners cheer loudly. Then comes the best part. Darkness falls. Boom! Fireworks shoot up! Lovely colors fill the sky. People cheer the brightness. Happiness shows on everyone's face. What a great day!

Work with a partner.

Find words with the suffixes *-ly* and *-ness*. Take turns using the words in sentences.

Read "An American Holiday" with a partner. Practice reading words with the suffixes *-ly* and *-ness*.

Read a Story

Genre

This story is **realistic fiction**. It tells about things that could really happen.

Features of Fiction

A fiction story has characters, a setting, and a plot.

The plot tells what happens.

The next morning, Cheng and his family enjoyed the delicious rice dumplings for breakfast.
"I helped make these," Cheng told his grandparents.
"They are the best I have ever tasted," said his grandmother.

The setting is in Hong Kong.

Cheng is a character in the story.

Something to Write About

by **Susan Henderson**

▸ **Set a Purpose**
What do you want to find out?

Cheng read the letter from his **pen pal** in New York. Max wrote about the fun he would have this summer during the **4th of July holiday**.

Cheng worried. Would he have fun things to say in his reply?

pen pal friend who writes letters
4th of July holiday a national holiday in the United States

"Come help me make **dumplings**," his mother called.

Cheng ran to the kitchen. His mother was making rice dumplings **wrapped** in bamboo leaves for the Dragon Boat Festival. Cheng loved those dumplings, with **sweet bean paste** or with meat.

dumplings traditional Chinese dish
wrapped covered
sweet bean paste a sweet filling

The Dragon Boat Festival is a special **holiday** in Hong Kong. It is held on the fifth day of the fifth month of the **lunar calendar**. It has a long **history**, going back thousands of years.

lunar calendar calendar based on the cycles of the moon

The next morning, Cheng and his family enjoyed the delicious rice dumplings for breakfast.

"I helped make these!" Cheng told his grandparents.

"They are the best I have ever tasted," said his grandmother.

▶ Before You Continue

1. **Clarify** How can you tell this story is fiction?
2. **Visualize** What do you see, hear, and smell when you read about the family's preparations for the festival?

▸ **Predict**
How do you think the family will **celebrate** the Dragon Boat Festival?

The family got ready to go. His dad hung **wormwood** on the door, a festival **tradition**. The **belief** is that it brings good health and **prosperity**.

"Hurry," said Cheng. "The festival starts soon."

"And I need to get ready for the race," said his dad.

wormwood a plant with woody branches

prosperity wealth and success

Cheng, his mother, and grandparents went to the **harbor**.

There were many things to do and see at the festival. There was lion dancing, music, and games. There were **stalls** selling a **variety** of different food. Everyone was having fun.

harbor place where boats stay
stalls stores

Next, the family lined up to watch the races. There were many boats in the water. Cheng thought the boats were beautiful with their **fierce** dragon heads. Cheng waited **anxiously** for his dad's race to begin.

fierce wild and strong
anxiously nervously

Then it was time for Cheng's dad to race. A man at the front of the boat **beat** out a **rhythm** on his drum. Water **splashed**. **People** shouted and clapped. Cheng's dad **paddled** as hard as he could.

beat played
rhythm song
splashed came up in a kind of spray
paddled pushed and pulled the water

Before You Continue

1. **Sequence** What happened before the dragon boat race?
2. **Describe** Look at the pictures on this page. What can you see? What are the **people** doing?

His dad's boat was **gliding** right next to another boat. The men paddled even harder. Cheng **held his breath**. Then he **cheered** as his dad's boat glided across the finish line just in front of the other boat.

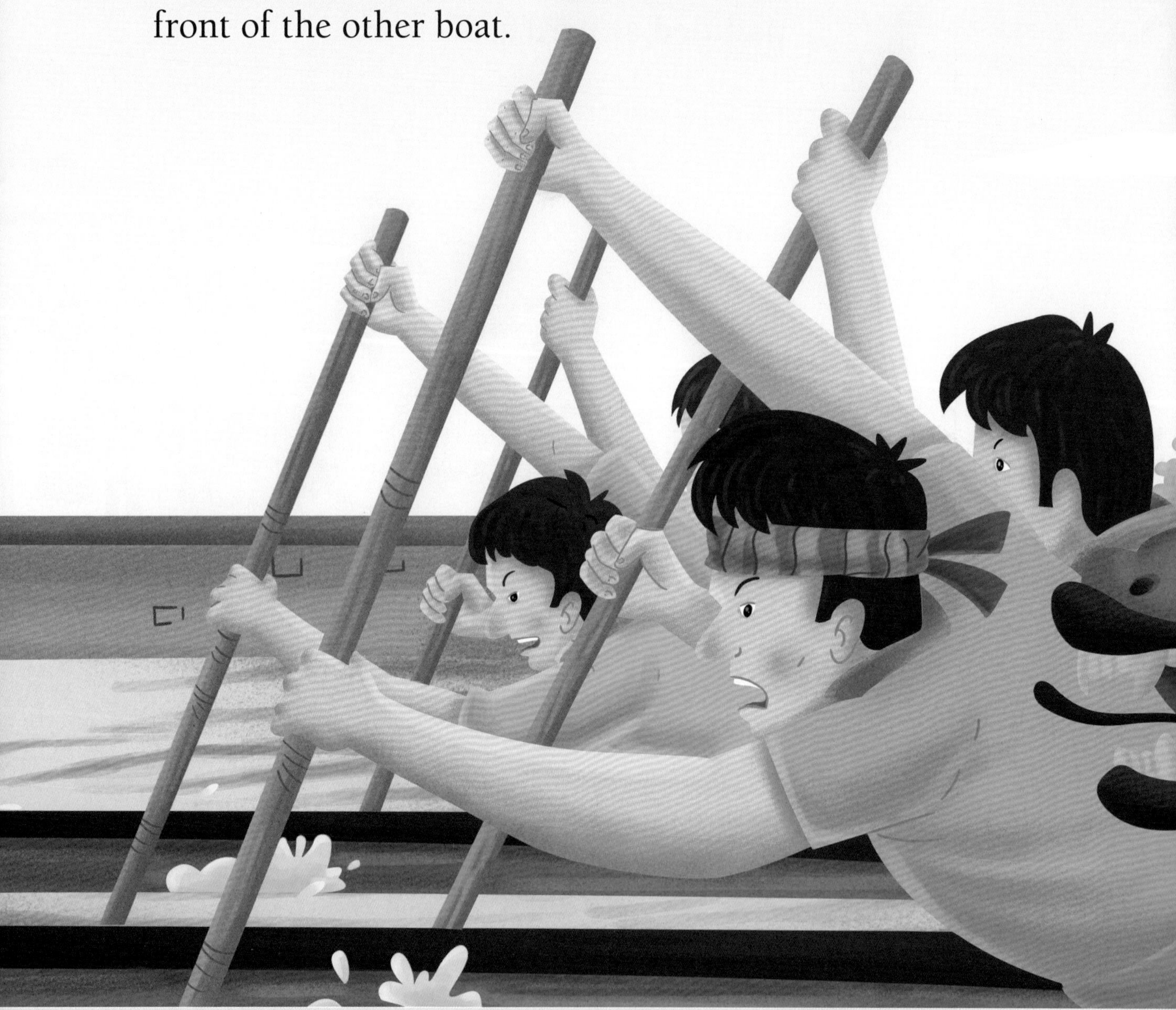

gliding moving across the water
held his breath didn't breathe for a moment
cheered shouted and clapped

After a day full of fun, the family **celebrated** his dad's win at their favorite restaurant. They **ordered** all the things that Cheng liked best—especially dumplings!

"What a great day! What a great festival!" Cheng said proudly.

ordered chose from a menu

Cheng knew that he shouldn't have worried about his letter. He would write about the dragon boats and the **variety** of ways to **celebrate** the festival. He would put in a photo of his dad's race. Max would like that. ❖

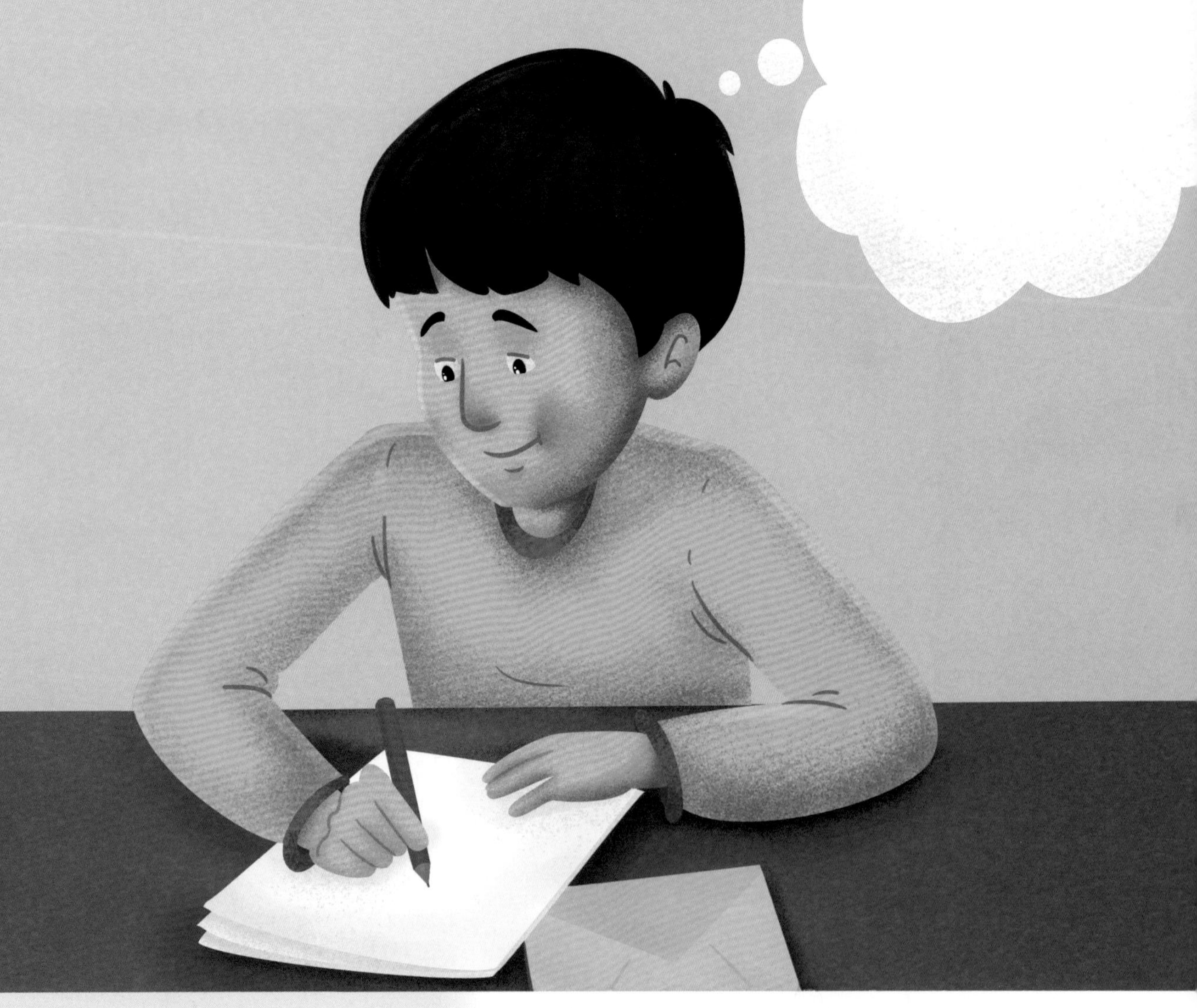

Before You Continue

1. **Confirm Prediction** Was your prediction correct? How did Cheng and his family **celebrate** the Dragon Boat Festival?
2. **Make Connections** Cheng is proud of the Dragon Boat Festival in Hong Kong. What makes you proud of your country?

Meet the Author

Susan Henderson

The author grew up in a small Scandinavian community in Wisconsin. She loved the traditional Norwegian and Danish foods and the holiday traditions.

Now, Susan lives in Seattle, where she can enjoy the wonderful artwork, food, and dances of the Pacific Northwest Native Americans. Susan believes that the best thing about living in the United States is being able to enjoy the traditions of so many cultures.

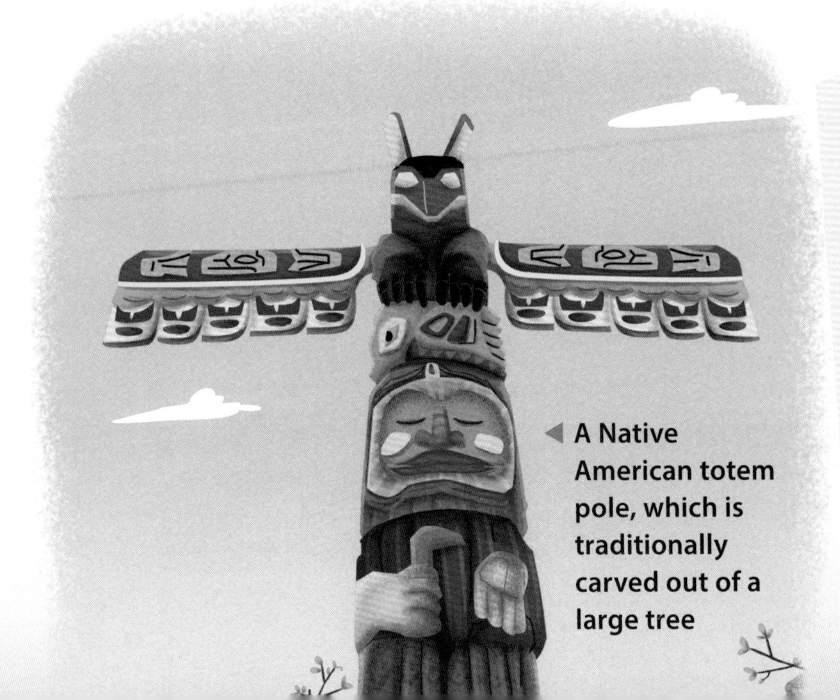

◀ A Native American totem pole, which is traditionally carved out of a large tree

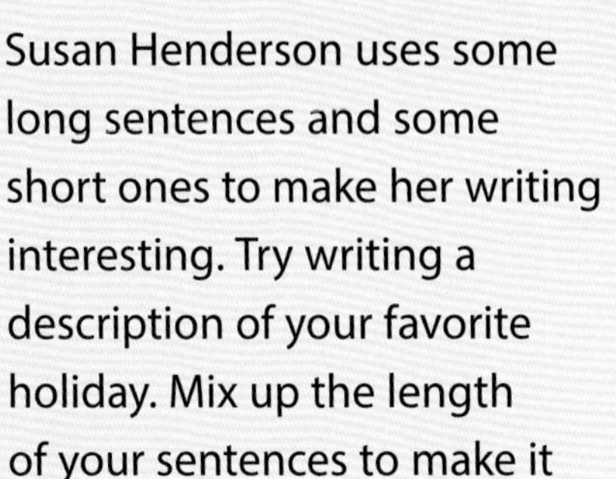

Writing Tip

Susan Henderson uses some long sentences and some short ones to make her writing interesting. Try writing a description of your favorite holiday. Mix up the length of your sentences to make it really interesting to read!

PART 1 **Think and Respond**

Talk About It 

1. What parts of this **realistic fiction** story could really happen?

   The parts that could really happen are ________________.

2. Imagine you are Cheng. Describe what you will do to **celebrate** The Dragon Boat Festival.

   Today we will ________________ and we will ________________.

3. How are Cheng and his pen pal's lives similar? How are they different?

   Their lives are similar because ________________.

   Their lives are different because ________________.

Write About It 

Think of a special day you celebrate in your country. Why is it important? How do you celebrate it? Write 3 sentences. Use **Key Words**.

In my country we celebrate ______.

It is important because ______.

To celebrate it we ______ and we ______.

Character's Feelings

Think about how the characters feel and why. Then fill in a character map for "Something to Write About."

Character Map

Character	How the Character Feels	Why the Character Feels This Way
Cheng	Worried	He doesn't know what to write in the letter to his pen pal.

Now use your character map. Tell your partner about the other characters in "Something to Write About."

The main character is ____.
He feels ____ because ____.

Fluency

Practice reading with the correct intonation. Rate your reading.

Use a Dictionary

You can **use a dictionary** to find out how to spell and say words. You can also learn what words mean. Use alphabetical order to find the word **culture** in the dictionary.

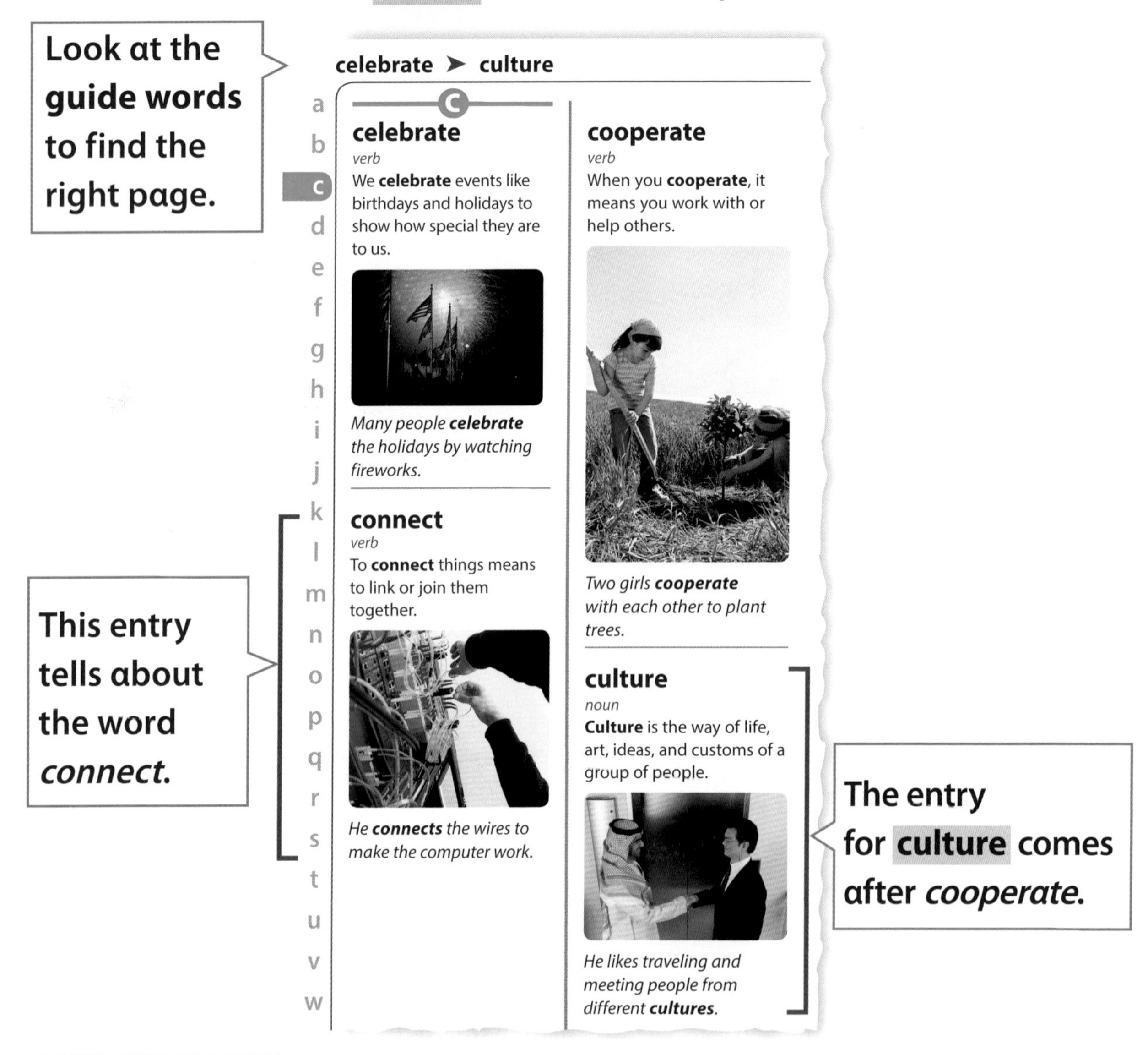

Try It Together

1. What word comes before **cooperate** on this dictionary page?
2. Where would you find the words **before** and **belong**? Between the guide words **beet ➤ begin** or **bell ➤ below**?

Making Connections Find out about **traditions** and customs in different parts of the world.

Genre A **poem** tells about feelings and ideas in a special way. Sometimes, the words don't mean exactly what they say.

OUR WORLD *Is Many Shades*

by Anna Goy

Our world is many **shades**

of **traditions** and **greetings**.

Some give gifts when they visit.

Others shake hands or take a deep **bow**.

A gentle touch to their fingertips.

Placing a hand on your heart.

We respect others' customs and habits.

We share.

shades light and dark colors
greetings ways to say "hello"
bow bend forward from the waist

Before You Continue

1. **Preview and Predict** What do you think the next part of the poem is going to be about?
2. **Make Connections** What kinds of greetings are described in the poem? How are they similar or different from the way you greet **people** in your country?

Our world is many shades

of the food we eat.

Dishes to **celebrate** **traditions** and **holidays**.

Sushi, tacos, kapsa, pizza.

Brigadeiros in Brazil, lefse in Norway.

A **variety** of tastes and **textures**,

yet we **break bread together**.

We share.

textures how the food feels in our mouth

break bread together sit down and eat with other **people**

Our world is many shades

of the **languages** we speak.

Mandarin, Swahili, Portuguese.

Hindi, Russian, French, Arabic.

Thousands of languages heard across the world,

yet we find a way of listening to others' stories.

To understand.

We share.

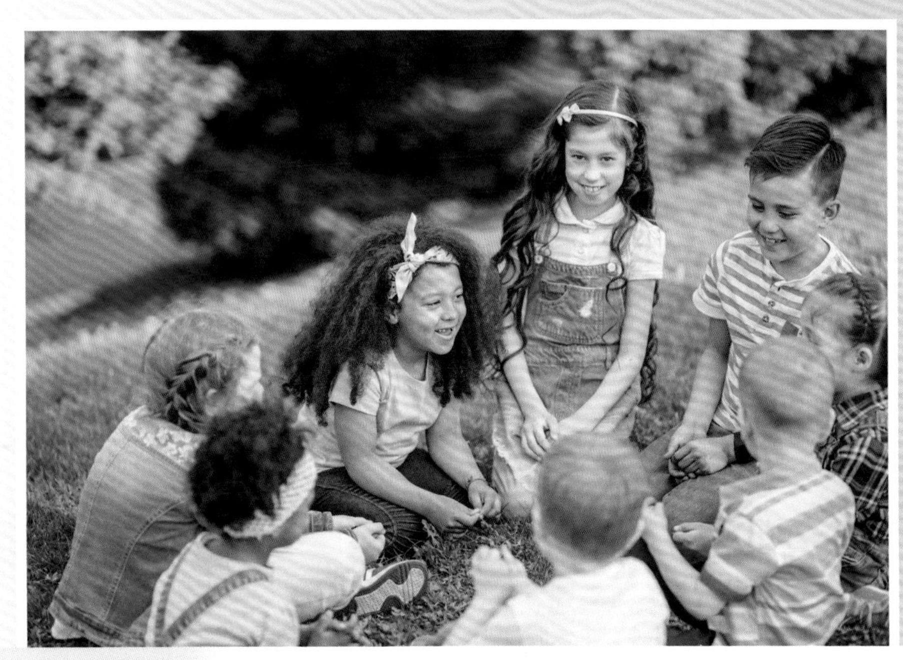

Before You Continue

1. **Make Connections** Think of **people** you have met who don't speak the same **language** as you. How do you understand each other?
2. **Context Clues** Look at page 250. What do you think brigadeiros and lefse are? How do the words around them help you understand?

Our world is many shades

of the families we live in.

A house full of brothers and sisters,

or just one or two.

Living with many **generations under one roof,**

or visiting the homes of those we love.

We spend time together.

We share.

generations young and old family members

under one roof living together in the same house

Our world is many shades

of **people** and ways of life.

Of **traditions**. Of **cultures**.

We **celebrate** our **differences**

and how **alike** we are.

Proud of our homes, and

opening them to our neighbors.

We look to connect.

We find **similarities.**

We share. ❖

similarities things we have in common

▸ Before You Continue

1. **Confirm Prediction** Was your prediction correct? What are the world's many shades?
2. **Theme** What's the poem about? In your own words, summarize the poem's main ideas.

Compare Language

Sometimes words mean exactly what they say. Sometimes they mean something else. Read the sentences from "Something to Write About" and "Our World Is Many Shades." Does each sentence mean exactly what it says? If not, tell what the sentence really means.

Comparison Chart

These words mean just what they say.

"Something to Write About"	"Our World Is Many Shades"
Cheng ran to the kitchen. This means exactly what it says.	Our world is many shades of the languages we speak. Meaning: There are many languages in the world.
	We find a way to listen to others' stories. Meaning: ________

These words do not mean exactly what they say.

Talk Together

Draw a picture that shows exactly what these words say:

"Proud of our homes, and opening them to our neighbors."

Then write a caption that tells what the words really mean. Try to use **Key Words**.

Prepositions

A **preposition** links a noun or pronoun to the other words in the sentence.

Grammar Rules Prepositions

• A preposition often tells where.	The fireworks burst **over** the buildings.
• Prepositions that are used often: *next to, in front of, over, under, beside, between, in, out, on, off, up, down, through, across, around,* and *into.*	Then the lights shine **in** the sky.

Read Prepositions

Read these sentences from "Something to Write About" with a partner. Find three prepositions. Explain or show what they mean.

A man at the front of the boat beat out a rhythm on his drum.
His dad's boat was gliding right next to another boat.
Then he cheered as his dad's boat glided across the finish line just in front of the other boat.

Write Prepositions 

Write two sentences about going to a fireworks show. Use prepositions to tell about a place or direction. Share your sentences with a partner.

PART 2 **Language Focus**

Words to Know
going
there
these

Express Intentions

Listen and read along.

Trips We'll Take

Poem 

One day I am **going** to Vietnam.
I plan to see Ha Long Bay **there**.
They say its landforms are amazing.
I'll be sure to take photos to share.

One day I am going to Egypt.
Where the Red Sea is deep and so clear.
You can swim in this body of water.
Its coral is super, I hear.

The world has **these** beautiful landforms.
There are mountains and deserts and more.
We are lucky to live on this earth
With such wonderful lands to explore!

Key Words

Look at the map. What things can you see?

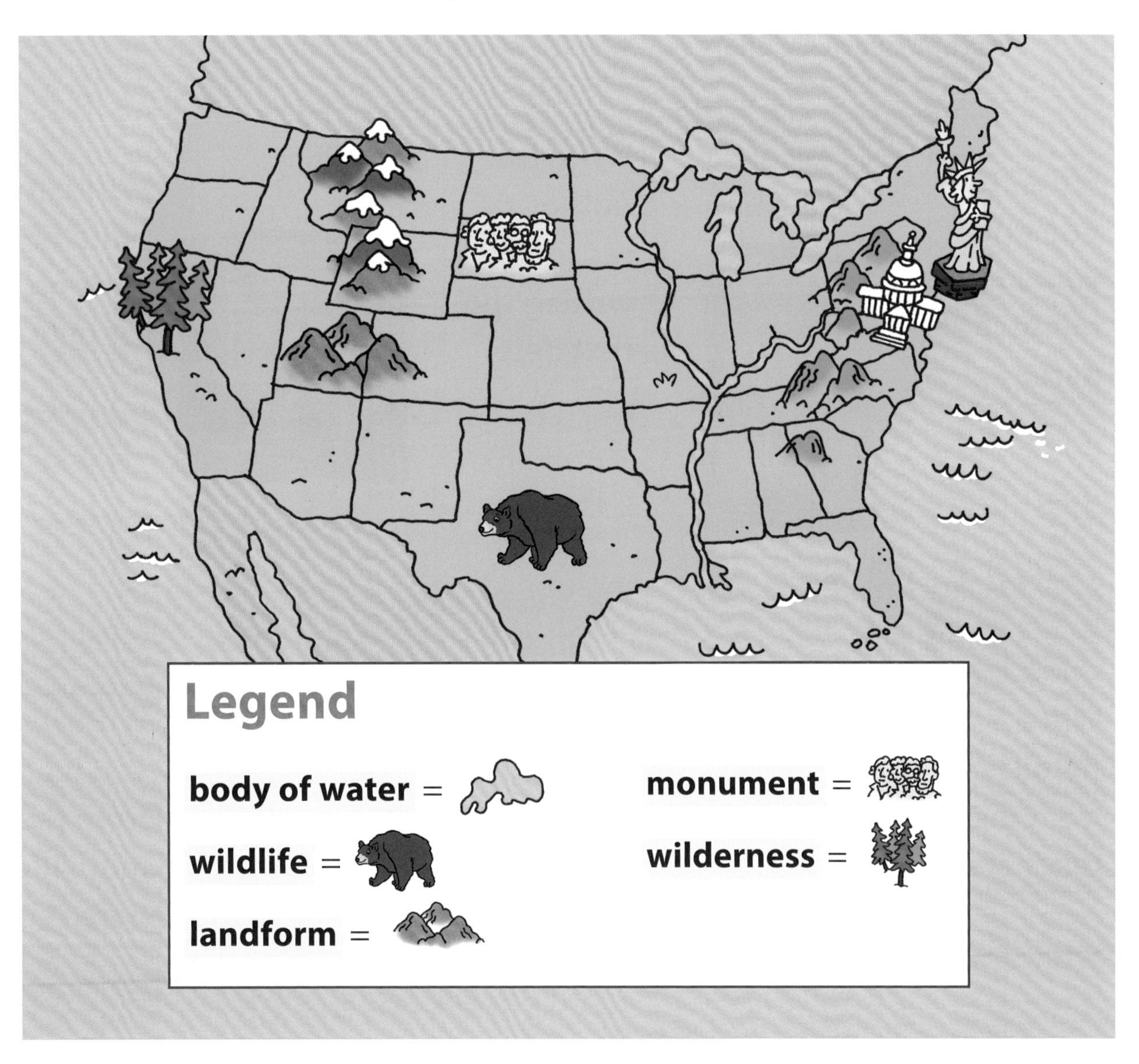

Talk Together

What places in the world would you like to visit? What landforms and animals would you like to see? Explain your answers to a partner.

Author's Purpose

The **author's purpose** tells why the author wrote the text.

Author's Purpose Chart

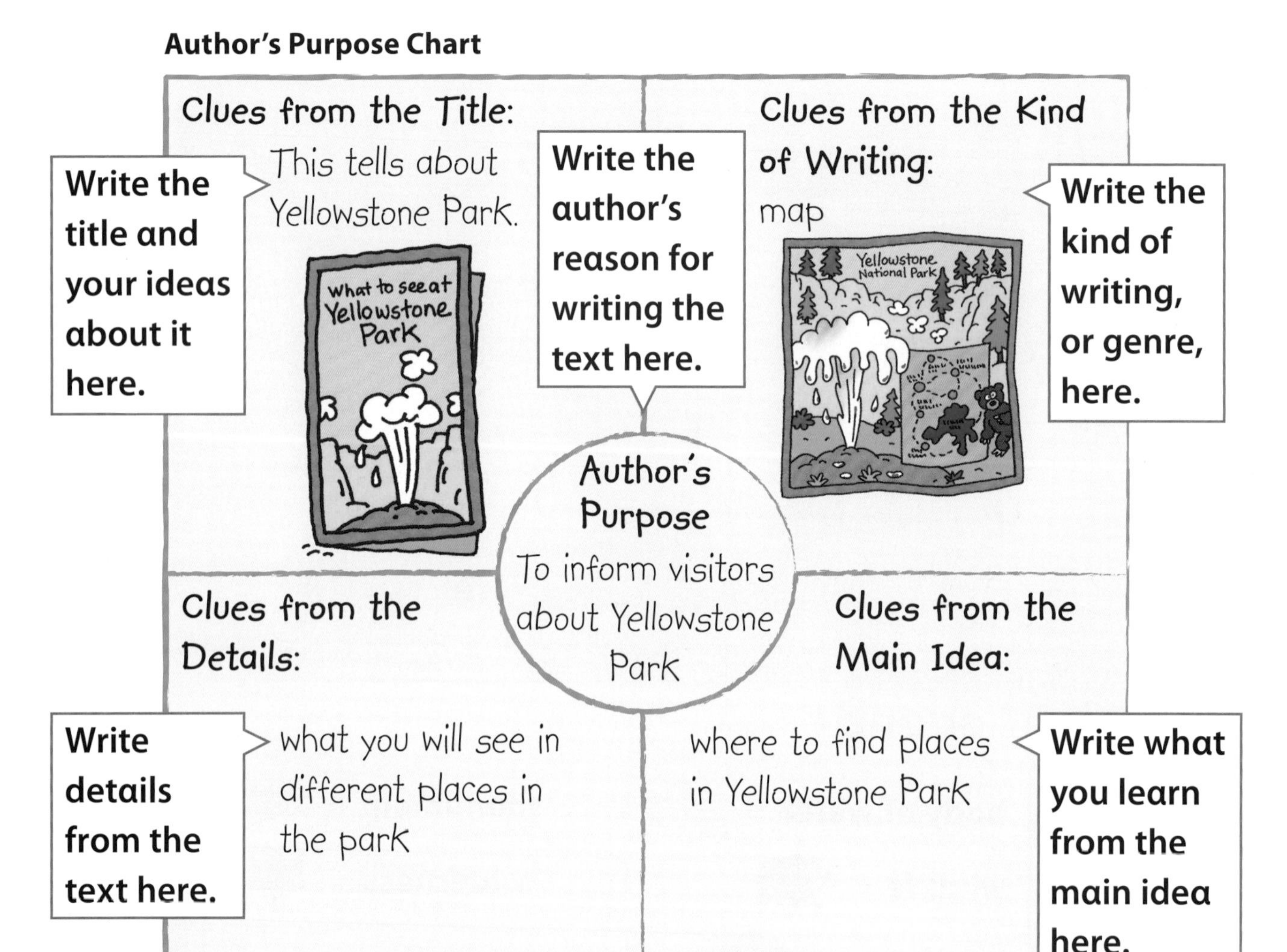

Talk Together

Read a magazine article or other nonfiction text with a partner. Then, use an author's purpose chart to figure out why the author wrote the text.

Academic Vocabulary

More Key Words

freedom
noun

We have the **freedom** to say what we want.

remember
verb

Remember to call and say, "Happy birthday!"

seek
verb

The girl **seeks** the piñata with a stick.

symbol
noun

Each candle on a birthday cake is a **symbol** for one year of your life.

united
adjective

When we play soccer, we are **united** as a team.

Talk Together

Tell a partner what a **Key Word** means. Then your partner uses the word in a sentence.

A **symbol** is something that stands for something else.

The Statue of Liberty is a **symbol** of the United States.

PART 2 **Reading Strategy**

Use Reading Strategies

Use reading strategies before, during, and after you read.

- Before: look through the text quickly. What is the text mostly about? Decide on your purpose, or reason, for reading.

- During: as you read, stop now and then. Ask yourself: *Does this make sense?* Use a reading strategy to help you understand better.
- After: when you finish reading, stop and think. Decide what you learned from reading the text. Share your ideas with others.

How to Use a Reading Strategy

1. Before you start to read, stop and ask: *What strategies will help me get ready to read?*

2. During reading, think about what strategies will help you understand.
3. After reading, ask yourself: *What strategies can I use? How will they help me think about what I read?*

Before I read
I will ____.

As I read,
I can ____.

Now that I'm done,
I think ____.

Reading Strategies

- Plan and Monitor
- Make Inferences
- Ask Questions
- Make Connections
- Visualize
- Draw Conclusions
- Summarize

Talk Together

Practice using at least two reading strategies.

Description

National Parks around the World

Did you know that there are more than 4,000 national parks around the world?

In some parks, you can see beautiful **bodies of water**. Jiuzhaigou National Park is in China. There are many waterfalls and lakes. Giant pandas, the international **symbol** of animal conservation, once lived here.

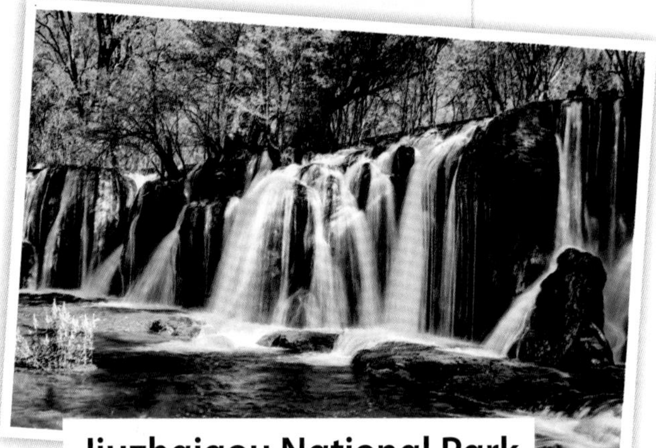

Jiuzhaigou National Park

Göreme National Park is in Turkey. Visitors come to **remember** ancient civilizations. You can see the ruins of their homes and cities. There are also unusual rock formations. These **landforms** are called "fairy chimneys."

National parks are important because they preserve **wilderness** areas and protect **wildlife**. Plus they are perfect places to go hiking and camping.

Millions of people visit national parks around the world. Which would you like to visit?

PART 2 **Phonics Focus**

Suffixes: *-ful*, *-less*

bowlful

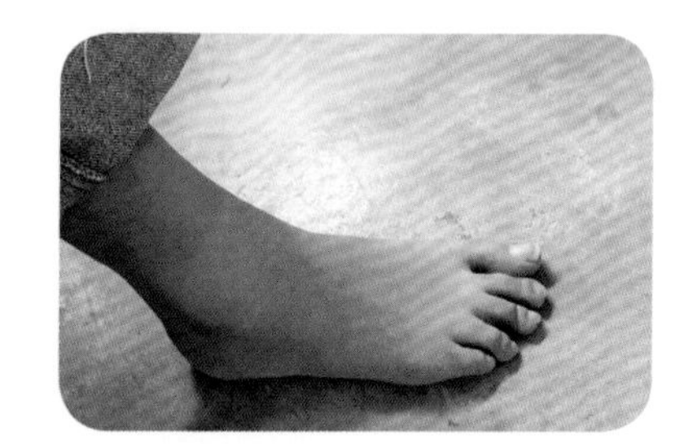

shoeless

Listen and Learn

Listen to the picture words for the suffix *-ful* or *-less*. Choose the same suffix from the box to complete each word.

ful	less

1.

The cloud______ sky was very blue.

2.

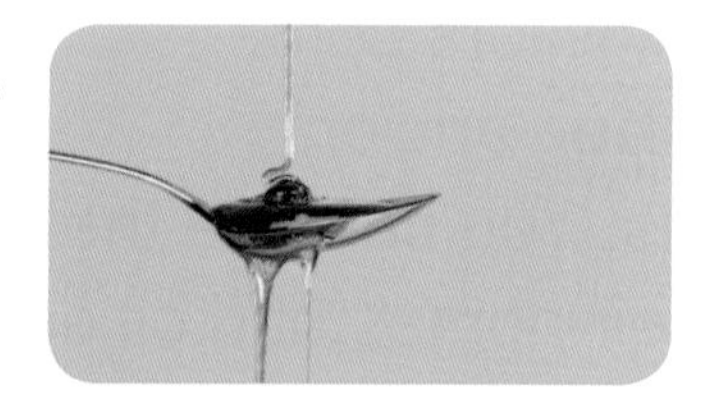

I like one spoon______ of honey in my tea.

3.

One hand______ of seeds will grow many plants.

4.

Some people like hair______ cats.

Talk Together

Listen and read. Find the words with the suffixes *-ful* and *-less*.

Over to You

A Long Journey

Many immigrants came to New York in the 1800s. They came on ships. They crossed a large body of water. The trip was long and hard. Some of these people wanted freedom. All wanted a better life. It was wonderful to see the Statue of Liberty. This monument was a symbol for them. It made them thankful. It made them hopeful. It meant their endless journey was over.

There was one more step, though. There were tests to take. Doctors checked for illness. Each person was checked. Some were too sick to come in. The doctors had to be careful. Only healthy people could come in. Most were welcomed happily. Finally, these fearless people could start their new life.

Work with a partner.

Say a word from the text with the suffix *-ful* or *-less*. Your partner then points to the word and uses it in a sentence.

Read "A Long Journey" with a partner. Practice reading words with the suffixes *-ful* and *-less*.

Read Literary Nonfiction

Genre

Literary nonfiction gives facts about a topic in a way that sounds like a story or a poem.

Features of Nonfiction

All **nonfiction** tells about real people, places, and events. It uses facts to explain or describe a topic.

Literary Nonfiction

Africa is home to many lands and many people. It stretches from the Sahara Desert in the north, through the rain forests of Central Africa, all the way to rocky Cape Town.

Textbook Nonfiction

Africa is the second-largest continent in the world. It has a diverse range of landforms and climate zones. With more than 1.2 billion people, it is also one of the most populated continents.

An Eagle's Eye

by **Anna Goy**

▸ Set a Purpose

Find out where the eagle goes.

Eagles fly across our skies. They look down onto the Earth. The Earth is their home. The Earth is our home, too. They see us moving quickly across the land, like **ants** in the distance. Our eyes look down. We don't look up.

ants small insects

In the distance, a wedge-tailed eagle sees the blue of the ocean. The sky and water meet; their colors **combine**. He sees the **corals** and fish of the Great Barrier Reef of Australia. It is a **monument** to the beauty of our oceans.

combine mix together

corals very small, invertebrate sea animals that live in compact colonies

A white-bellied sea eagle flies over an island, resting in the calm waters of the Indian Ocean. Orangutans and elephants enjoy **freedom** in the island's forests. White sands paint its beaches. Monkeys play on its **shores**. He **soars** over the biggest island in Asia, Borneo.

shores beaches
soars flies

An eastern steppe eagle sees a great and ancient wall. Like a **powerful** dragon, it travels through China. It climbs up and over mountains. It falls down into deserts. The eagle follows its **path** for thousands of kilometers.

powerful strong
path line

Before You Continue

1. **Imagery** Why does the writer describe people as "ants" and China's Great Wall as a "dragon"?
2. **Describe** Look at the photo on page 268. What **landforms** can you see?

Predict
What do the photos on pages 270–271 show?

The Himalayan golden eagle pushes through the clouds to the **peak** of Mount Everest, or Qomolangma. Standing proud, it **seeks** the sun. It is the king of **landforms**. It is the king of the skies. It is the highest mountain in the world.

peak top

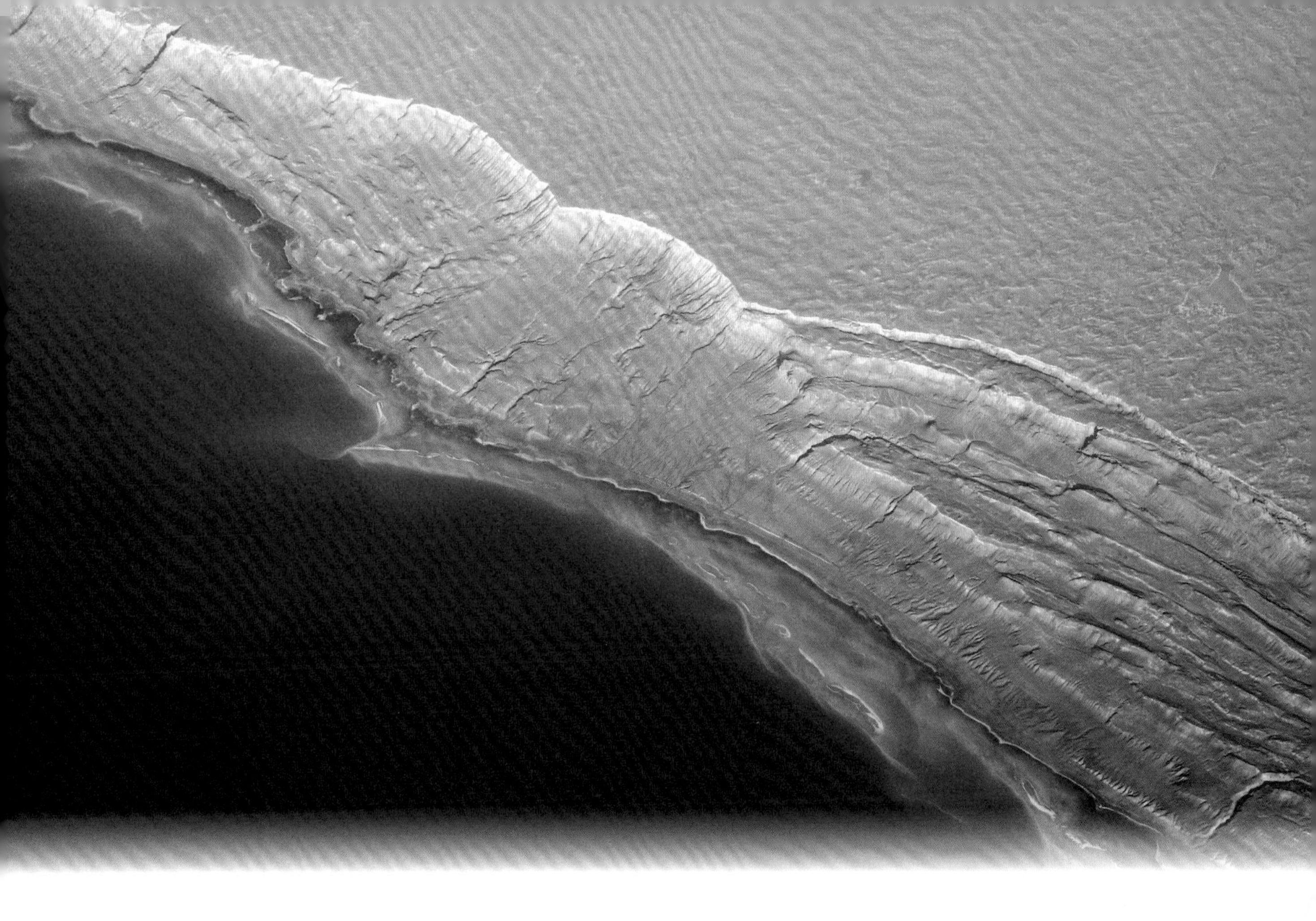

The pallas's fish eagle sees the waters of the Caspian Sea. **Lying** between Europe and Asia, it is **trapped** on all sides. This **body of water** is the largest lake in the world. The eagle flies high above the water. He celebrates his **freedom**.

Lying Located
trapped surrounded by land

Before You Continue

1. **Confirm Prediction** What do the photos show on pages 270–271? Was your prediction correct?
2. **Detail** What do we learn about the height of Mount Everest (Qomolangma) and the size of the Caspian Sea?

A spotted eagle **pauses** as he flies through the Middle East. He **remembers** an ancient civilization. Their **tombs** and **monuments** are hidden in the deserts of Jordan. It is the city of Petra, built deep into the mountain behind. It **glows** as the sun rises into the sky.

pauses stops
tombs a special place built in rock where people are buried
glows lights up

A crowned eagle flies fast. He crosses the grasslands and deserts of Africa. He hears the sound of water before he arrives. He sees the Zambezi River, more than 2 kilometers wide. Feeling water on his **feathers**, he flies down into Victoria Falls.

feathers body

The white-tailed eagle flies over Europe, to the Colosseum of Rome in Italy. Its empty windows welcome the eagle inside. He flies around the **amphitheater**. He imagines people shouting as they watch **wild animals** face each other. He imagines their **symbols** of power.

amphitheater stadium
wild animals animals that live in natural environments

Before You Continue

1. **Clarify** Look at the photos on pages 272–274. Which of these show man-made structures?
2. **Make Connections** Do you have important buildings and structures in your country? Describe them.

A bald eagle enjoys his **freedom** in the **wilderness** of Alaska. **Icy** mountains, rivers, and forests cover the land. The eagle sees bright colors dancing in the sky. He flies high and is **united** with the greens of Aurora, the Northern Lights.

Icy Frozen

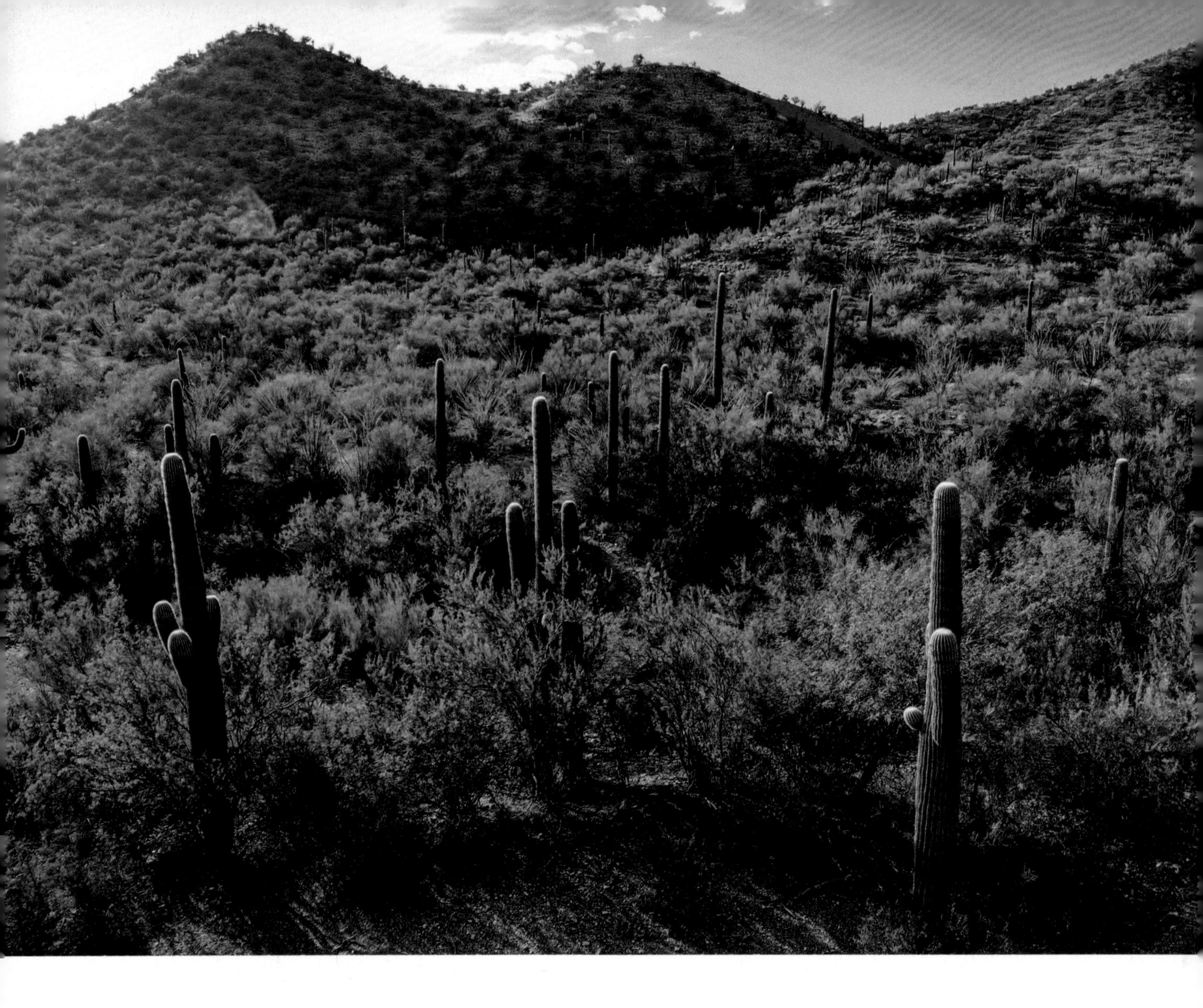

The golden eagle flies south over the **continent of North America**. He feels the heat of the Sonora Desert. It **extends** from the state of Arizona to Mexico. He sees coyotes and mountain lions. He sees cacti, like **needles** in the hot, dry earth.

continent of North America land mass that includes Canada, the U.S., and Mexico

extends continues

needles sharp tools ▶

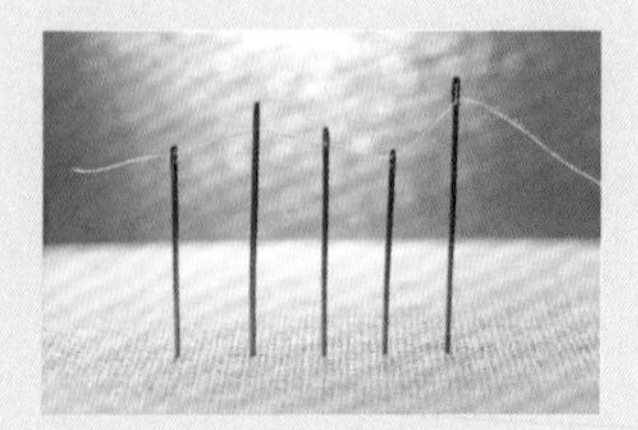

Crossing the mountains of Mexico, a black hawk eagle flies towards the **magnificent ruins** of Chichén Itzá. It was the **ceremonial capital** of the Maya civilization. Enormous pyramids rise above the forest around it. Snakes and jaguars decorate its walls. They are **symbols** of a great past.

magnificent great
ruins remains of very old structures
ceremonial capital center of the ancient culture

▶ Before You Continue

1. **Make Comparisons** Look at pages 275–276. How is the climate different in Alaska and in the Sonora Desert? Which words in the text help you know this?
2. **Detail** Which different types of **landforms** are listed on pages 275–277?

The black-and-white hawk eagle flies **seeking** the South American winds. He finds a **blanket** of forest below him, crossing into Brazil. It is the great Amazon rain forest. It is a celebration of nature. The calls of its **wildlife** unite, welcoming the eagle to their home.

blanket large area

Eagles see our cities. They see us. Our eyes look down. They cry out. They tell us to enjoy the natural beauty of our earth. They tell us to **admire** the **monuments** of its people. To look up. ❖

admire look at with pride

▸ Before You Continue

1. **Clarify** What does the eagle tell us to do?
2. **Author's Purpose** What is the writer's purpose in this selection? How does the author want us to feel?

PART 2 **Think and Respond**

Talk About It 

1. How do you know this selection is **nonfiction**?

   It is nonfiction because ______________________.

2. The selection tells about some of the world's **landforms**, buildings, and structures. Describe one that you would like to visit. **Give a reason why** you want to go there.

   One of the world's landforms/famous structures is __________.
   I want to go because ______________________.

3. What does this selection teach us? Where in the text does it say this?

   This selection teaches us that ______________________.
   The text says ______________________.

Write About It 

Write a brief poem that describes what an eagle would see, hear, smell, and feel in your country. Use **Key Words** in your poem.

An eagle flies in my country's sky.
He sees ________.
He hears ________.
He smells ________.
He feels ________.

Author's Purpose

Think about the author's reasons for writing "An Eagle's Eye."

Author's Purpose Chart

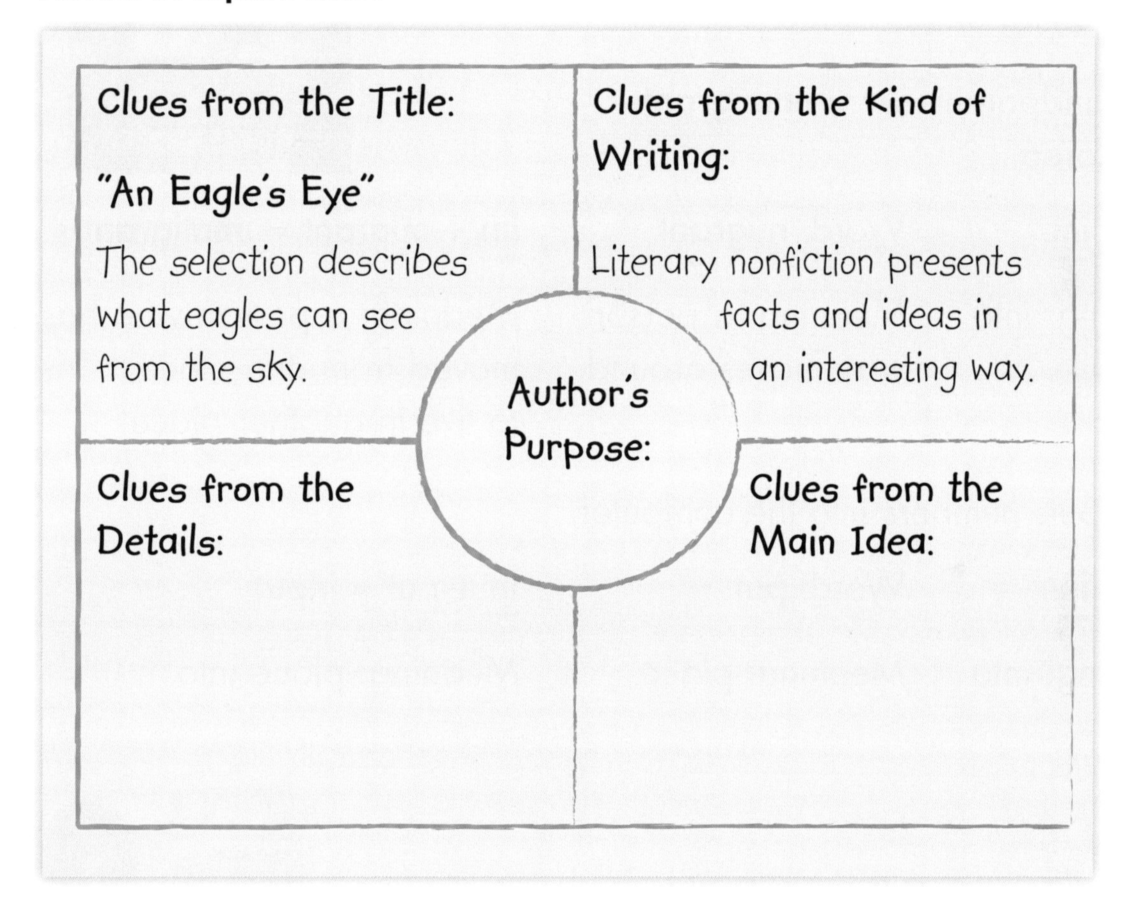

Now work with a partner and use your author's purpose chart to figure out the author's reason for writing "An Eagle's Eye."

The author tells me ______.
The author wrote this selection to ______.
The author's purpose is ______.

Fluency

Practice reading with correct phrasing. Rate your reading.

PART 2 **Word Work**

Prefixes

A **prefix** is a word part that is added to the beginning of a word. A prefix can change the meaning of the word.

My grandparents were **immigrants** from Korea.

Prefix: im-	Word: **migrant**	im + migrant = **immigrant**
Meaning: into	Meaning: a person who moves around	Meaning: a person who has moved from one place to live in another place

She inputs numbers into the computer.

Prefix: in-	Word: **put**	in + put = **input**
Meaning: into	Meaning: place	Meaning: place into

Try It Together

Read the sentences. Then answer the questions.

Our family comes together during reunions.

1. The prefix re- means again. What does the word **reunion** mean?
2. Write a sentence with a word that begins with a prefix.

Making Connections Find out what the people of the United States share.

Genre Song lyrics are the words of a song. They often use rhyme, rhythm, and repetition like poems do.

This Land Is Your Land

words and music by **Woody Guthrie**
photos on pages 283, 285–289
by **Sam Abell**

This land is your land. This land is my land.

From California to the New York Island.

From **the Redwood Forest** to the **Gulf Stream waters**

This land was made for you and me.

the Redwood Forest a big park in California full of redwood trees

Gulf Stream waters warm Atlantic Ocean waters

Before You Continue

1. **Analyze Genre** Read the song lyrics aloud. How are they like a poem?
2. **Main Idea** What is the most important idea of this verse? Tell it in your own words.

As I was walking **that ribbon of highway**,

I saw above me **that endless skyway**.

I saw below me that golden valley.

This land was made for you and me.

that ribbon of highway on a road that looked like a long, thin piece of cloth

that endless skyway the sky

▶ Before You Continue

1. **Ask Questions** What question do you have about this verse of the song? Look for an answer in the text or photos.
2. **Figurative Language** Reread the first line on page 284. Was the speaker really walking on a ribbon? Explain.

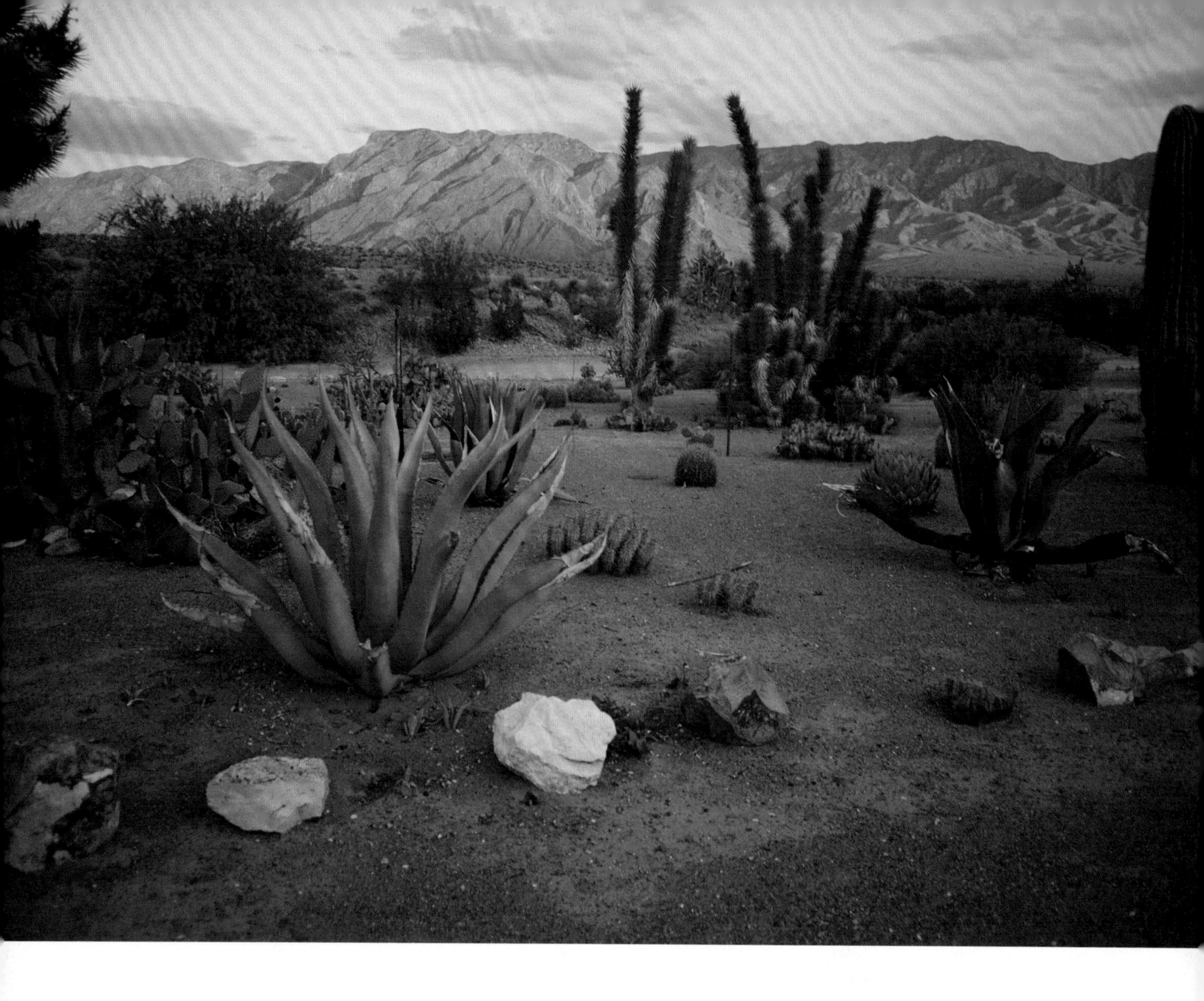

I've **roamed and rambled** and I followed my footsteps

To the **sparkling sands of her diamond deserts**;

And all around me a voice was **sounding**:

This land was made for you and me.

roamed and rambled gone to many places
sparkling sands of her diamond deserts dry, sandy areas of land that shine brightly in the sun
sounding singing

Before You Continue

1. **Make Inferences** What can you tell about the speaker from the song lyrics? How does he feel about his country?
2. **Visualize** Which words help you see, feel, and hear the places the song describes?

When the sun came shining, and I was **strolling**,

And the wheat fields waving and the dust
 clouds rolling,

As the fog **was lifting** a voice was **chanting**:

This land was made for you and me. ❖

strolling walking
was lifting leaving
chanting singing

More About Sam Abell

Sam Abell travels across the United States and around the world, taking photos of many places and people. He has provided photos for National Geographic Society for almost 40 years.

Mr. Abell learned **photography** from his father when he was very young.

"For me, photography means, '***Andiamo!***'" he said. "It's what gets me out the door."

photography how to take photos
Andiamo! *Let's go!* (in Italian)

▸ Before You Continue

1. **Make Inferences** The song tells about a singing voice. What do you think the speaker means?
2. **Draw Conclusions** How are the speaker and Sam Abell alike?

Compare Author's Purpose

Authors have a purpose, or reason, for writing texts. What do you think the authors of "An Eagle's Eye" and "This Land is Your Land" are trying to do?

Comparison Chart

	"An Eagle's Eye" by Anna Goy	"This Land Is Your Land" by Woody Guthrie
persuade readers		✔
inform readers	✔	
entertain readers		
share experiences		
express feelings		
express creativity		

Authors can have more than one purpose.

Put a check if the statement is true for the selection.

Talk Together

With your partner, take turns choosing picture cards. Use the cards and **Key Words** to tell about America.

Prepositional Phrases

A **prepositional phrase** starts with a preposition and ends with a noun or pronoun. Prepositional phrases add details to a sentence.

Grammar Rules Prepositional Phrases

Use prepositional phrases	
• to show where something is *above, below, between, in, out*	**in** Yosemite National Park **below** the waterfall
• to show direction *up, down, through, around, into*	**through** the woods **around** the big boulder
• to show time *before, during, after, until*	**until** our next visit **during** summer vacation
• to add details *at, for, of, to, about, with, without*	**about** the park **without** our backpack

Read Prepositional Phrases

Read these sentences from "This Land is Your Land" with a partner. Identify two prepositional phrases.

I saw above me
that endless skyway.
I saw below me that
golden valley.
This land was made for you and me.

Use Prepositional Phrases

Write two sentences using the two prepositional phrases you found in the song above.

Writing Project

Write about Yourself

Write a Personal Narrative 

Tell what the world means to you or someone you know. Put your story into a class scrapbook.

Study a Model

A personal narrative tells about a real event that means a lot to you. Read about how Ömer celebrated Earth Day.

The beginning tells what **event** Ömer is writing about.

Together We Care

by Ömer Aksoy

Last year I saw a lot of trash in my neighborhood. I felt sad, so I decided to clean up the streets **on Earth Day**.

I asked for help at my school. I didn't think anyone would come, but **I was in for a big surprise!** Around 50 kids came. They brought their families, too.

We picked up more than 100 bags of trash in the streets. **It was awesome!**

That day I learned that **together, we can help our world**. My mom was happy, too. She said my small idea made a big difference.

The middle tells more about what happened. Ömer uses **words that sound like him.** He writes using his own voice.

The end tells why it was **important**.

Prewrite

1. **Choose a Topic** What will you write about? Talk with a partner. Choose an event from your life that is important to you.

Language Frames	
Tell Your Ideas	**Respond to Ideas**
I remember when ______.	Tell me why ______ is important to you.
One of the most important things that ever happened to me is ______.	______ sounds interesting! What details will you use?
I believe ______.	I don't think this is a good topic because ______.

2. **Gather Information** Think about the event. What happened? Who was there? What did you see, hear, and feel?

3. **Get Organized** Use a Feelings Chart to help you organize details.

Feelings Chart

Character	How the Character Feels	Why the Character Feels This Way
My mom	She is happy.	

Draft

Use your details and chart to write your draft. Remember to tell why the event is important. Use words and sentences that sound like you.

Revise

1. **Read, Retell, Respond** Read your draft aloud to a partner. Your partner listens and then retells the story. Next, talk about ways to make your writing better.

Language Frames	
Retell You tell about ______. I think this story is important to you because ______.	**Make Suggestions** I'm not sure why ______ is special. Can you explain that more? The writing doesn't sound like you. Maybe you could change ______.

2. **Make Changes** Think about your draft and your partner's ideas. Then use revision marks to make your changes.

   - Do your words and sentences sound like you? If not, change some.

     I was in for a big surprise!
     ~~More people came than I thought.~~

   - Do you tell why the event is important? Add details that will help your reader understand.

     that together, we can help our world.
     That day I learned ~~how people work together.~~

Spelling Tip

Watch out for words that sound alike: *through* is a preposition, but *threw* is a verb.

Edit and Proofread

Work with a partner to edit and proofread your personal narrative. Look for prepositional phrases. If a prepositional phrase starts a sentence, you may need to add a comma after it. Use revision marks to show your changes.

Present

On Your Own Make a final copy of your personal narrative. Read it aloud to your classmates. You could also send it in an e-mail to a friend or family member.

Presentation Tips	
If you are the speaker...	**If you are the listener...**
Listen to how you're telling the story. You should sound like you're talking to a friend.	As you listen, think of something similar that happened to you.
Change your voice when events are funny or sad or serious.	Think about why the event is important to the reader.

With a Group Collect all of the personal narratives. Put them in a scrapbook. Add photographs, drawings, and decorations. Take turns bringing the book home to share with your families.

Talk Together

In this unit, you found lots of answers to the **Big Question**. Now, use your concept map to discuss the **Big Question** with the class.

Concept Map

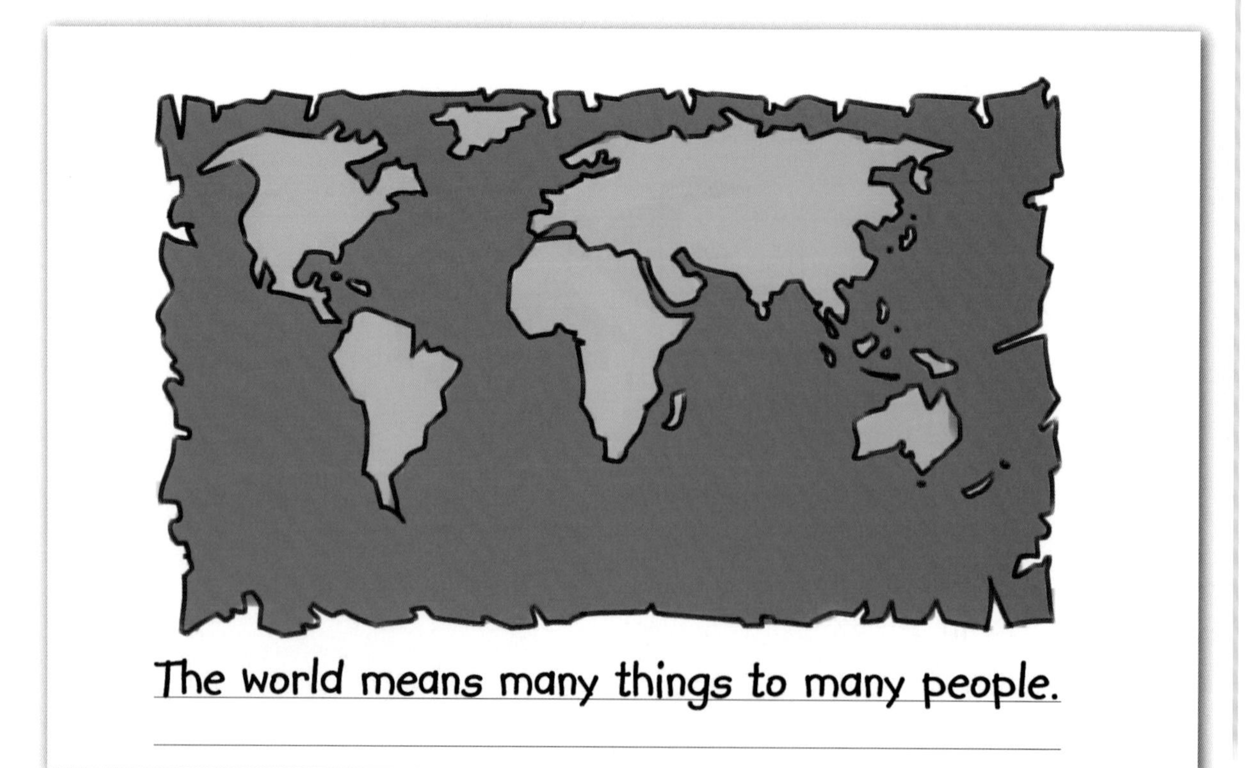

Share Your Ideas

Choose one of these ways to share your ideas about the **Big Question**.

Write It!

Write a Song

Work with a partner to write your own song about the world we live in. Perform your song for the class. Tell what the world means to you.

Talk About It!

Give a News Report

Pretend that you and your partner are reporters on the local news. Give a news report about a famous landmark close to where you live. Share your report with the class.

Do It!

Perform a Skit

Make up a skit about another holiday. Use the characters from "Something to Write About." Assign roles and think of lines for each character to say. Make props to use in the skit. Then perform the skit for your class.

Write It!

Write a Recipe

Write the recipe for a favorite meal that you enjoy at home.

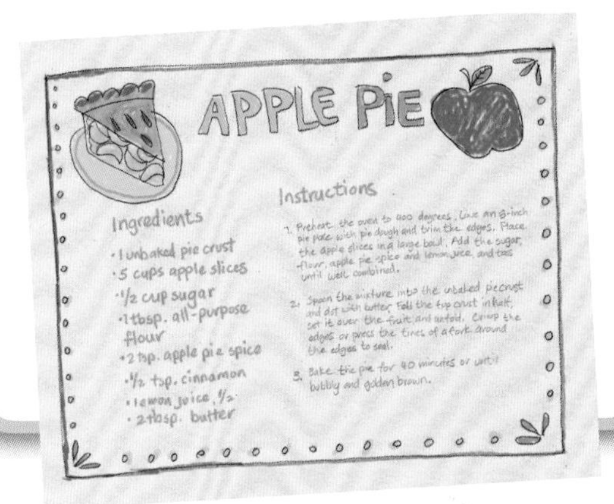

APPLE PIE

Ingredients
- 1 unbaked pie crust
- 5 cups apple slices
- 1/2 cup sugar
- 1 tbsp. all-purpose flour
- 2 tsp. apple pie spice
- 1/2 tsp. cinnamon
- lemon juice, 1/2
- 2 tbsp. butter

Instructions
1. Preheat the oven to 400 degrees. Line an 8-inch pie plate with pie dough and trim the edges. Place the apple slices in a large bowl. Add the sugar, flour, apple pie spice and lemon juice, and toss until well combined.
2. Spoon the mixture into the unbaked piecrust and dot with butter. Fold the top crust in half, set it over the fruit and unfold. Crimp the edges or press the tines of a fork around the edges to seal.
3. Bake the pie for 40 minutes or until bubbly and golden brown.

Picture Dictionary

The definitions are for the words as they are introduced in the selections of this book.

Parts of an Entry

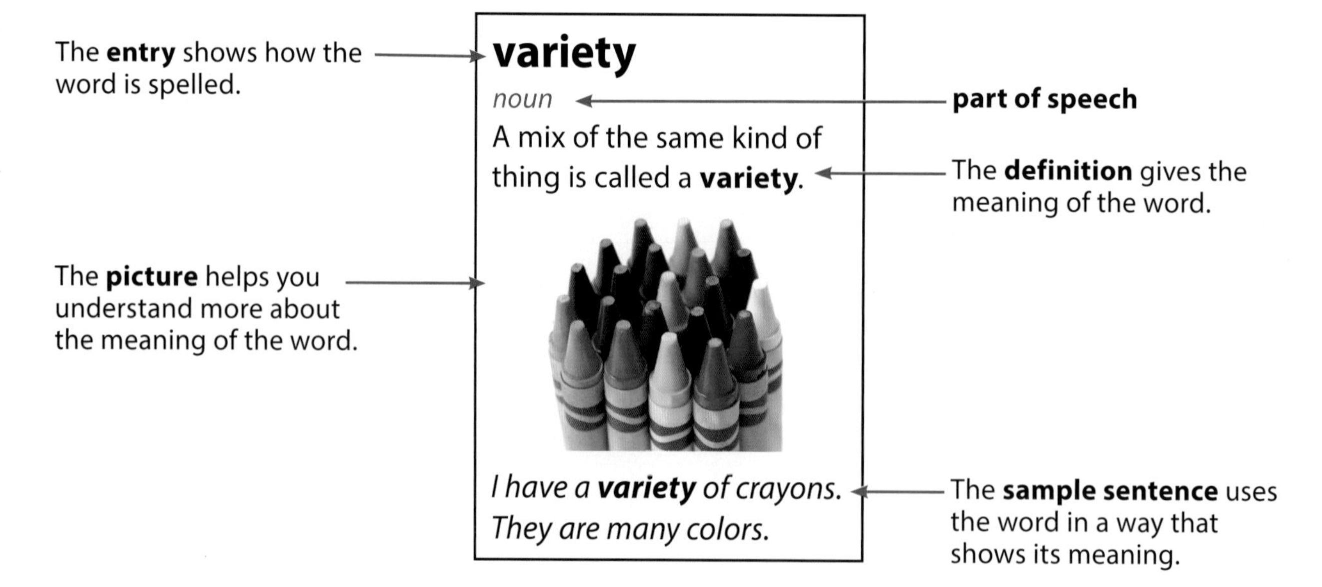

A

ability

noun

When you are able to do something, you have an **ability**.

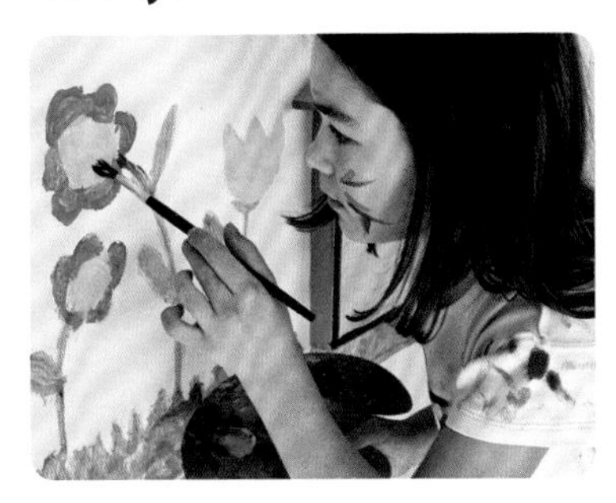

*She has great **ability** in art.*

accept

verb

When you **accept** something, you take a thing that is offered to you.

*Her mother **accepts** the flowers and a hug.*

add

verb

To **add** means to put things together.

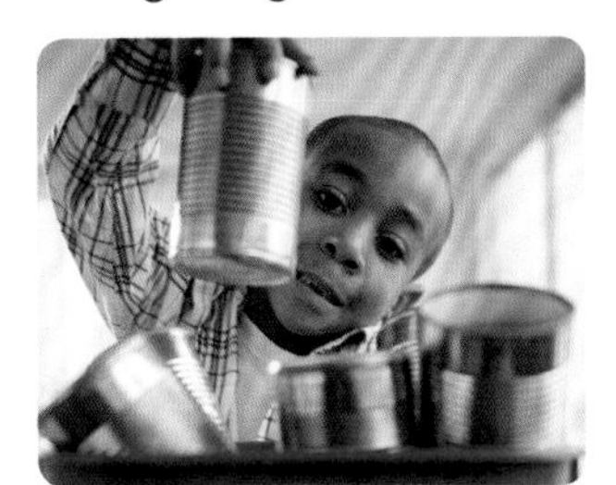

*When you **add** things to a group, you make the group bigger.*

affect

verb

When you **affect** something, you change it.

*The hot sun **affects** ice cream. It makes ice cream melt.*

alike

adjective

Things that are **alike** look the same.

*These dogs look **alike**.*

alone

adverb

Alone means to be without anyone else.

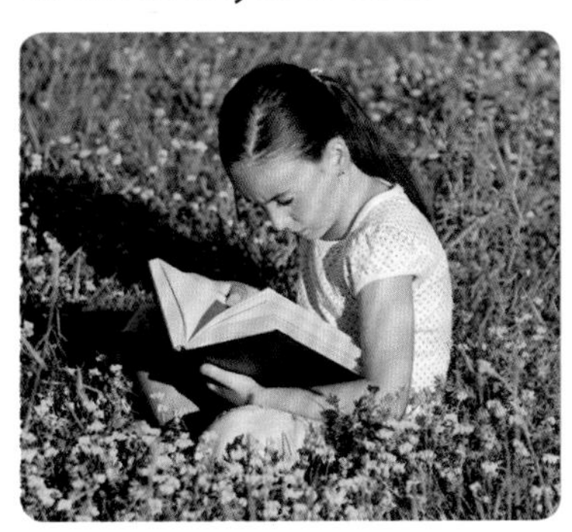

*She likes to be **alone**.*

appear

verb

When something **appears**, it comes into sight.

*The whale **appears** above the water.*

autumn

noun

Autumn is the season between summer and winter. It is also called "fall."

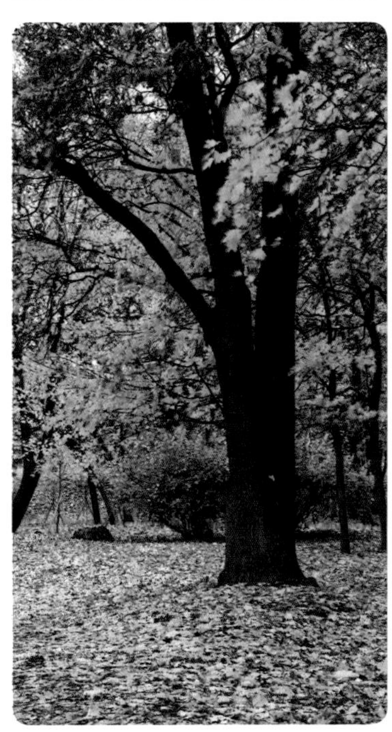

***Autumn** is when the leaves on trees change color and fall to the ground.*

B

begin

verb

To **begin** means to start.

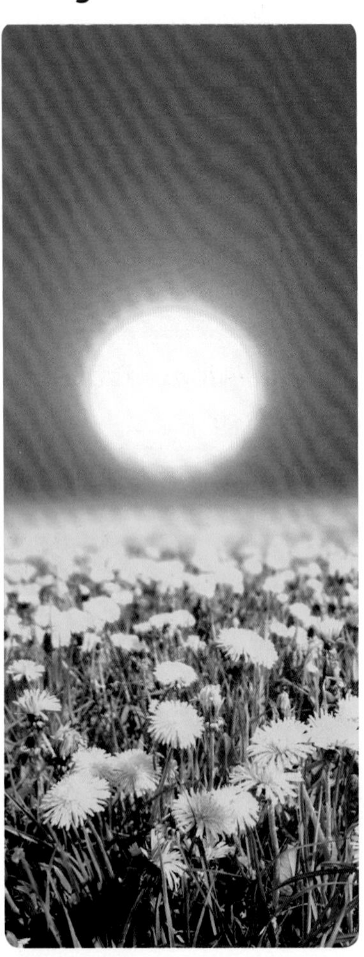

*When the sun rises, the day **begins**.*

belief

noun

A **belief** is a strong feeling that something is true.

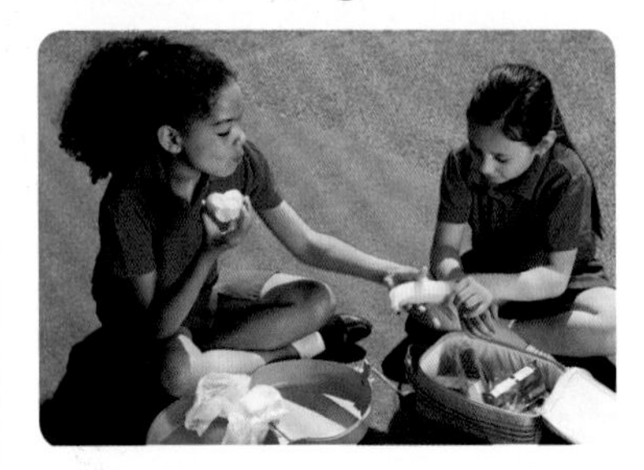

*Her **belief** that people should share helped her to give half of her lunch to her friend.*

body of water

noun

A **body of water** is a large amount of water, such as an ocean, lake, or river.

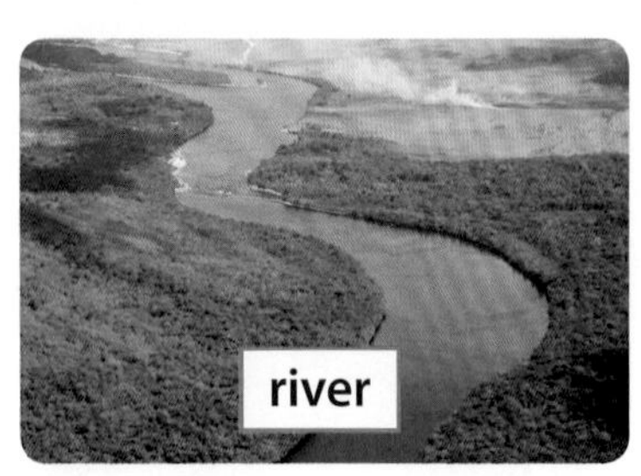

*The Pacific Ocean is the largest **body of water** on Earth.*

C

celebrate

verb

We **celebrate** events like birthdays and holidays to show how special they are to us.

*Many people **celebrate** the holidays by watching fireworks.*

chain

noun

A **chain** is a series of things that are connected.

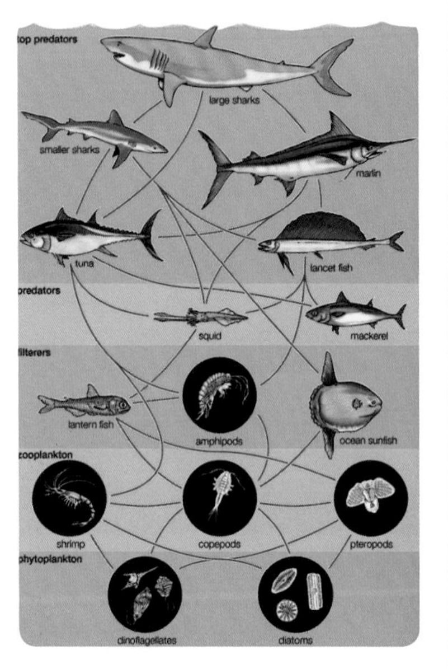

*Food **chains** show how animals and plants are connected.*

connect

verb

To **connect** things means to link or join them together.

*He **connects** the wires to make the computer work.*

D

cooperate
verb
When you **cooperate**, it means you work with or help others.

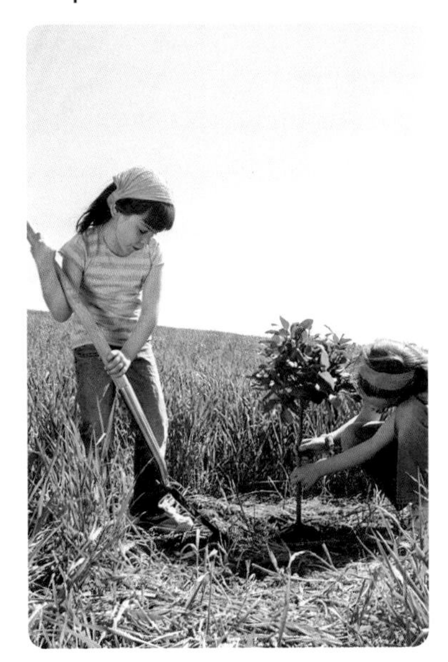

*Two girls **cooperate** with each other to plant trees.*

culture
noun
Culture is the way of life, art, ideas, and customs of a group of people.

*He likes traveling and meeting people from different **cultures**.*

danger
noun
Something is a **danger** when it can hurt you.

*If you walk too close to the edge, you are in **danger** of falling.*

day
noun
The time between sunrise and sunset is **day**.

*The sun can be seen in the sky during the **day**.*

difference
noun
The **difference** is the way that one thing is not the same as the other thing.

*One apple is red. That is the **difference**.*

difficult
adjective
When something is **difficult**, it is hard to do.

*It can be **difficult** to learn some new things.*

dream
noun
A **dream** is something you hope to do or succeed at in the future.

*Her **dream** is to win a medal at the track meet.*

a b c d e f g h i j k l m n o p q r s t u v w x y z

E

Earth

noun

Earth is the planet we live on.

*What does **Earth** look like from space?*

education

noun

To get an **education** means to learn things you didn't know before.

*You go to school to get an **education**.*

end

verb

The **end** is the last part of something.

*We turned off the TV at the **end** of the program.*

enemy

noun

An **enemy** is someone who hates you and wants to harm you.

*The opposite of an **enemy** is a friend.*

enough

adjective

To say you have **enough** means you have all that you need.

*There is just **enough** milk to fill the glass.*

expect

verb

When you **expect** something, you think it is likely to happen.

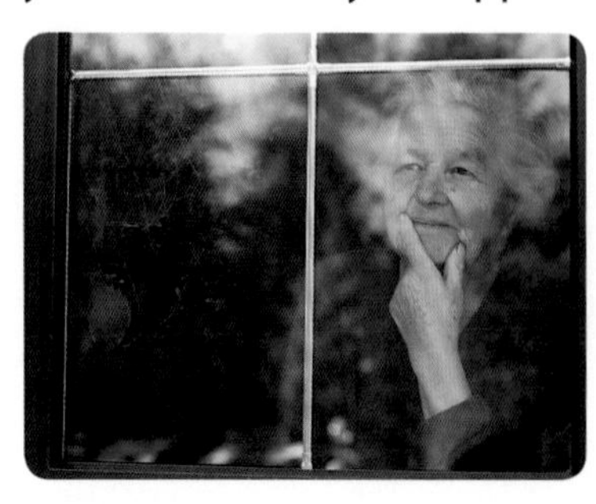

*I **expect** the clouds will turn into rain today.*

explain

verb

To **explain** is to talk about an idea so that someone else can understand it.

*She **explains** the math problem to her student.*

F

fall

noun

Fall is another word for "autumn." It is the season between summer and winter.

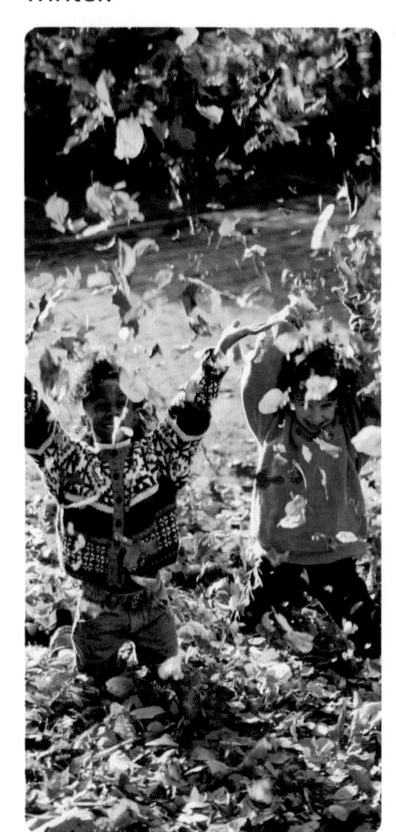

*In the **fall,** children like to play in piles of leaves.*

freedom

noun

Freedom means you can do the things you want to do.

*We have the **freedom** to say what we want.*

H

happen

verb

*When something **happens**, it takes place.*

*They watch what **happens** in the game.*

history

noun

History is the study of people and events from the past.

*George Washington was the first president in U.S. **history**.*

holiday

noun

A **holiday** is a special day when many people do not work.

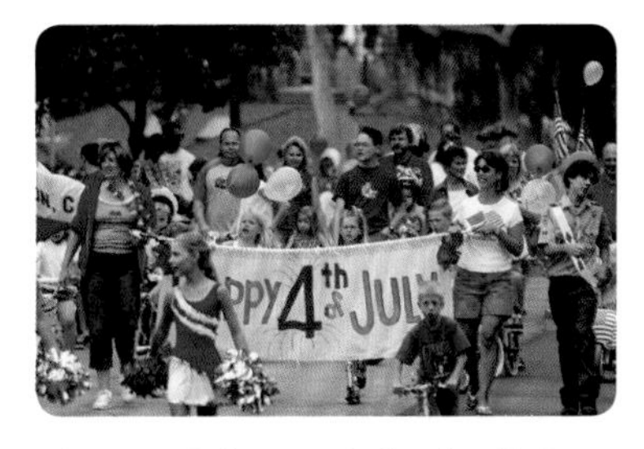

*They celebrated the **holiday** by having a parade.*

I

important

adjective

If something is **important**, you care about it a lot.

*Firefighters have an **important** job.*

J

join

verb

To **join** means to become a member of a group.

*He was happy to **join** a Little League team.*

L

landform

noun

A **landform** is the way that the surface of the land is shaped.

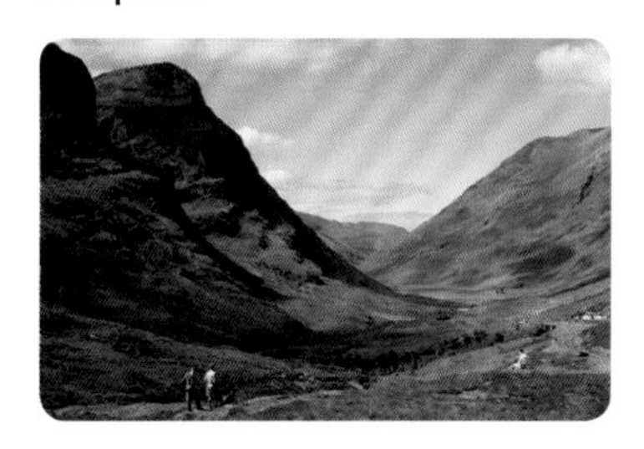

*This **landform** is called a valley.*

language
noun
A **language** is a system of words and grammar used by people to talk and write to each other.

*These people are using sign **language**.*

M

measure
verb
To **measure** is to figure out the size or amount of something.

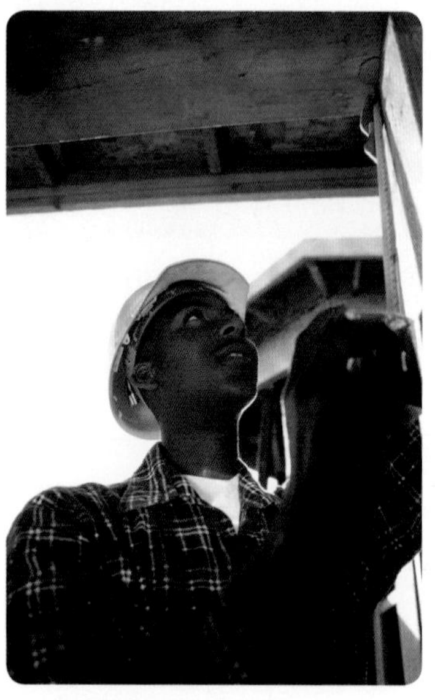

*He **measures** the doorway to see how big it is.*

monument
noun
A **monument** is something that is built so that people remember something important.

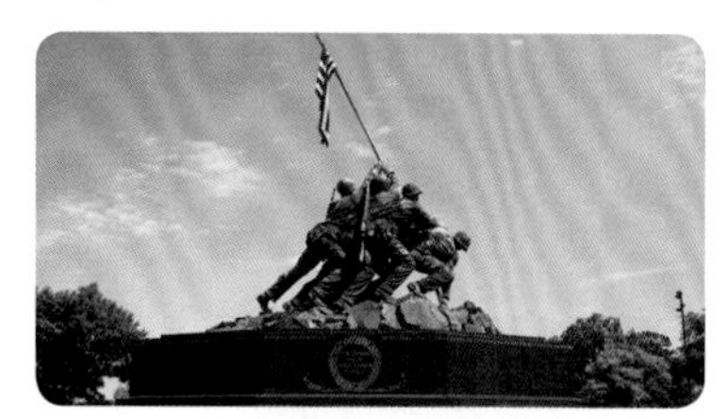

*This is a **monument** to war heroes.*

moon
noun
A **moon** is a natural satellite that travels around, or orbits, a planet.

*You can see our **moon** from Earth.*

motion
noun
If something is in **motion**, it is moving.

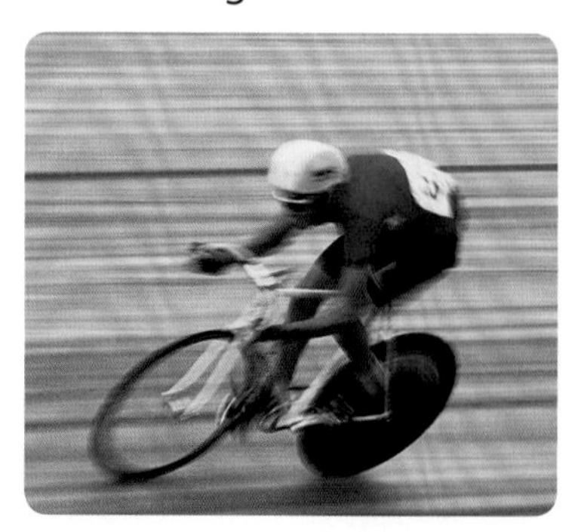

*The man is in **motion**.*

N

necessary
adjective
When something is **necessary**, it is absolutely needed.

*A seatbelt is **necessary** to stay safe in a car.*

night
noun
Night is the time between sunset and sunrise.

*It is dark outside at **night**.*

O

observe
verb
When you **observe** something, you watch it.

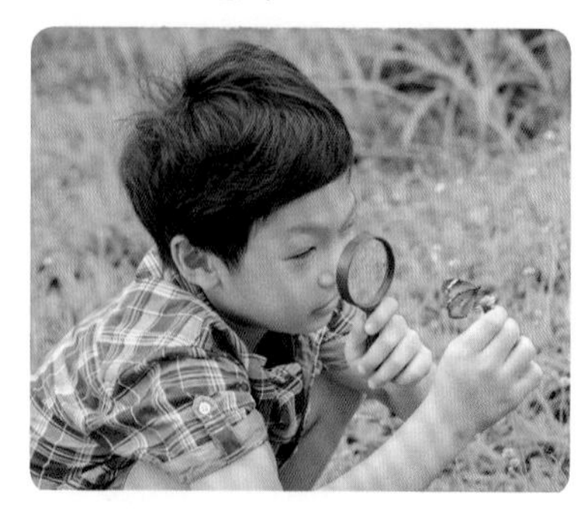

*He **observes** the insect.*

opportunity
noun
An **opportunity** is a chance to do something.

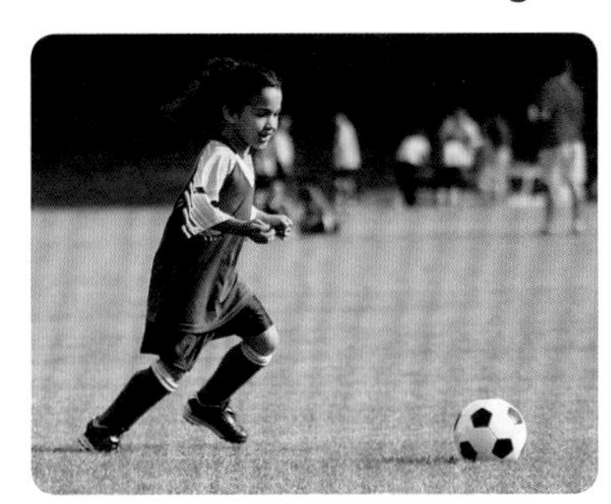

*She has an **opportunity** to kick the ball.*

organize
verb
To **organize** means to put things neatly in order.

*She **organized** the robots on her shelf.*

others
noun
Others are people apart from you.

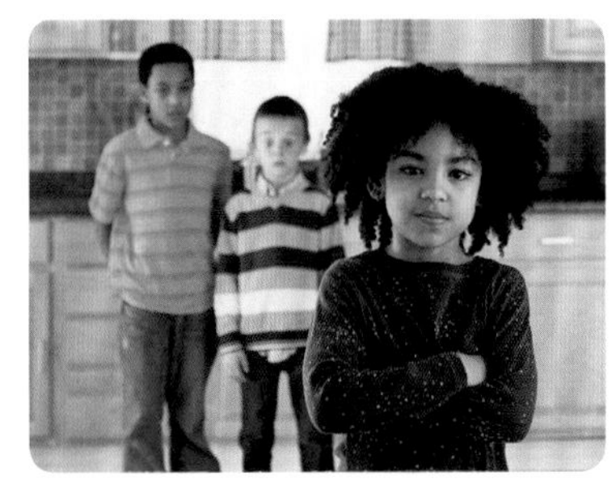

*Casey stands away from the **others**.*

P

partner
noun
A **partner** is someone you do something with, such as dancing.

*These people were famous dance **partners** in the movies.*

pattern
noun
When things are done in a **pattern**, they are done again and again in the same order or way.

*Orange, gray, and blue tiles make a **pattern** on this floor.*

people
noun
People are groups of men, women, and/or children.

*These **people** are students in a school.*

plan
noun
A **plan** is a set of organized ideas that help you reach a goal.

Plan to Clean My Room
1. Make bed.
2. Fold clothes.
3. Put away clothes.
4. Clean desk.

*This is a **plan** to clean my room.*

possible
adjective
If something is **possible**, it means it could happen.

*Airplanes make it **possible** for people to fly.*

project
noun
A **project** is work that you plan carefully.

*His school science **project** took a long time to finish.*

a b c d e f g h i j k l m n o p q r s t u v w x y z

R

reason

noun

A **reason** is why something is a certain way.

*Hard work and practice are the **reasons** she is a good musician.*

relate

verb

When things **relate** to each other, there is a connection between them.

*All the questions **relate** to what our teacher said in class.*

remember

verb

To **remember** something means to think of it again or have a memory of it.

***Remember** to call and say, "Happy birthday!"*

repeat

verb

To **repeat** means to do or say the same thing again.

*She has to **repeat** what she said because her teacher did not hear her.*

respond

verb

To **respond** is to answer someone by speaking or writing.

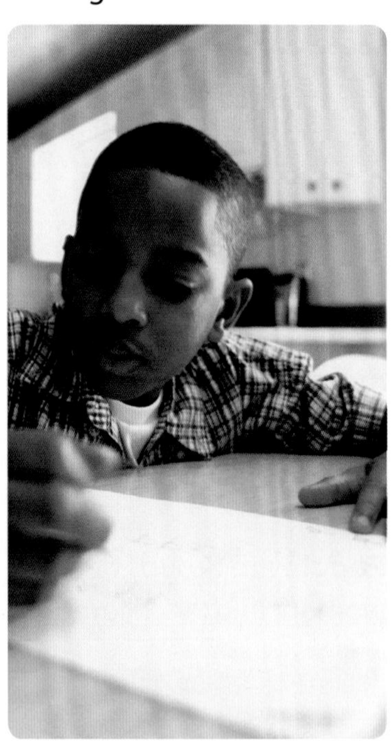

*He **responds** to the letter from his friend.*

result

noun

The **result** is what happens after a series of actions.

*If you trip and drop a cup, the **result** is broken pieces.*

role

noun

Something's **role** is its job or its purpose.

*A guide dog's **role** is to help blind people walk from one place to another.*

S

season

noun

A **season** is one of the four parts of the year. The seasons are spring, summer, autumn or fall, and winter.

spring

summer

fall

winter

*Which one is your favorite **season**?*

seek

verb

When you **seek** something, you are trying to find it.

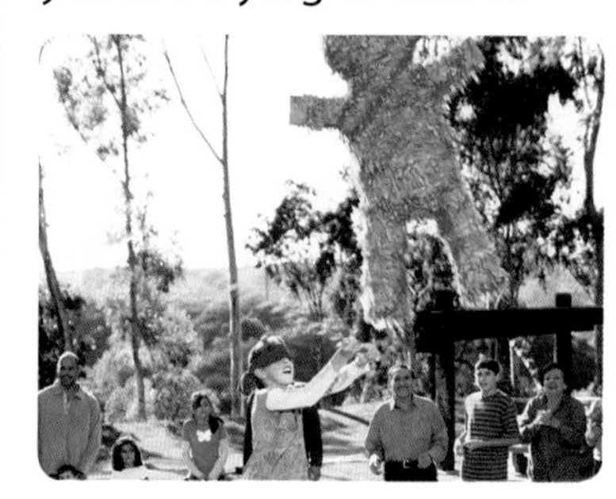

*The girl **seeks** the piñata with a stick.*

shadow

noun

A **shadow** is a dark area that is made when something blocks the light.

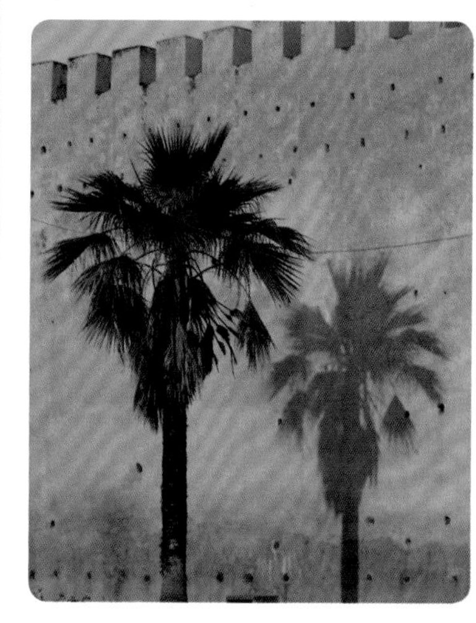

*You can see the **shadow** of the palm tree on the wall.*

share

verb

When you **share**, you give someone part of something you have.

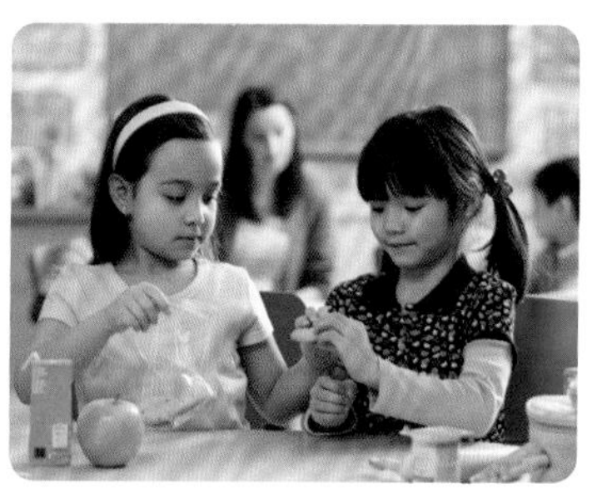

*The two girls **share** their lunch.*

skill

noun

A **skill** is the ability to do something well.

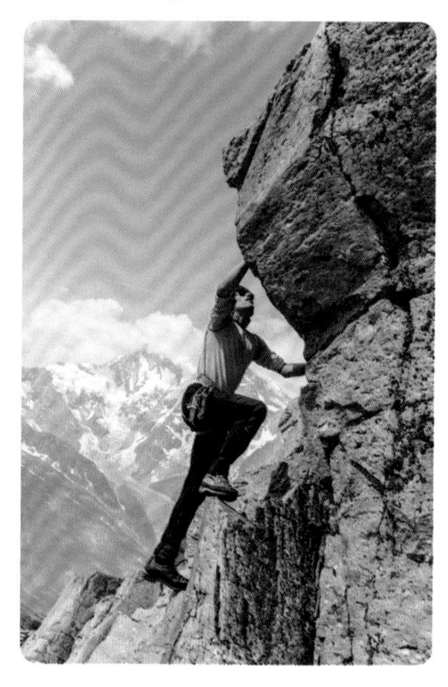

*Rock climbing takes a lot of **skill**.*

society

noun

A **society** is a group of people who live in the same area or country. It can also be a group of people with the same interests and hobbies.

*In our **society**, we salute the flag.*

society (continued)

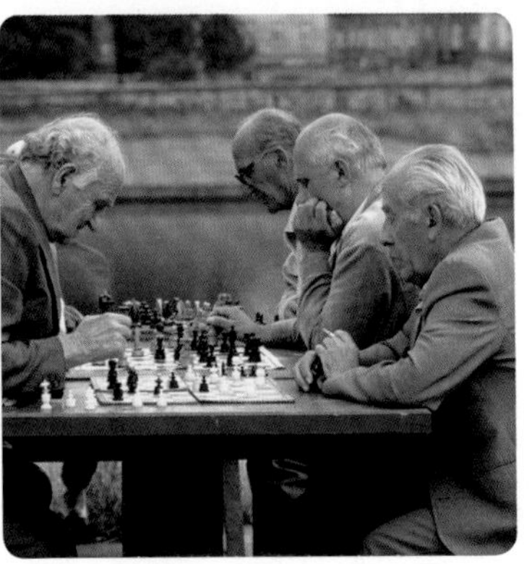

*This chess **society** meets on Wednesdays.*

species

noun

A **species** is a group of animals or plants that have similar characteristics.

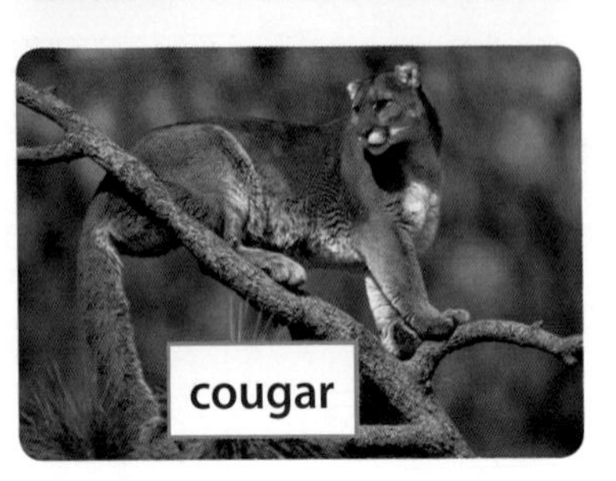

*There are many different **species** of cats.*

spring

noun

Spring is one of the four seasons of the year. It comes between winter and summer.

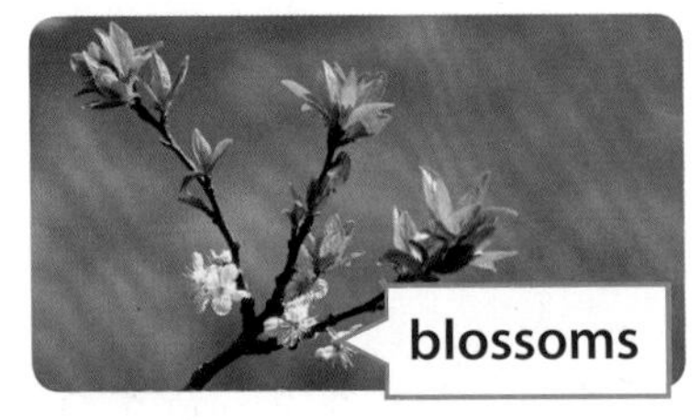

***Spring** is a time of regrowth.*

stars

noun

Stars are very large balls of gas. From Earth, **stars** look like points of light in the night sky.

*The **stars** shine brightly at night.*

success

noun

Success is when you set out to do something and you get it done.

*They win the game. It is a big **success**!*

summer

noun

Summer is one of the four seasons of the year.

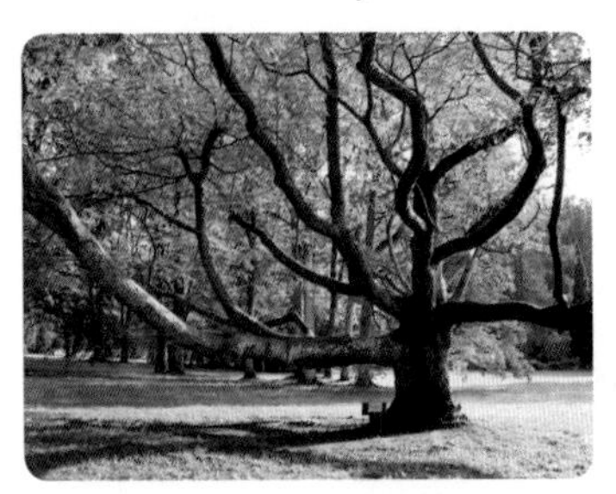

***Summer** comes after spring and before autumn.*

symbol

noun

A **symbol** is something that represents something else.

*Each candle on a birthday cake is a **symbol** for one year of your life.*

T

team member

noun

Team members are the people who work together to get something done.

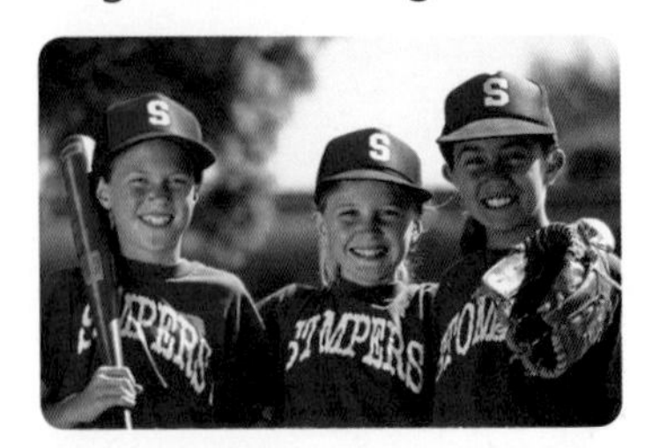

*These **team members** work together to win the game.*

teamwork
noun
When people work well together, they are using **teamwork**.

*It takes **teamwork** to build a house.*

threaten
verb
If something or someone **threatens** you, it causes you to feel afraid or in danger.

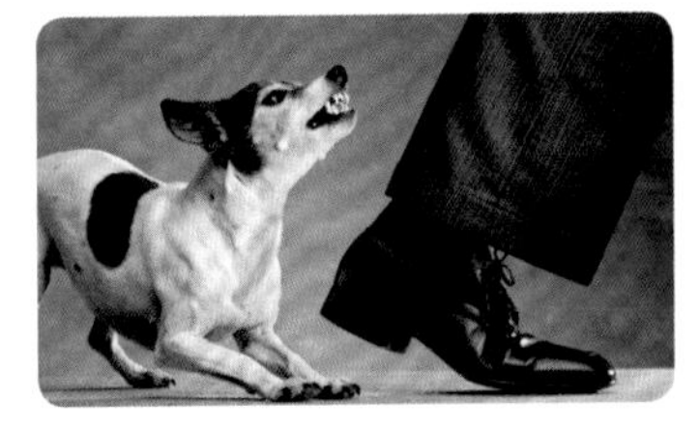

*The angry dog **threatens** by barking.*

together
adverb
People are **together** when they are in the same place at the same time.

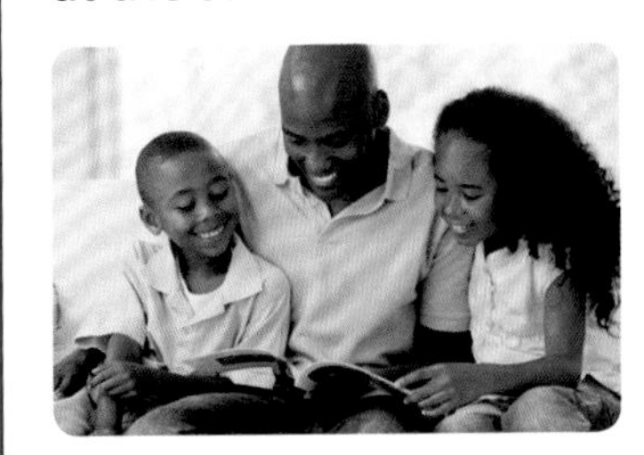

*This family likes to spend time **together**.*

tradition
noun
A **tradition** is a custom or belief that is shared by a group of people.

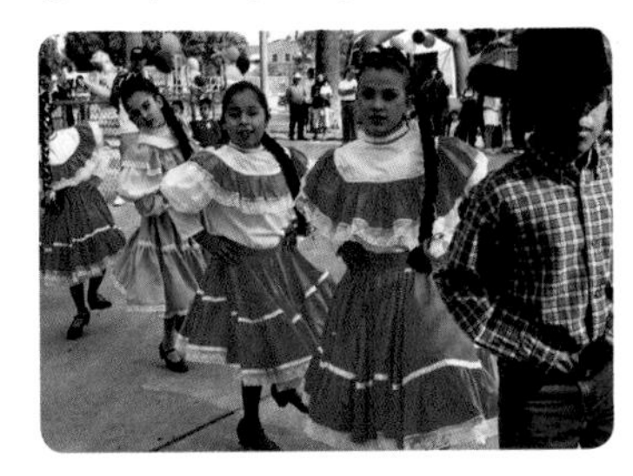

*Dancing is part of their **tradition**.*

U

united
adjective
When a group is **united**, the people agree and work together.

*When we play soccer, we are **united** as a team.*

unusual
adjective
Something **unusual** is odd or uncommon.

*This tiny animal is very **unusual**.*

useful
adjective
When something is **useful**, it helps you.

*Tools are **useful** for fixing broken things.*

V

variety
noun
A mix of the same kind of thing is called a **variety**.

*I have a **variety** of crayons. They are many colors.*

vegetation
noun
Vegetation is all the plants of an area.

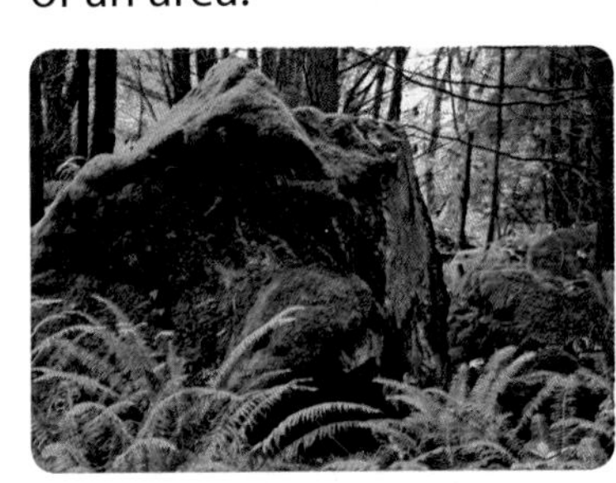

*Can you name the different kinds of **vegetation**?*

a b c d e f g h i j k l m n o p q r s t u v w x y z

a b c d e f g h i j k l m n o p q r s t u v w x y z

W

weather

noun

Weather is the current condition of the air. Weather is how cold or hot it is or if it is raining, snowing, or sunny.

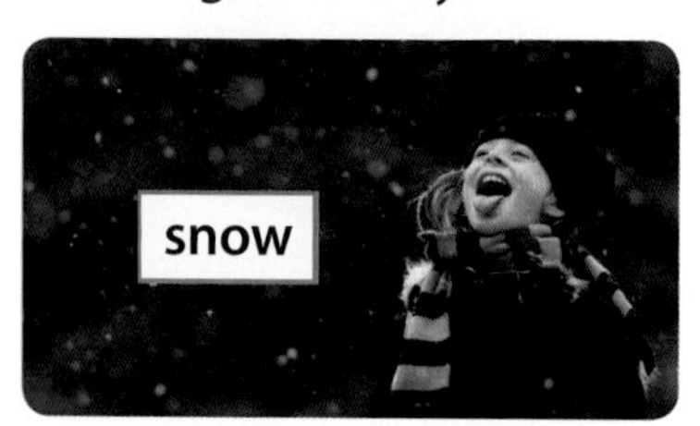

*The **weather** is cold today.*

wilderness

noun

A **wilderness** is an area of natural land which is not used by people.

*We can only find wild animals and plants in the **wilderness**.*

wildlife

noun

Animals that live in their natural environment are **wildlife**.

*Different **wildlife** live in different parts of the world.*

winter

noun

Winter is one of the four seasons of the year. Winter comes after autumn and before the spring.

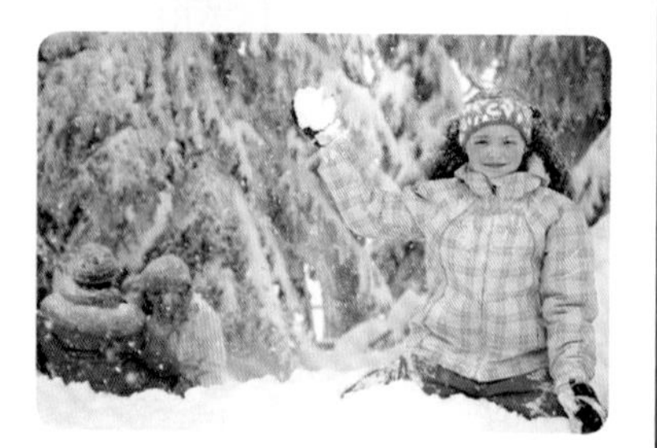

*There are many fun things we can do in **winter**.*

Index

T

V

Index of Authors

Index of Illustrators

Index of Photographers

Text and Illustrator Credits

Unit Five

HarperCollins Publishers: *WHEN THE WIND STOPS* by Charlotte Zolotow. ©1962, renewed 1990 Charlotte Zolotow Trust. By permission of Edite Kroll Literary Agency, Inc. Illustrations copyright © 1995 by Stefano Vitale. Used by permission of HarperCollins Publishers.

Penguin Random House: Illustrations and entire text from *WHAT MAKES THE SEASONS?* by Megan Montague Cash, copyright © 2003 by Megan Montague Cash. Used by permission of Viking Children's Books, an imprint of Penguin Young Readers Group, a division of Penguin Random House LLC. All rights reserved. Any third party use of this material, outside of this publication, is prohibited. Interested parties must apply directly to Penguin Random House LLC for permission.

Unit Six

John Forster and Tom Chapin: Excerpt from the lyrics of "Stone Soup" by John Forster and Tom Chapin. Copyright © 1990 by Limousine Music Company and The Last Music Co. (ASCAP). Reprinted by permission of the authors.

Scholastic, Inc: Reprinted from *Mi Barrio (My Neighborhood)* by George Ancona, published by Children's Press. Used with permission of Scholastic.

Unit Seven

Marian Reiner Literary Agent: Excerpt from *Go to Sleep, Gecko* by Margaret Read MacDonald, illustrated by Geraldo Valério. Text copyright © 2006 by Margaret Read MacDonald. Illustrations © 2006 by Geraldo Valério. Published by August House Publishers Inc. Used by permission of Marian Reiner.

Unit Eight

Ludlow Music Inc.: Excerpt from the lyrics of "This Land is Your Land", words and music by Woody Guthrie. Copyright © 1956 (renewed), 1958 (renewed), 1970 (renewed), 1972 (renewed), Ludlow Music, Inc. International copyright secured. Made in U.S.A. Used by permission of TRO. All rights reserved including public performance for profit.

Photographic Credits

Cover Sevenkingdom/Dreamstime. iii (tl) 2–3 Vast Photography/Getty Images (tr) David Ramos/Getty Images (bl) Heini Wehrle/Minden Pictures (br) NASA Photo/Alamy Stock Photo. iv Angus McComiskey/ Alamy Stock Photo. vii Angus McComiskey/Alamy Stock Photo. ix Jeff Hunter/ Stone/Getty Images. xi aabejon/iStock/Getty Images. 2–3 Vast Photography/Getty Images. 5 (tc) James P. Blair/National Geographic Image Collection (tr) Creative Travel Projects/Shutterstock (br) Martin Maun/Shutterstock.com (bc) John Foxx/Stockbyte/Getty Images (bl) Veni/E+/Getty Images (tl) Media Union/Shutterstock.com. 7 (tl) Tory Kallman/Shutterstock.com (tc) J&L Images/Photodisc/Getty Images (tr) all_about_ people/Shutterstock.com (bl) apdesign/ Shutterstock.com (bc) Africa Studio/Shutterstock. 10 (tl) Siyapath/Shutterstock.com (tc) Simon Bratt/ Shutterstock.com (tr) Michele Aldeghi/Shutterstock. com. 11 Craig Heath/Shutterstock.com. 19 Don Farrall/Photodisc/Getty Images. 34–35 TSI Incorporated. 35 (l) Klaus Tiedge/Blend Images/ Getty Images (r) Image Source/Photodisc/Getty Images. 39 (tl) Amehime/Shutterstock.com (tr) FamVeld/Shutterstock.com (bl) John Foxx/ Stockbyte/Getty Images (br) IdeaBug Inc/ Shutterstock.com (r) Steve Wisbauer/Photodisc/ Getty Images. 40 (tl) Matthias Breiter/Minden Pictures (tr) Igor Shpilenok/Minden Pictures (cl) Minden Pictures/Masterfile (cr) Arterra/Getty Images (bl) MILLARD H. SHARP/Science Source (br) M & J Bloomfield/Alamy Stock Photo. 41 (tl) moira lovell/Alamy Stock Photo (tc) GoGo Images Corporation/Alamy Stock Photo (tr) Rawpixel.com/ Shutterstock.com (bl) SW Productions/Getty Images (bc) T.TATSU/Shutterstock. 44 (tl) anela.k/ Shutterstock.com (tr) Elvira Koneva/Shutterstock. com (cl) Tobias Arhelger/Shutterstock.com (cr) froggyimage/Shutterstock.com (bl) Africa Studio/ Shutterstock.com (br) Drpnncpptak/Shutterstock. com. 45 elod_pali/Shutterstock.com. 62 (l) Compass Productions/Alamy Stock Photo (r) Steve Debenport/iStock/Getty Images. 63 (tr) Peg Skorpinski (bc) focus35/iStock/Getty Images. 64 (bc) istock.com/VLIET (inset) J. M. Storey/ Carleton University. 65 (c) stevegeer/iStock/Getty Images (inset) Joel Sartore Photography/National Geographic Image Collection. 72 Vast Photography/ Getty Images 74–75 David Ramos/Getty Images. 75 (br) George Rudy/Shutterstock.com. 77 (tl) Jim West/Alamy Stock Photo (tr) Jupiterimages/ Photolibrary/Getty Images (b) Ariel Skelley/Getty Images. 79 (tl) JGI/Jamie Grill/Getty Images (tc) Maica/E+/Getty Images (tr) Robert Byron/ Dreamstime.com (bl) Denise Kappa/Shutterstock. com (bc) Jose Luis Pelaez Inc/DigitalVision/Getty Images. 82 (tl) Pozdeyev Vitaly/Shutterstock.com (tr) Asier Romero/Shutterstock.com (cl) mrs/ moment/Getty Images (cr) arrowsmith2/ Shutterstock.com (bl) Gavran333/Shutterstock.com (br) Mriya Wildlife/Shutterstock.com 83 Michael Gancharuk/Shutterstock.com. 99 Peachtree Publishers. 100 Jose Luis Pelaez Inc/DigitalVision/ Getty Images. 113 (tl) Monkey Business Images/ Dreamstime.com (tr) Monkey Business Images/ Getty Images (cl) Monkey Business Images/ Dreamstime.com (cr) Monkey Business Images/ Getty Images (bc) Monkeybusinessimages/ Dreamstime LLC. 115 (tl) Jun Tsukuda/Aflo/Getty Images (tc) Digital Vision/Getty Images (tr) Rob Marmion/Shutterstock.com (bl) jacglad/ Shutterstock.com (bc) Brand X Pictures/Stockbyte/ Getty Images. 118 (tl) Craig Heath/Shutterstock. com (tr) Gayvoronskaya_Yana/Shutterstock.com (cl) Sabir Babayev/Shutterstock.com (cr) michaeljung/Shutterstock.com (bl) Erickson Stock/ Shutterstock.com (br) bondvit/Shutterstock. 119 Roel Slootweg/Shutterstock.com 120–121 Alexis TOUREAU/Getty Images. 122 Angus McComiskey/Alamy Stock Photo. 123 (t) Stephen Butler/Shutterstock.com (b) Tim Graham/Getty Images. 124 (c) Per-Anders Pettersson/Getty Images (inset) Pajac Slovensky/Shutterstock (b) Zoonar GmbH/Alamy Stock Photo. 125 Alexis TOUREAU/ Getty Images. 126 (c) DrimaFilm/Shutterstock.com (b) bluedog studio/Shutterstock.com. 127 (t) Tim Graham/Getty Images (inset) Alexis TOUREAU/ Getty Images. 128 (t) oneworld picture/Getty Images (b) Dan Kitwood/Getty Images. 129 oneworld picture/Getty Images. 130 Elena-Grishina/Shutterstock.com 131santypan/ Shutterstock.com. 132 Angus McComiskey/Alamy Stock Photo. 133 oneworld picture/Getty Images. 134 Pajac Slovensky/Shutterstock.com. 136 Alexis TOUREAU/Getty Images. 140–141 meunierd/ Shutterstock.com. 148 David Ramos/Getty Images. 150–151 Heini Wehrle/Minden Pictures. 153 (tl) Vishnevskiy Vasily/Shutterstock.com (tr) Peter Steiner/Alamy Stock Photo (bl) Tamara Kulikova/ Shutterstock.com (br) Ross Jolliffe/Alamy Stock Photo. 155 (tl) Comstock Images/Stockbyte/Getty Images (tc) Yurchyks/Shutterstock.com (tr) John A. Rizzo/Photodisc/Getty Images (bl) diego_cervo/ iStock/Getty Images (bc) Jupiterimages/Stockbyte/ Getty Images. 158 (tl) Mega Pixel/Shutterstock.com (tr) Natpant Prommanee/Shutterstock.com (tcl) polarpig/Shutterstock.com (tcr) Evano/ Shutterstock.com (cl) kristiillustra/Shutterstock. com (cr) KK Tan/Shutterstock.com (bcl) Colin Hui/ Shutterstock (bcr) Itchy Feet/Shutterstock.com (bl) Colin Hui/Shutterstock.com (br) Peetz/ Shutterstock.com. 159 R. Maximiliane/ Shutterstock.com. 175 Marian Reiner. 178 (tl) Jacek Chabraszewski/Shutterstock (tr) R. Maximiliane/Shutterstock.com (bl) Comstock Images/Stockbyte/Getty Image (br) Duskbabe/Dreamstime.com. 179 Zafer Kizilkaya/ Images & Stories. 180 James Watt/Perspectives/ Getty Images. 181 Paul Kay/Oxford Scientific/Getty Images. 182–183 Octavio Aburto. 184 Zafer Kizilkaya/Images & Stories. 187 (t) Prasanth Aravindakshan/Shutterstock.com (bl) waniuszka/ Shutterstock.com (br) Pal Teravagimov Photography/Moment/Getty Images. 188 (tl) Johan Swanepoel/Shutterstock.com (tr) NIGEL DENNIS/ Science Source (bl) Tropical Marine Reef Fish and Invertebrates/Alamy Stock Photo (br) Stephen Frink/Photodisc/Getty Images. 189 (tl) Jacek Chabraszewski/Shutterstock.com (tc) Mostovyi Sergii Igorevich/Shutterstock.com (tr) Steve Smith/ DigitalVision/Getty Images (bl) Vitaly Titov/ Shutterstock.com (br) microstocker/Shutterstock. com. 190 (l) Dr Morley Read/Science Source (r) Mark Moffett/Minden Pictures. 192 (l) subbotina/ 123RF (cl) science photo/Shutterstock.com (cr) Vitaly Zorkin/Shutterstock.com (r) aimy27feb/ Shutterstock.com. 193 paula french/Shutterstock. com. 194–195 Jeff Hunter/Stone/Getty Images. 194 Tim Laman/National Geographic Image Collection. 196–197 Beverly Joubert/National Geographic Image Collection. 198–199 Tim Laman/National Geographic Image Collection. 198 Gerard Soury/The Image Bank/Getty Images. 199 (r) Federico Cabello/SuperStock (inset) David Hosking/Alamy Stock Photo. 200–201 Reinhard Dirscherl/WaterFrame/Getty Images. 200 age fotostock/Alamy Stock Photo. 202 (t) NIGEL DENNIS/Science Source (bl) Doug Cheeseman/ Photolibrary/Getty Images (br) Steve Cukrov/ Shutterstock.com. 203 (c) Jeremy Woodhouse/ DigitalVision/Getty Images (inset) Fuse/Corbis/ Getty Images. 204 Prisma by Dukas/Universal Images Group/Getty Images. 205 Oxford Scientific/ Photodisc/Getty Images. 206–207 Reinhard Dirscherl/WaterFrame/Getty Images. 206 Tim Laman/National Geographic Image Collection. 207 Steffen Foerster/Shutterstock.com. 208 Paul Banton/Shutterstock.com. 210 (tl) Tim Laman/ National Geographic Image Collection (br) Ian Shaw/Alamy Stock Photo. 211 Primož Cigler/ Shutterstock.com. 212–213 Steve Hopkin/The Image Bank/Getty Images. 213 Konrad Wothe/ Minden Pictures. 215 namibelephant/iStock/Getty Images. 220 Heini Wehrle/Minden Pictures. 222–223 NASA Photo/Alamy Stock Photo. 224 catherine lucas/Alamy Stock Photo. 225 (tl) Darrenp/Shutterstock (tr) Bettmann/Getty Images (cl) Lane Oatey/Blue Jean Images/Getty Images (cr) Matt Moyer (bl) Cade Martin/UpperCut Images/ Getty Images (br) Lane Oatey/Blue Jean Images/ Getty Images. 227 (tl) Shutterschock/Shutterstock. com (tc) Nathan Guinn/Shutterstock.com (tr) CharlieAJA/iStock/Getty Images (bl) absolut/ Shutterstock.com (bc) David P. Smith/Shutterstock. com. 230 (tl) Jaromir Chalabala/Shutterstock.com (tr) Monkey Business Images/Shutterstock.com (cl) Lopolo/Shutterstock.com (cr) kate_sept2004/E+/ Getty Images (bl) Kokhanchikov/Shutterstock.com (br) Tmild/Shutterstock.com. 231 Debra Anderson/ Shutterstock.com. 248 (tl) Nathan Guinn/ Shutterstock.com (tr) Maica/E+/Getty Images (bl) Yurchyks/Shutterstock.com (br) Gallo Images/ ROOTS RF collection/Getty Images. 249 szefei/ Shutterstock.com. 250 (l) Dragon Images/ Shutterstock.com (r) Zurijeta/Shutterstock. 251 (tr) Photographee.eu/Shutterstock.com (br) UfaBizPhoto/Shutterstock.com. 252 (tr) PixieMe/ Shutterstock.com (br) Monkey Business Images/ Shutterstock.com. 253 (tr) Rawpixel.com/ Shutterstock (br) Photographee.eu/Shutterstock. com. 255 (t) Galyna Andrushko/Shutterstock.com (b) anopdesignstock/iStock/Getty Images. 256 (b) John_Walker/Shutterstock.com (inset) PhotoRoman/Shutterstock. 259 (tl) Bruce C.

Murray/Shutterstock.com (tcl) Monkey Business Images/Shutterstock.com (tcr) digitalskillet/Shutterstock.com (tr) Siri Stafford/DigitalVision/Getty Images (bl) Denise Kappa/Shutterstock.com (bc) aabejon/iStock/Getty Images. 261 Efired/Shutterstock. 262 (tl) baibaz/Shutterstock.com (tr) MoreGallery/Shutterstock.com (cl) photolinc/Shutterstock.com (cr) Sepp photography/Shutterstock.com (bl) Narsil/Shutterstock.com (br) Tanee/Shutterstock.com. 263 byvalet/Shutterstock.com. 264–265 Patrick Rolands/Shutterstock.com. 266 StockIllustrations.com/Alamy Stock Photo. 267 Larissa Dening/Shutterstock.com. 268 LENSAMCC/Shutterstock.com. 269 Hendi Sujatmiko/Shutterstock. 270 Vixit/Shutterstock.com. 271 Boris Rezvantsev/Shutterstock.com. 272 Travel Wild/Alamy Stock Photo. 273 Torsten Reuter/Shutterstock.com. 274 SF photo/Shutterstock.com. 275 Christopher Boswell/Shutterstock.com. 276 (t) NortePhoto/Alamy Stock Photo (b) badboydt7/Shutterstock.com. 277 Hemis/Alamy Stock Photo. 278 Octavio Campos Salles/Alamy Stock Photo. 279 worledit/Shutterstock.com. 280 worledit/Shutterstock.com. 282 (t) Horizon International Images Limited/Alamy Stock Photo (b) carlosseller/Shutterstock.com. 283 Sam Abell/National Geographic Image Collection. 284 Oscity/Shutterstock.com. 285 Sam Abell/National Geographic Image Collection. 286 Sam Abell/National Geographic Image Collection. 287 Sam Abell/National Geographic Image Collection. 288 Sam Abell/National Geographic Image Collection. 289 (bkgd) Sam Abell/Nation Geographic Image Collection (inset) Sam Abell/National Geographic Image Collection. 291 Sam Abell/National Geographic Image Collection. 296 NASA Photo/Alamy Stock Photo. 298 David P. Smith/Shutterstock. 299 (tl) Jacek Chabraszewski/Shutterstock (tc) moira lovell/Alamy Stock Photo (tr) Tory Kallman/Shutterstock (cl) Comstock Images/Stockbyte/Getty Images (c) Shutterstock/Shutterstock.com (br) Duskbabe/Dreamstime.com (bl) JGI/Jamie Grill/Getty Images (bc) Gelpi/Shutterstock.com 300 (tl) Yellowj/Shutterstock.com (tc-ocean) Image Farm Inc./Alamy Stock Photo (tc-lake) 2009fotofriends/Shutterstock.com (tc-river) Janne Hamalainen/Shutterstock.com (tr) Encyclopaedia Britannica/UIG/Getty Images (bl) Jupiterimages/The Image Bank/Getty Images (bc) Nathan Guinn/Shutterstock.com (br) Yurchyks/Shutterstock. 301 (tl) Maica/E+/Getty Images (tc) Sergey Mostovoy/Dreamstime.com (tr) CharlieAJA/iStock/Getty Images (cr) Steve Smith/DigitalVision/Getty Images (bl) Gallo Images/ROOTS RF collection/Getty Images (bc) Ldambies/Dreamstime.com (br) Jun Tsukuda/Aflo/Getty Images. 302 (tl) Stocktrek/Photodisc/Getty Images (tc) ERproductions Ltd/Blend Images/Getty Images (tr) GoGo Images Corporation/Alamy Stock Photo (cl) Digital Vision/Getty Images (c) Robert Byron/Dreamstime.com (br) Donna Day/The Image Bank/Getty Images (bl) Marc Bruxelle/Shutterstock.com (bc) absolut/Shutterstock.com. 303 (tl) Bruce C. Murray/Shutterstock.com (tc) North Wind Picture Archives/Alamy Stock Photo (tr) John A. Rizzo/Photodisc/Getty Images (cr) Fuse/Corbis/Getty Images (bl) Rawpixel.com/Shutterstock.com (bc) Davis Barber/PhotoEdit (br) KATHLEEN REVIS/National Geographic Image Collection. 304 (tl) Lokibaho/E+/Getty Images (tc) robertharding/Alamy Stock Photo (tr) Diego Vito Cervo/Dreamstime.com (c) Media Union/Shutterstock.com (cr) Frank Schiefelbein EyeEm/Getty Images (bl) SW Productions/Getty Images (bc) J&L Images/Photodisc/Getty Images (br) all_about_people/Shutterstock.com. 305 (tl) Rob Marmion/Shutterstock.com (tc) Michael Ochs Archives/Moviepix/Getty Images (cl) Martin Poole/DigitalVision/Getty Images (c) apdesign/Shutterstock.com (cr) Denise Kappa/Shutterstock.com (bl) Jupiterimages/Stockbyte/Getty Images (bc) Matt Moyer (br) Ted Horowitz/Corbis/Getty Images. 306 (tl) T.TATSU/Shutterstock (tc) Africa Studio/Shutterstock (tr) jacglad/Shutterstock.com (cl) Cleve Bryant/PhotoEdit (bc) Jim Arbogast/Photodisc/Getty Images (br) Jim Craigmyle/First Light/Getty Images (bl) Monkey Business Images/Shutterstock.com (blc) digitalskillet/Shutterstock.com. 307 (tl) rotofrank/iStock/Getty Images (tc) Tomasz Adameczek | Dreamstime.com (tr) Buena Vista Images/DigitalVision/Getty Images (bc) Jose Luis Pelaez Inc/DigitalVision/Getty Images (bl) Siri Stafford/DigitalVision/Getty Images (br) Andersen Ross/Stockbyte/Getty Images. 308 (tl) Peter Horree/Alamy Stock Photo (tc) John Foxx/Stockbyte/Getty Images (tr) Jareso | Dreamstime.com (tcl) Jeremy Woodhouse/DigitalVision/Getty Images (bcl) John Foxx/Stockbyte/Getty Images (c) OHishiapply/Shutterstock.com (cr) Denise Kappa/Shutterstock.com (bl) NICK NORMAN/Media Bakery (bc) Brand X Pictures/Stockbyte/Getty Images (br) Brand X Pictures/Stockbyte/Getty Images. 309 (tl) Dennis MacDonald/PhotoEdit (tc) Kayte Deioma/PhotoEdit (tr) microstocker/Shutterstock.com (cl) GK Hart/Vikki Hart/Getty Images (c) aabejon/iStock/Getty Images (cr) David P. Smith/Shutterstock.com (bl) Monkey Business Images/Getty Images (bc) Vitaly Titov/Shutterstock.com (br) Tracy Ferrero/Alamy Stock Photo. 310 (tl) JOEL SARTORE/Media Bakery (tc) Erhard Nerger/Getty Images (tr) John Rizzo/Photolibrary/Getty Images (bc) Mogens Trolle/Shutterstock.com (bl) Martin Maun/Shutterstock.com (br) XiXinXing/Shutterstock.com. (cr) indykb/Shutterstock.com.

Acknowledgments

The Authors and Publisher would like to thank the following reviewers and teaching professionals for their valuable feedback during the development of the series.

Literature Reviewers

Carmen Agra Deedy, Grace Lin, Jonda C. McNair, Anastasia Suen

Global Reviewers

USA:

Blanca L. Campillo, Reading Coach, Chicago Public Schools, Chicago, IL; **Carla Chavez,** Language Arts Specialist, Galena Park Independent School District, Houston, TX; **Annena Z. McCleskey,** ELA Consultant/Regional Literacy Training Center Director, Wayne RESA, Lathrup, MI; **Sashi Rayasam,** Director of ESL Services K-12, Durham Public Schools, Durham, NC; **Robin Rivas,** Curriculum Specialist ESL/EFL; Milwaukee Public Schools, Milwaukee, WI; **Shareeica Roberts,** ESL Teacher, Carroll Academy for International Studies, Aldine, TX; **Cynthia Rodriguez,** Bilingual Teacher, Brill Elementary, Klein ISD, TX; **Julie Sanabria,** ESOL Teacher, Mamaroneck Avenue School, New Rochelle, NY; **Jennifer Slater-Sanchez,** Educator, Palmdale School District, Palmdale, CA/Adjunct Professor, Brandman University, Antelope Valley, CA; **Georgia Thompson,** Literacy Coach, Esperanza Hope Medrano Elementary School, Dallas, TX

Asia:

Mohan Aiyer, School Principal, Brainworks International School, Yangon; **Andrew Chuang,** Weige Primary School, Taipei; **Sherefa Dickson,** Head Teacher, SMIC, Beijing; **Ms Hien,** IP Manager, IPS Vietnam, Ho Chi Minh; **Christine Huang,** Principal, The International Bilingual School at the Hsinchu Science Park (IBSH), Hsinchu; **Julie Hwang,** Academic Consultant, Seoul; **David Kwok,** CEO, Englit Enterprise, Guangzhou; **Emily Li,** Teaching Assistant, SMIC, Beijing; **Warren Martin,** English Teacher, Houhai English, Beijing; **Bongse Memba,** Academic Coordinator, SMIC, Beijing; **Hoai Minh Nguyen,** Wellspring International Bilingual School, Ho Chi Minh; **Mark Robertson,** Elementary School Principal, Yangon Academy, Yangon; **Daphne Tseng,** American Eagle Institute, Hsinchu; **Amanda Xu,** Director of Teaching and Research, Englit Enterprise, Guangzhou; **Alice Yamamoto,** ALT, PL Gakuen Elementary School, Osaka; **Yan Yang,** Director of Research Development, Houhai English, Beijing

Middle East:

Lisa Olsen, Teacher, GEMS World Academy, Dubai, United Arab Emirates; **Erin Witthoft,** Curriculum Coordinator, Universal American School, Kuwait

Latin America:

Federico Brull, Academic Director, Cambridge School of Monterrey, Mexico; **Elizabeth Caballero,** English Coordinator, Ramiro Kolbe Campus Otay, Mexico; **Renata Callipo,** Teacher, CEI Romualdo, Brazil; **Lilia Huerta,** General Supervisor, Ramiro Kolbe Campus Presidentes, Mexico; **Rosalba Millán,** English Coordinator Primary, Instituto Cenca, Mexico; **Ann Marie Moreira,** Academic Consultant, Brazil; **Raúl Rivera,** English Coordinator, Ramiro Kolbe Campus Santa Fe, Mexico; **Leonardo Xavier,** Teacher, CEI Romualdo, Brazil

The Publisher gratefully acknowledges the contributions of the following National Geographic Explorers and photographers to our program and planet:

Tyrone Hayes, Enric Sala, and Sam Abell